Essential Reads *on* Family Offices

AF736615

Contents

Foreword — 3

Family office profiles — 5

Family office profile: Rodolfo Paiz, CEO of the PT Family Office (Miami and Guatemala) — 7
Interview by Suzy Peterfriend

Family office profile: Northwood Family Office — 10
Interview with Tom McCullough by Barbara R Hauser

An interview with Sue Nickason of Dart Family Office — 15

Governance, entrepreneurship, resilience and reinvention on the five-generation journey of a family enterprise — 17
Dennis T Jaffe, Maya Prabhu and Carolina Cintra

Family office profile: VALUEworks AG, Zurich/Switzerland — 26
Interview with Kecia Barkawi, CEO and founder of VALUEworks AG by Barbara R Hauser

Family business, family office and next gen — 30
Fabrizio Arengi Bentivoglio

Single-family offices in the 21st century – remaining fit for purpose — 33
Iraj Ispahani and Carl Sjöström

Governance — 41

Case study – design and set up of a family investment office — 42
Guillermo Barandalla

Family mission vision and values statements: the essential foundation of an effective family governance system or just another form that cannot function? — 45
Christian Stewart

The three family constitution archetypes and a wise alternative — 53
Christian Stewart

Family constitutions, the rule of law and happiness — 60
Barbara R Hauser

Stress tests – building resilience in the face of a crisis — 68
David Werdiger

The benefits of applying the rule of law in family governance — 74
Barbara R Hauser

The great man fallacy and family governance — 79
Franklin J Parker

NextGen 85

Family office succession planning 86
Susan R Schoenfeld

The right time to involve the next generation 94
Antoaneta Proctor

Parental expectations: effective guidelines or messy messages? 99
Raimund Kamp

Not the founder's family office: evolving to meet the needs of rising generations 106
Amelia Renkert-Thomas

Let's do it the SMART way: a practical guide for the raising of affluent children 115
Philippe J Weil

The importance of financial education for securing wealth transfer across generations 122
Peter Brock

I'm successful, but can't talk to my children about money! Help! 128
Maya Prabhu

The hows and whys of enterprising families reinterpreting timeless tales for their NextGen 133
Asher Noor

Generational resilience through the integration of governance into structure 140
Carly E Doshi, William J Kambas and Michael S Schwartz

Reframing succession in a disruptive era – a business family perspective 148
Roger King and Jeremy Cheng

Five things wealthy families can learn from Lee Man Tat 154
Russell Cohen

The next generation of strategic cultural philanthropy – impact, social justice and the opportunities for nextgen donors in the arts 156
Melissa Cowley Wolf

Effective mentoring for the next generation 165
Jessica McGawley

Women: wealth and self-reliance 185
Philip Marcovici and Caroline Underwood

Safeguarding the family's digital narrative: how to navigate the challenges of the social media revolution 209
Charlie Bain

About Globe Law and Business 225

Foreword

Barbara R Hauser
Founding editor, *The International Family Offices Journal*

Nicola Saccardo
Editor, *The International Family Offices Journal*

As founding editor and current editor of *The International Family Offices Journal*, we have had the pleasure of reading a number of outstanding articles over the years on a diverse range of topics. It is therefore a pleasure to introduce this collection of authoritative materials carefully curated from the prestigious archives of the journal and from the Special Report, *Family Business and Responsible Wealth Ownership*, edited by Iraj Ispahani.

This volume focuses on three key themes:

- **Family office profiles:** Learn from family offices themselves about their unique structures and outlooks, as well as their best practices.
- **Family governance:** Understand the essential principles and practices of effective family governance, which is critical for preserving family harmony and ensuring the long-term success of the family office.
- **NextGen and succession:** Explore the all-important and ever-relevant topic of how to successfully transition family wealth and leadership to the next generation.

Contributions to this volume have been written by a range of leading family office members and their advisers. We hope that you find the contributions as informative and insightful as we have, and we would welcome your feedback.

Essential Reads *on* Family office profiles

Our long-term and trusted relationship with a family-business consultant was absolutely priceless, and its importance and value to both the family's emotional and financial well-being cannot possibly be overstated.

Family office profile: Rodolfo Paiz, CEO of the PT Family Office (Miami and Guatemala)

Interview by Suzy Peterfriend

Q: How regularly did you have family meetings while you were setting up the business, growing the business, and while you were in the process of selling and after you sold the business?

A: The earliest structured meetings of which I am aware date back to the 1970s, when my family's second generation (my father and his siblings, then in their thirties) began to meet every Tuesday morning for several hours. All important issues, whether family or business-related, were addressed at that meeting, which they called 'PC' meaning 'Paiz Consultants' as a humorous reference to a short-lived business venture. Anyone could bring an issue to PC, but only the G2 siblings and our CFO could stay for the entire meeting. At that point, our supermarket business, founded in 1928 but limited to a single store until 1960, had expanded to a dozen locations.

In the early 1980s, my family was blessed by a chance encounter with a young Ivan Lansberg – a family business consultant focused on Latin America; we became one of his earliest clients, and have worked with him continuously since then. Soon after we began working with Ivan we began a tradition of annual or semi-annual structured family meetings, and we became more diligent about protecting and preserving the various 'family spaces' like the family vacations, the family discussions, and the special occasions like Christmas dinner. All of those practices continued as the business grew, outside partners joined, and the company merged with a competing chain.

Our long-term and trusted relationship with a family-business consultant was absolutely priceless, and its importance and value to both the family's emotional and financial well-being cannot possibly be overstated. Many potential problems were proactively prevented, and many more were easily solved when they occurred, because for so many years Ivan had taught us proven best practices and we had continued investing in the family's dialogue on governance and family systems.

Upon the sale of the business in 2010, it became clear to all that the five branches had evolved different characters and preferences for their future entrepreneurial and financial strategies, and that reinvesting everything into a single holding company for the entire family was not the right path.

We distributed the proceeds among the five branches of the family, and each branch has since then followed its own strategy. Shared investments are welcome, but not required. Each branch has taken the 30 years of systemic governance experience and used it to design their own new and independent governance structures.

We still enjoy 'family time' and all get along beautifully, but the majority of our operating businesses and investments are on a per-branch basis and not a whole-family basis.

Q. What was the role of the family office throughout that time, and what role does it have now?

A: Today there is a widespread misconception that family offices are primarily wealth management entities for families that have large and liquid fortunes. Since the early 1980s our family created a true family office to provide (and/or source) a variety of services that the family needed. We had accountants to manage the books for several of our smaller family businesses and to prepare the tax returns for members of the family with confidentiality and discretion.

Our family office either provided or oversaw services related to property management, document management (indexing and safe-keeping of critical papers), financial and company reporting, individual and shared insurance policies, security, and quite a few others. These services both reduced our workload (allowing more time to grow the business and more time to spend with family) and increased our capability to operate complex structures or manage sophisticated projects since we had an executive capacity dedicated to the family.

That collective family office served us well until the sale of the supermarket chain in 2010, and continues to serve us well for some things; but the new per-branch paradigm has led each family branch to create their own family office infrastructure to fit their needs and strategies, and those are gradually taking over all functionality and services from the collective.

At this point, each branch of the family has some level of in-house family-office capability providing a significant executive capability. Some services are provided in-house and some are outsourced, but the whole of what the family offices do provides the backbone of what all these families require in terms of governance and ownership of some fairly complex projects, operating businesses and projects.

Q: What was/is your role in this process?
A: After working in several industries from commercial real-estate development to telecommunications, I gravitated to management consulting. From there, convinced that our long relationship with Ivan had been critical to our survival (as both a happy family and successful business), I developed a passion for family business consulting myself and specialised in that field as of 2006. I also began to invest heavily of my time and energy into the Family Firm Institute (FFI), which I see as the heart of family-business knowledge around the globe, both for my own education and in order to give back to other families and advisers some of the benefits that we had received from working with Ivan for so long.

After the sale in February 2010 and my father's tragic accident in August of that same year, I took responsibility for creating and leading my branch's family office while continuing to consult for several other families. I continued to increase my involvement with FFI, becoming the first person to contribute funds for the new GEN Programme in late 2009 and eventually joining the Board of Directors in 2014. I have been teaching families and other advisers about the nature and composition of family offices since 2012, and in 2016 grew and rebranded my consulting company to become 55 Fidelius, a true, service-focused multi-family office for the Americas.

Q: What do you see as the future of your family office?
A: I constantly tell families that there is no universal right answer. Rather, the goal is to discover what the right answer is for them at this stage in their lives. It has been fascinating to watch as each branch's family office has evolved in a different way. My own branch of the family has shown a strong preference for individual ownership but collective governance, so our family office is particularly strong at reporting and executive services related to our individual holdings and at project management for the investments we undertake together.

However, experience has taught me that it is not cost-effective to provide in-house financial wealth management services for families with less than US$300 million in liquid, investable assets, so we have outsourced our financial asset management to another multi-family office that specialises in only those types of services.

Our family office will continue to be the core of our family's executive capacity. In the end, that is essentially what every family office is – the ability to do whatever the family needs done. However, my personal belief is that my sisters will, in the long term, prefer to have our branch become a client of 55 Fidelius in order to gain from economies of scale while reducing the risk and workload of being responsible for a single family office.

But whether we remain a single family office or join 55 Fidelius, the family office will continue to provide the operational and executive 'glue' that will keep us working together for decades more to come, and enjoying it!

Our family office relationships start with a conversation. We sit down with each family and talk about their hopes, their goals, the resources they have at their disposal, and the constraints and challenges they face.

Family office profile: Northwood Family Office

Interview with Tom McCullough by Barbara R Hauser

How and why did you start it? Describe the firm's history?
I was a frustrated consumer!

I had worked for over 20 years in senior executive roles in wealth management at a large Canadian bank, and I realised that there was a gap in the market for clients like me. Families of wealth had accountants, lawyers, investment managers and bankers, but they did not have anyone to create a central strategic plan, tie everything together, and make sure it actually happened. I started Northwood Family Office in 2003 with my co-founder Scott Hayman to try and address this gap in the market (and solve my own family's problems).

The family office concept was virtually non-existent in Canada when we started, and up until four to five years ago it remained an idea unfamiliar to many wealthy Canadians. My family was Northwood's first client, and we have now grown our practice to serve approximately 60 families of wealth across Canada. Our 14-year history is a testament to the need for family office services.

How did you choose the name?
The name Northwood actually has an interesting origin. It was certainly meant to evoke the iconic northern forests in Canada, but it was mostly based on the three benefits we want to contribute to the lives and financial affairs of our client families – *direction, perspective* and *confidence*. These three attributes are represented by the three trees in the Northwood logo.

Direction. The first part of our name – 'north' – evokes a picture of a compass, with the needle pointing up to the 'N'. Our experience is that if a person knows their 'north point' – in other words, if they have thought through what is most important to them and their family, including their principles, their goals, and what they really believe in – they are less likely to get lost on their way there. All other decisions become easier and make more sense when you have truly understood what is 'north' for you. We help our clients do this and thereby achieve clear *Direction.*

Perspective. The second part of our name, 'wood', suggests a picture of a forest. If you are standing in the middle of a forest, it is easy to get overwhelmed by the individual trees and not see the forest as a whole. At Northwood, we help our clients by shining the light on the whole 'forest' of their financial affairs. Most people's financial lives are made up of a collection of standalone advisers and products, such as tax, investment, insurance, philanthropy and legal, among others. Because these areas are often kept separate, like individual trees in a forest, the clients are often faced with making 'one-off' decisions that do not necessarily fit in with the whole picture. We help our clients to see the whole proverbial 'forest, and not just the trees' and thereby gain proper *Perspective.*

The family office concept was virtually non-existent in Canada when we started, and up until four to five years ago it remained an idea unfamiliar to many wealthy Canadians.

Confidence. If you have a clear understanding of your *Direction* (knowing what 'north' is for you) and a good sense of *Perspective* (seeing the big picture and not missing the 'forest for the trees'), it leads to a sense of *Confidence* – the confidence that you have a sensible plan, you have made the best decisions you can, and things are well looked after.

This is our name and it is also the promise we wanted to make to our client families.

How do you operate and what services are offered?

Our family office relationships start with a conversation. We sit down with each family and talk about their hopes, their goals, the resources they have at their disposal, and the constraints and challenges they face. We also undertake a full net-worth review, including reviewing all key financial documents, so we can get an accurate picture of the family's current situation. We then discuss what they are looking for from their family office and, together, we tailor a service plan that will work for them.

The services we offer fall into three main categories:

Integrated planning

After the initial client discovery meeting, integrated planning is the next step. Northwood works with the family and their other key advisers to identify priority issues, map out a game plan and develop solutions together to meet the family's objectives. This can include family governance, risk management, and tax and estate planning, among other topics. Our integrated approach allows us to see the big picture and manage all aspects of our clients' net worth.

Northwood's breadth and depth of experience in all key financial disciplines makes us uniquely positioned to pull all the pieces of the puzzle together. In a sense, we act as the 'architect and general contractor' for each family, coordinating all the expert 'trades' and making sure the financial 'house' gets built to the right specifications.

Investment management

A second major area of responsibility is investment management. Our approach to family investment management is founded on five objectives:

- Meeting client goals – we set a sensible investment policy based on our calculation of the capital that will be required to meet each of the family's goals and then work to ensure clients' investments are managed in a manner consistent with those goals.
- Capital preservation – we aim to protect client investments through a conservative approach with appropriate balance between risk and reward.
- Diversification – we ensure client portfolios are well diversified – by asset class, region, manager style, industry group and security – which tends to reduce volatility and increases the probability of goal achievement.
- Superior risk-adjusted returns – we search for, select and combine boutique-style, value-oriented investment managers, who are specialists in their fields and have the potential to deliver superior risk-adjusted returns.
- Tax and fee efficiency – taxes eat away significantly at investors' returns, particularly in a low-yield environment. We take advantage of the tools and structures that can reduce the negative impact taxes have on investment performance. We also use our economies of scale to help reduce fees for clients whenever possible.

Implementation

The third area of focus is implementation. We believe that the finest plans in the world are not worth the paper they are printed on unless they are successfully executed. We focus much of our time and attention on this responsibility on behalf of our clients, which typically includes consolidated reporting, administration, task management and generally making sure the trains run on time and nothing falls through the cracks.

Describe the firm's core value proposition and differentiating factors?

Our core value proposition is that we are an independently owned firm that provides objective, integrated advice and management to families of wealth. We do not have proprietary products to sell to clients, nor do we have incentives to put them into any specific investment vehicles. We simply help our clients see the big picture of their financial affairs and provide them with the implementation expertise that we have developed over many years of advising families of wealth.

Most families already have access to advisers in specific disciplines, such as tax, legal, insurance and investments. However, there is often very little coordination among these professionals, often resulting in an unconnected mix of investments, strategies and services that may not meet the family's objectives. Our role, as a family office, is to develop an integrated plan for family wealth, to identify areas requiring specific expertise and attention, and to direct and manage them in a sensible manner.

When it comes to differentiating factors, the following attributes come to mind:

Independent and nimble

We have always held firmly to our objectivity and our client-first focus. Our boutique nature allows us to respond quickly to client needs and has led us to develop a very close-knit client service team of professionals who know each client family intimately. At the same time, we have developed global reach and a network of independent experts through our founding membership in the Wigmore Association. The Wigmore Association is a collaboration of eight leading family offices from around the world. Our membership in this association helps enhance our understanding of the issues that are most important to the families we serve, and gives us access to significant global resources. [Note from the Editor: See our article on the Wigmore Association in the first issue of the Family Offices Journal.]

Built to last

At Northwood, we have always felt a responsibility to be a family office firm that is built to last and serve both current and future generations of our client families. Our families understand that we need to be profitable and sustainable with a diversified client base, in order to ensure that we will thrive in the future, and can be there for them when they need us. We have always been focused on our succession plan and on building up our younger staff to eventually manage the firm and look after clients. Half of our client service team is under 40 years old, and each member is well-credentialled in the key technical areas of importance to clients. This is of significant benefit to our client families who are interested in a strong and stable family office with the ability to stay independent and objective and to look after the family over multiple generations.

Thought leadership

Family wealth is a complex and ever-changing field and it is important not just to stay current, but to get ahead of the curve on behalf of our client families. We have always strived to differentiate ourselves by seeking out ongoing learning opportunities and sharing the knowledge base that we have built. In 2013, I co-authored a book titled *Family Wealth Management: 7 Imperatives for Successful Investing in the New World Order.* I am an Adjunct Professor and Executive-in-Residence at the University of Toronto's Rotman School of Management where I teach Private Wealth to MBA students. I am also a member of the Editorial Board of the *Journal of Wealth Management* and an Entrepreneur-in-Residence at Western University's Ivey School of Business. My partners and staff are similarly active in the family wealth field. As is often the case in these types of situations, I receive as much or more than I give. But, most importantly, it has allowed us the opportunity to exchange ideas with the best thinkers in the world on topics of critical importance to our families, and to help build up the next generation of integrated family wealth advisers.

Describe the firm's investment philosophy?

We always undertake investing in the context of an overall plan for the family net worth which takes into account all of the other relevant aspects including tax planning, estate and succession planning, philanthropy and family goals and dynamics. We then go through the process of understanding and quantifying the spending goals (both lifetime and legacy) of each client family. We then determine how each of the financial goals is going to be funded and what kind of asset classes are most appropriate to ensure that the goals will be met, with a minimum of risk. Nearer-term and 'must-have' goals will be funded with lower-risk, more-liquid assets, and longer-term or more 'aspirational' goals can be funded with assets that may have more risk and less liquidity, along with a higher expected return.

We then choose external managers in each asset class, with a focus on quality and risk mitigation, and monitor them on an ongoing basis. We are highly sensitive to taxes and fees, which can reduce a family's net worth, and we work to reduce them wherever possible.

What have been some of the challenges?

As with any growing business, we have dealt with several challenges since starting Northwood Family Office in 2003. A few that stand out over the years include:

Explaining the concept

When we started Northwood, the concept of a multi-family office was not well known in Canada. Awareness has increased over the last decade and a half (in no small part due to our active education activities), as we have grown Northwood into the leading multi-family office in the Canadian market. Northwood has been routinely selected as the No 1 independent family office in Canada in *Euromoney*'s Global Private Banking survey. However, in a country where the six big banks have historically dominated the market, we still encounter families of wealth who have never heard of the multi-family office concept.

Finding the right staff

Managing the lives and complex financial affairs of multi-generational families of wealth is challenging and demanding work. It requires a very special type of adviser – one with a wide range of knowledge, significant experience, quiet confidence and an even temperament. Not surprisingly, it can be difficult to find and hire top-quality employees with all of the skills that a multi-family office demands.

This has always been a challenge, but we have also viewed it as an opportunity. The financial and professional services industries tend to operate in silos, so we have had to create our own 'expert

As any entrepreneur knows, you have to be careful not to become bogged down in details. It is all too easy just to keep 'working in *the practice' as opposed to 'working* on *the practice'.*

generalist' family office advisers. Instead of recruiting established silo advisers, we have tried to hire smart and credentialled younger professionals, and then build up their integrated skill-sets over time. This has worked well for us and it has created a very cohesive team with a long-term focus. When you have employees who are invested in the long-term success of the family office, it makes succession planning and continuity of service for our families much easier.

Keeping your eyes on the 'big picture'

As any entrepreneur knows, you have to be careful not to become bogged down in details. It is all too easy just to keep 'working *in* the practice' as opposed to 'working *on* the practice'. As a family office, our number one priority is our clients, and this means being proactive in their lives and responsive to their needs above all else. This focus has served us (and them) well, but if we are not careful, a solely inward focus can lead to myopia. Being conscious of this challenge, we always set aside time each month, quarter, and year to think about the 'big picture' and what client families will need in the future and what we want our practice to look like in the years ahead.

What trends do you see? What are your predictions for the family office market?

The family office industry continues to evolve as more and more wealthy families become aware of the service and of the benefits of objective, integrated financial and life management. I might be biased, but I think that family offices will continue to grow in Canada and globally as the affairs of families of wealth become increasingly complex. At the same time, the interconnection between families and finance has never been stronger. The coming wealth transition from the baby boomers to their offspring will only further highlight the importance of thoughtful succession planning and solid family governance during multi-generational wealth transfers.

As someone who has worked in senior wealth management roles at banks and now runs a family office, I am very aware of the different areas of focus at the two institutions. A family office is easily able to take a consistent client-first approach, but this is not always possible at a bank where the firm's interests often take priority. I believe that to objectively advise families you have to have independent ownership and independent thought. I think it is much more difficult to do that if you are part of a large public financial services company.

What advice would you give?

Over the last 14 years I hope we have learned a few things about how to build and run a successful multi-family office. Below are a few of my most important takeaways.

Start with family goals, not financial solutions

It is tempting (and sometimes even more fulfilling) to jump right into investment or technical solutions early on in a client relationship. At Northwood, we resist that temptation. Everything – and I mean everything – starts with what the family has and wants to accomplish – long before we get to discussing specific investment strategies or planning ideas. We ask fundamental questions like: "*What* is the money for?", "*Who* is it for?", "*When* will it be needed?" and "How high a *priority* is the particular goal?" Only once we have clear and detailed answers to these questions can we move on to the implementation stage of our process. They can be hard questions to answer, but it is worth the effort. They are the critical foundations of a goals-based wealth management philosophy and to making sure we help families accomplish what is most important to them.

Fact-based decision making

The financial services industry is filled with forecasters and prognosticators. There are thousands of people making predictions on everything from stock markets to GDP growth rates to currency movements. While it is good to be aware of and have an opinion on these statistics, we have always focused most of our time and effort on fact-based decision making. Using facts (that can be corroborated) versus predictions (that can't) to guide decision making provides better, more certain outcomes for clients and helps them focus on the most important factors. I can't guarantee you where the S&P 500 is going to be a year from now (and neither can anyone else), but I can tell you what your spending rate is and how likely you are to be able to maintain it over a long period of time.

Control what you can and conservatively estimate the rest

In an uncertain and volatile global investing environment, it is more important than ever to focus on the items that you *can* control. Taxes are controllable, in the sense that every dollar saved in taxes provides a 'certain' additional return with no added risk. Investment costs are another area where we can work to minimise the costs to clients and thus increase their overall returns. Some other areas that we view as controllable are personal spending, how long you will work, when you will sell your business, ensuring a margin of safety in your investment portfolio and the amount of investment risk you choose to take. For the things that no one can reliably control, like investment returns, we use conservative estimates in our planning models. Positive surprises are rarely a problem, whereas negative surprises can play havoc with family plans.

How many employees do you have?

We have 15 employees at Northwood Family Office and are continuing to grow quickly. Of the 15 staff, nine are client facing, including the three partners in the business. Partners are responsible for all client relationships, with support provided by our client management associates. It is important for us to continue to grow staff levels as we grow our client base, to ensure that our clients continue to receive the highest level of responsive service and advice. Considering we started this company 14 years ago with two people working together in one office, I am proud of the success we have been able to achieve and the confidence we have been able to bring to our client families.

An interview with Sue Nickason of Dart Family Office

Q: Can you give us some background to the Dart Family Office?
A: The Dart Family Office was established in the Cayman Islands in 1993. Ken Dart and his family first visited Grand Cayman in the late 1980s and fell in love with the island. Recognising the opportunities Cayman could offer, both as a place to make his family's home and base his family office, he opened a small investment office in 1993 with three employees. Some 28 years later that investment office has grown to become the base of Ken Dart's global operations and Grand Cayman continues to be home to his family.

Q: How many jurisdictions did they consider, and what were the factors in favour of Cayman?
A: The Dart family considered a number of jurisdictions, including the Bahamas and Cayman. After researching the various locations, the family visited the shortlisted jurisdictions. When they visited Grand Cayman, the decision to choose the Cayman Islands was immediate. While it offered the same easy access to the United States with English as the official language as did the Bahamas, Cayman's robust infrastructure seemed far superior and its status as a British Overseas Territory was advantageous (with a sound judiciary). Further, the lack of direct taxation and no restrictions on foreign ownership of property were important considerations when choosing Cayman.

Q: Is Cayman the location of several family offices?
Yes, there are several single-family offices located in the Cayman Islands. Most of these families choose Cayman for the same reasons as did the Dart family. Cayman's wealth management/estate planning legislation (such as the Star Trust and the new Foundation law), safety, high standard of living, stable government and welcoming community are among the reasons why family offices have chosen the Cayman Islands as an address.

> *"On a personal level – for the families and also their core group of employees – Cayman's lifestyle is very attractive."*

Q: Where are the families based, and why did they choose Cayman? Do they have another branch in their home jurisdiction?
A: The families come from around the world – other island nations in the Caribbean, Canada, the United States, Latin America, United Kingdom and Europe in particular. Some have another office in their home jurisdiction, while others only have an office in Cayman. Some initially start with a satellite office in Cayman but then relocate here completely. The move often occurs because the families realise how easy it is to do business in Cayman and the world-class professional service providers that are based here negate the need to deal with time zone changes or travel to other jurisdictions to attend to family office matters. On a personal level – for the families and also their core group of employees – Cayman's lifestyle is very attractive. Excellent schools, reliable healthcare, tropical year-round climate, a sophisticated community of globally mobile individuals and professionals, and superb recreational opportunities all make Cayman very liveable.

Q: How many people work in the Dart office and what roles do they have?
A: We do not provide specific family office details, but Dart global headquarters as well as its Cayman-based development company is based in Cayman and collectively they employ around 1,000 people.

To date, the Dart group have invested over US$1.6 billion in the Cayman Islands and we are proud of the positive impact this makes on the local economy. In addition, the Dart group invest in the community, with a focus on education and developing the future leadership of Cayman though a portfolio of scholarship and mentoring programmes.

Q: What challenges do you see for the future?
A: There is heightened regulatory scrutiny of single-family offices globally, due to a lack of understanding of what a single family does and how it operates. This poses additional – and unnecessary – admin work for families going forward. Family offices in general face

increasingly complex security, investment, ESG and succession planning considerations, and these show no sign of abating in the near future.

The Cayman government has a robust consultation process when amending existing or introducing new legislation, and through Cayman Finance, Cayman-based family offices and their advisers are able to provide feedback and collaborate with the Cayman government and the regulator to ensure Cayman remains a competitive and innovative jurisdiction that adheres to global standards.

Q: What is the network of family offices that you are considering founding? What advantages will it offer?

A: The Cayman Islands Family Office Association will provide thought leadership and best practices sharing opportunities for families, an opportunity for coordinated advocacy efforts and a private network for new families who are relocating to Cayman to join. This association will help raise the profile of the Cayman Islands as a jurisdiction of choice for family offices.

Q: If other family offices are interested in Cayman, what steps would you recommend to help them find out more?

A: We have a team at Dart who assist other families and high-net-worth individuals who are considering a move to Cayman. Our founder, Ken Dart, believes that 'a rising tide raises all ships' and we are committed to the long-term, sustainable future of the Cayman Islands. This includes attracting other family offices, quality businesses and discerning individuals to bring further diversity and opportunity to the Cayman economy.

Our team's extensive experience in the Cayman Islands and relationships with qualified service providers and professionals enables us to assist. Our complimentary services include: meeting with family office representatives to understand their needs and timeframe, assistance with planning a visit – extending preferred rates at our hotels (The Ritz-Carlton Grand Cayman, Kimpton Seafire Resort & Spa and Palm Heights), making restaurant reservations, suggesting activities and neighbourhoods to tour, providing a list of professional service advisers (law firms, banks, etc) and personal introductions to the same, providing information on relevant government services and departments including turnkey services through InvestCayman, sharing customised real estate market data reports, hosting VIP residential and commercial property tours and recommending opportunities on how to enjoy the best of Cayman's fantastic, cosmopolitan lifestyle. To arrange an initial meeting, we look forward to being contacted at relocate@dart.ky.

Governance, entrepreneurship, resilience and reinvention on the five-generation journey of a family enterprise

Dennis T Jaffe, Maya Prabhu and Carolina Cintra

In 1920, Arthur Tavares de Melo acquired his sister's shares in a sugar mill they inherited, which he turned into a sugar and alcohol plant with his wife Helena's eldest brother José Hardman, and her father, Samuel Hardman. Unfortunately, soon after they started, the depression hit. From 1933, the Brazilian government heavily regulated the sugar industry (which they did for 55 years, until 1989). Arthur and Helena had three older sons, followed by a daughter, and several years later by four more sons, who formed the second generation of the family business.

Over four generations, their business overcame its early austerity to become a huge family-owned conglomerate, comprising many businesses and investments. Their family grew to include 27 cousins in the third generation to 63 blood members – ranging in age from five to 47 – in the fourth, and many more being born into the fifth generation. Their public story includes many business sales and acquisitions leading to a family enterprise with many businesses and investments.

This huge success would not have been possible without their family story – of generational transitions and a shared family culture that developed as each business challenge was responded to by an evolving family partnership based on the legacy values espoused from their humble beginning by Arthur and Helena. While their values are at the centre of their story, they were brought to life and revitalised by the emerging family teams in each generation.

The family has always been very private, but they agreed to share the personal story of how their family values, culture and governance developed from a simple partnership to increasingly complex arrangements in each new generation. We interviewed Eduardo and Marcos, third generation family members, Andre, from the fourth generation, and Marcelo Reis, who runs their family office investment and governance entities.

The family developed from its founding to its current place as a family conglomerate, with many entities and shared family leadership. We tell the story through the major transitions in their business and within the family, and how the family faced each one by rethinking their business and family organisation. Their experience suggests there is no single 'secret' to long-term success. Rather, we uncover common principles developed as they moved from the first to the now fifth generation. After each crisis point, the family reemerged with a revitalised governance platform that enabled the business to adapt and grow with the family.

As they prepare to celebrate their 100th year, they identified the principles that anchor their family culture:

- A strong positive family culture of cooperation and common purpose starting in their 1st generation;
- Family members who know and deeply trust each other;
- An ability to anticipate and face new realities, make decisions that may depart from long-standing features of their business; and
- Involving new leaders in each new generation and passing leadership across generations without losing the wisdom of the older generation.

We present each major transformation over four generations, exploring how changes within the family – deaths, decisions to leave, and the presence of new leadership – along with business shifts – sales, acquisitions and diversification – interconnected to create inner and outer reinvention of their structure and governance. The family succeeded because of the engagement and cooperation of three major groups of stakeholders: the elders and their legacy of values and business wisdom; business builders who developed business discipline and focus; and the entrepreneurial energy of each new generation.

First transformation – shift to cooperative business leadership by second generation brothers

After 15 years of partnership, in 1943, Jose died suddenly. It was the middle of the Second World War, and a difficult time for the business. Arthur was now burdened with the entire responsibility of running the business. He and his father-in-law decided to sell the business. That might have been the end of it. But his three eldest sons – Vinicio, Virgilio and Murilo – wanted to run the business themselves. With hard work, they bought shares in the business from their parents, who in turn delegated the administration of the business to them. This was the first sign that there was a special drive for a family partnership: the sons were still teenagers – aged 17 to 21. Only Vinicio, the oldest, had finished college! Thus, the business swiftly passed to a second generation. They succeeded because of their hard work, along with support and advice from the patriarchs and Samuel Hardman.

After the war, they expanded by purchasing and building new businesses, so that each brother was able to run one of them. The mills were their life; each brother lived on the land near his mill. The younger brothers eventually joined them and worked at the mills as well. While having space for each to run their own mill, the brothers met weekly and saw themselves as stewards for the growing family. They had a strong commitment to shared values and collaboration which became the core of their family culture.

Matriarch's influence

Family members can exert informal influence behind the scenes that play a key supportive role in the business and the family. While the brothers and their sister were the shareholders, they drew support and learned values from their mother Helena, a force in their lives until she passed away in 2000. The third generation remember that grandma was a silent partner, playing a strong role in aligning everyone. Major decisions were all shared and approved by her. One third-generation family member recalls, "My grandfather delegated very young, and my grandmother had great influence on decisions. She had a really strong personality".

Her strong and quiet presence was seen as helping the family avoid the tradition in Latin families to appoint a single strong single patriarch. Instead, they created trusting, highly engaged cooperation and shared leadership. Her great-grandson Andre feels that her example set up a cooperative ethic for successive generations that enabled them to work together and resolve problems without escalating conflict:

I like to think of her as the Chief Trust Officer. She was the person that would evaluate and coordinate people, it is not a formal position. [She told us] it's better for you to think of business first and family second because as you do something that is good for the business then the business goes well, and the family plays well alongside. If you start doing things to accommodate your family situation and that starts to interfere with the business, then it's a major limitation for the future of the business and the family itself. You must be very pragmatic on that. You cannot allow yourself to do things to accommodate this person or that person but to try to do it in a consensus way is always better.

The family had a Sunday lunch at her house, which helped keep the family connected to each other. But the family wondered what would happen when the grandparents were no longer with them, and their numbers increased beyond a single dinner table.

Business acquisitions

As a result of family growth, the new second-generation members wanted to expand and diversify by seeking new businesses. In 1953, the family founded a fruit juice business, Maguary, managed by three of the younger brothers, until its sale in 1984.

The sugar business was moving from the northeast, starting mills in the south centre of Brazil where the climate was better, and production costs lower. They decided to invest in this new region and used proceeds from selling Maguary for purchases.

During the 1960s and 70s, the sugar industry was very profitable, allowing the family to expand and diversify by starting and buying other companies. In the early 70s they bought more alcohol distillers and created an ice cream company, years later joining Kibon (Philip Morris Group) in a joint venture. The family now owned faster-growing and more profitable businesses along with their sugar cane roots.

They recognised that the company had expanded far beyond a trio of sugar mills, and that they needed to professionalise and clarify their structure and decision-making process. The family engaged an adviser to strengthen their governance, guide the succession of the eldest ones and keep the transparency of the process (something that they've always valued). This exemplifies the family pragmatism to keep the family together by anticipating future moves. The consultant made several proposals which became their initial governance, consisting of a shareholder's agreement and rules for family employment. Specifically, they created:

Family members can exert informal influence behind the scenes that play a key supportive role in the business and the family.

Since the family had a collaborative culture that emphasised consensus, the trio of family leaders wanted to listen to and include their younger siblings, who they realised would soon be their successors.

- a new and more centralised organogram of the decision-making process and policies; and
- new and clear rules about the relationship between family and business, and how family members would enter the business.

Second transformation – departure of a business leader; splitting the business

With their acquisitions, the family enterprise was thriving into the 1990s. The growth and increasing complexity and the involvement of the third generation, led to a need for further change in their business governance and ownership. Since the family had a collaborative culture that emphasised consensus, the trio of family leaders wanted to listen to and include their younger siblings, who they realised would soon be their successors. They wanted to avoid potential conflict and competition for positions and provide a fair and clear roadmap for entry.

For this reason, they developed policies and practices around transparency, making decisions and defining ownership and business roles for each of them, as well as their soon-to-be adult children.

The second-generation younger brothers were many years younger. Some of the 27 third-generation cousins worked in the business. After decades of working together, different branches of the family had different agendas. It was clear the family would benefit from clearer policies about future ownership and management.

Leadership was also in flux. In 1993, the three eldest members from the second generation passed leadership to one of their younger brothers – Romildo – who became President. He saw himself as the bridge to the next generation.

In 1994, after nearly a generation where the three uncles worked in their mills every day, they were presented with a huge dilemma. Murilo, the youngest member of the trio of elder brothers, announced that he wanted to leave the company and the remaining brothers agreed to split the business to allow this to happen.

Another third-generation family member recalls: *I believe all these decisions were hard for everybody, they worked together for 50 years and suddenly they had to split the business and leave ... but I believe this was very smooth. I do not remember any big problem in this; we presented the values of the companies to my uncle and his sons, they decided to take the sugar mill and that was it. We separated the business. The family is very pragmatic in these situations; we decide always not to compromise, to affect the business; you must decide what's best for the family but also what's best for the business.*

It is unusual for a family to manage such a split cooperatively and in a way that everyone feels is fair. The younger family members attribute their success to their ethic of cooperation, established by their grandparents. Instead of a structure where there was a single patriarchal founder, the family had a deep culture that stressed cooperation for business success for everybody.

Third transformation – entry of the third generation

At the turn of the century, the family faced a major shift of their business and generational succession. The five remaining brothers and their sister had 27 children, ranging from 20 to over 50 years old. Their holdings were taking a very different form from the sugar mills and related companies run by their fathers. The family had professional structures in place, so the third generation faced a family enterprise no longer owner-operated.

Some third-generation family members worked in the business. They expected to become the new leaders, but with so much talent and dedication, the second-generation brothers wanted to ensure that the process of succession was fair, organised and inclusive. This is the point where many successful families face business and leadership challenges as the new generation has different capabilities, values and agendas. Conflict and competition can easily arise. They wanted the process to be as professional and independent as possible, so in 2002 they engaged another outside consultant to work with them to organise succession.

The consultant was asked to 'evaluate' each third-generation family executive and propose changes to the company structure and who would best succeed Romildo. The new structure, announced in mid-2003,

It can be awkward when family members, who have already made a commitment to the family enterprise by choosing to work there, are asked to shift roles, responsibility and authority.

was implemented with the next generation taking control. New leaders were selected based on capacity and qualifications, irrespective of their family branch. The eldest cousin, Carlos, was named President, Eduardo was named commercial VP, Marcos became financial and business VP and Mauricio was the operational VP.

The business environment was strong and vibrant. Brazil was thriving and restrictions on businesses were being eliminated. After a decade of accumulating businesses in the 90s, the rise of competition and the entry into the market by huge multi-national businesses led the family to decide to sell some of their older, maturing businesses. Other companies they knew, including COSAN, Brazil's largest sugar mill company, had just gone public with an IPO. The family explored a joint venture in some new areas, or sale of part of their business, to a larger firm. This didn't work out, and in 2007 this process culminated in a huge milestone event for the family: they sold their legacy ethanol and sugarcane plants to Louis Dreyfus Commodities.

Fourth transformation: selling legacy business; establishing the family office

With the sale, the family moved beyond a 90-year legacy into new territory. The second and third generation would come into an inheritance of substantial resources that needed to be invested. With one move, the family was transformed from a manufacturing to a financial family. They had to decide their next step, and whether they would remain together as a family. They realised that they once again had to improve/adjust/adapt their governance policies for how they made decisions, who would participate in the move forward, and what form that would take.

How did the sale affect generational and role transition as ownership and management passed to their third generation? It can be awkward when family members, who have already made a commitment to the family enterprise by choosing to work there, are asked to shift roles, responsibility and authority. While they may have been successful and mastered their role in the business, now they had to manage the shift from being owner-operators of huge industrial businesses to that of a financial family. Everyone had to learn and change.

The family took a huge deep breath, as they made sense of their new reality. Before they could act, family members had to decide what they wanted to do and whether to remain together, or each branch go their own way.

Sale of the legacy business is a major turning point for a business family – with the huge liquidity, many families choose separation. This makes sense especially if their identity as a family was with their operating business; without it, their interests separated and there was no need to remain in business together. But there is another path, taken by a minority of families – to remain together and develop a new focus and identity. With their shared history and culture of collaboration, the Tavares de Melo family chose to continue together. The creative task they faced was how to do that.

The new identity for the family enterprise was contained in their family office. Marcelo Reis joined the family to help organise, implement and head up their new investment structure, a position where he remains today.

Marcos described the transition after the sale:

We knew we had to have an office to manage the real estate and all these things, so we brought in some people that used to work with us at the sugar mill, opened a new office, sat with our uncles, and created some rules for the family office to work in the beginning, very basic rules. In 2007, after we sold the business, we hired an adviser here, to guide us about how to structure the liquidity so we could meet the family goals, objectives and give the freedom for (everyone) to leave or stay as they pleased. We created a structure that we have today. Of course, it changed a little bit, so most of the people invest the liquidity together but they have the freedom to leave if they want. We are now 14 years later but most of the family still invest together. We are partners, we have real estate and companies together, up to today.

The new family office enabled them to pursue other investments. Given their commitment to collaboration, as they considered each new investment, individual family branches and sometimes individuals, could decide whether they wanted to be part of each new venture. The choice continues to this day. They worked actively to sustain their shared family identity. While they retained some shared ventures in land, as they embarked on new ventures, they allowed households to opt in or out of each new opportunity. For example, a venture called Sensatto, owned by three of the six family branches, invested in new ventures. They formed what could be called 'a family marketplace', in which the family shared opportunities as they met regularly.

The family now owns or has large investments in over 50 companies. The family is hugely entrepreneurial, generating new ideas and pursuing new investments continually. With their liquidity, several branches began passing ownership to the third generation. As each brother passed ownership to his offspring, the nature of the board, decision making by the owners, and their new business entity, was in flux. The third generation had their own ideas, and everyone was involved.

As branches and households invested separately, the family was organised as a holding company containing all family owners. Their legacy values were updated into a unique and special culture with three core principles:

- *Freedom to choose to invest.* While every family member had a share of ownership in the family office, everyone had a portfolio of investments. When there were new liquidity opportunities, each person decided whether and how much to invest. So, ownership in the office portfolio began to differ for each family.
- *Consensus decision making.* The family was democratic and collaborative; every choice was collaborative.
- *Separation of family and business activities.* Creating a family assembly and council that sustained the history and legacy of the family and developed the values, skills and commitment of the new generation to them. The emerging governance structure divided family from business activities, with clear links and interconnections between the two:

Fifth transformation – sustaining family identity and resilience through family governance

As the family office developed, and a new generation acquired ownership, there was a need for further development of family relationships in the new generations. After a generation of brothers as owners, now each family branch contained several owners, with different amounts of ownership. Despite the ownership differences, as a family they wanted to treat everyone equally. Like many evolving family enterprises, there was a difference in rights and responsibilities for each family member as a member of the family and as an owner of the business. Alongside their portfolio of businesses and investments, there were family-based activities that had nothing to do with the business, in which everyone participated.

The six branches now contain 174 second to fifth-generation family members, representing a diversity of views, concerns and familiarity with the business. Andre remembers that when the business was sold "80% of the fourth generation family members didn't have a clear idea who their cousins were, or the family history". Only he and his cousin Mauricio Filho worked for the family. Since they wanted to be a trusting and collaborative family as well as an

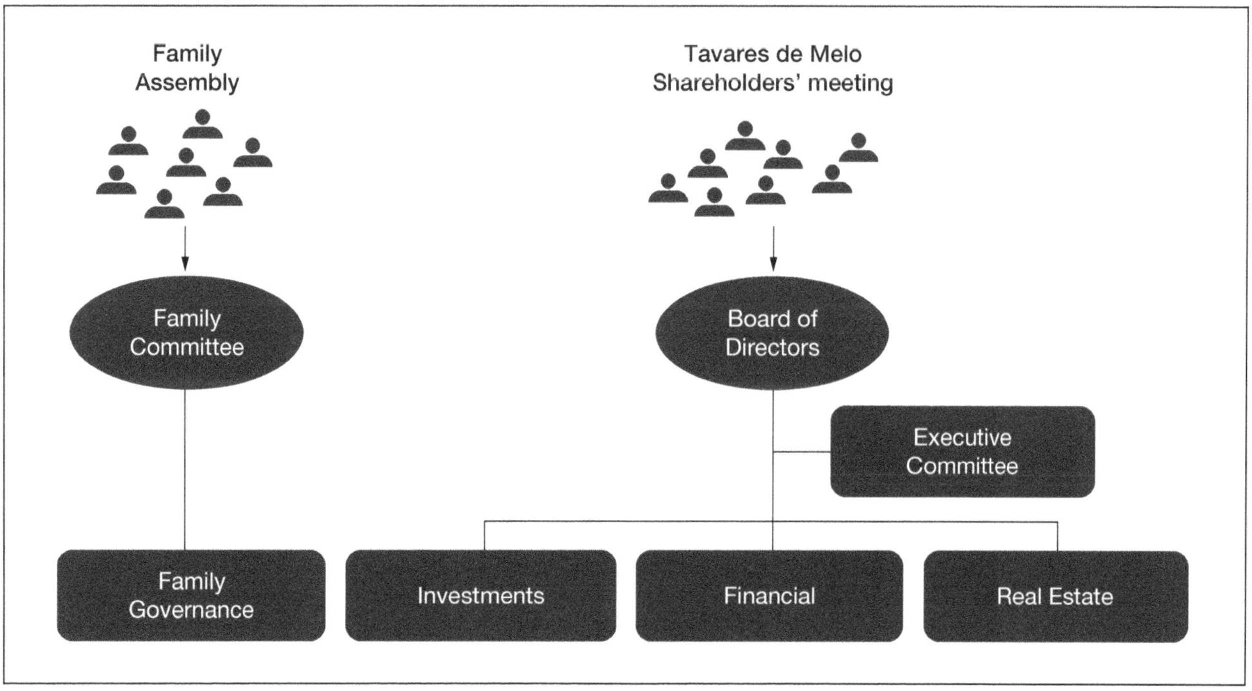

investment group, they had to build a structure, policies and activities that sustained the family alongside their business board. Their governance defined a clear organisation for the 'tribe' of family households that expressed their legacy values.

In 2012 they convened a large family meeting for members of the six family branches. When they were smaller, they remembered having family dinners, but now they were spread out, with many households, some living in different countries. To get to know each other, they had name tags with their family branch. As they got to know each other and imagined their shared future into new generations, they shared information about family finances and businesses, and what they were doing personally and in their careers.

Their family governance contained two entities:

- An annual family meeting, where the entire family got together to celebrate their family history, build personal relationships, educate and prepare their rising generations and have fun together.
- A family council – the executive committee of the family – that represented each family member – young, old, married-in – to define and set up shared non-financial family activities.

The family council represented the family, operating alongside the business board of directors. It met monthly and contained a family member from the older and younger members of each of the family branches, for a total of 12. The council saw itself as the legacy keeper of the family values.

The council and assembly identified four goals to guide the family:

- Keep the legacy and transmit this *legacy* to the next generation, not only the next generation, but all family members.
- *Provide the best communication* to the 122 family members of the second to fifth generation (or by including spouses the number goes to 174 and growing every day). They contain divergent people, branches, opinions, values and interests.
- *Integration of the family members.* With fourth and fifth generation members living abroad (US, Europe, Canada), they are no longer a Brazilian family. It's a worldwide family.
- *Educating and preparing* the next generation for involvement and leadership.

Project Legacy develops capability within the rising generation

To sustain the family legacy, the family initiated an all-encompassing initiative, Project Legacy, an ambitious programme that consisted of three levels. A family member had to complete the first level before they could go on to the next.

As Andre, one of the fourth generation working in the business, explains:

Level I focused on the family's values, with a strong content of storytelling. The younger ones would gather to hear the histories to the foundation of the business from one of their uncles, they've got to hear ... most of them did not hear these stories because the business was sold about 15 years ago and some of them were younger ... they didn't have time to feel that experience ... the first part was really focused on values and storytelling. This value and communication and storytelling part lasted for about six months with several meetings; we even displayed some movies from my grandfather and others. All of them were stored online so they can be seen again or by people who have not seen them before. A family member had to complete this programme before they could advance to the other stages.

Marcelo continues:

Level II focused on technical and soft skills, governance. The idea was to make sure that everybody had the minimum content in their heads to become a responsible stockholder. Even though they didn't want to run or take part in running some business ... they need to know the importance of governance and financial planning and leadership and things like that.

Level III was the entrepreneurial part, to develop and stimulate the entrepreneurial aspects of each family member. We assembled teams that came up with new ideas for business. Each team had to develop a business plan and go though every step of developing a business plan, so we did it for another year. There were six groups with six different projects, almost 20 members involved. One of the groups was living in Portugal. They shared their business plans with the family and got feedback. One of them was even selected for implementation.

Coming transformation – succession to fourth generation leadership

As members of the fourth generation reach their 40s, some have begun to work in the family enterprise, and others may enter. Now three generations from the

---

The challenge is to get each new family member committed to the shared enterprise and prepare them for the complex roles of leadership in both family and business governance.

Challenges never end. A family can never coast and relax very long before they must consider new ways.

founding members, the challenge is to get each new family member committed to the shared enterprise and prepare them for the complex roles of leadership in both family and business governance.

As Andre notes:

We have some different challenges. The first was about the structure and the value of sticking together. As the new generation has a different way to see the world, they still should see the value of staying together. I worked in the company for about seven years then went on to work at other companies, as an executive, and rejoined the family business four years ago.

It was more straightforward when we used to run actual businesses, because there were more transactions going on and by the time we sold and transitioned from operators to investors it became more of a challenge. Things are not tangible as they used to be. The main topic now is how to align and engage these newer generations with the company and its values.

In the Tavares de Melo Group, we have four fourth-generation family members working together, three of us without executive positions (between executive committee and the board). We talk a lot about how to engage our cousins, how to work with them, how to open communication channels, how to bring their backgrounds to the business. We have capable people that are not directly involved with the business, but we want to use their experience, to leverage their knowledge from being in other businesses into our families.

Leveraging the learning of the rising generation

Project Legacy is not their only effort. It will lead to other programmes, adding to the development of each new generation, as Andre explains:

We are now creating a new programme for carrying on. The original Project Legacy is now giving birth to two new programmes, one that is more focused in content and it's open for every family member and another one that is more focused on the business so we want to capture these experiences these other family members have, but cannot give it back because they are running their own businesses ... my brother, for instance, works for JPMorgan, my cousin, Mauricio, works in a commodities company, we do have a real estate company ... and everybody is scattered in a different business ... so we want now to capture their experiences and bring it back to the business. We, ourselves, are going to present the business as we run it today and then they are going to evaluate and fix it and we'll have some assemblies and webinars and things like that. We want to capture their experience and bring it to the family business.

Marcelo commented:

With the pandemic we are discussing new projects, Project Future, that we are telling, and communication and the main topic is to continue this formation and this training, and we are having online classes, webinars to tell the story and the next webinar will be an interfamilial webinar ... we are inviting another large multi-generational family from Recife to join and exchange experiences with us.

What can we learn from this history?

The five-generation, 100-year journey of the Tavares de Melo family is a story of each generation adding both financial and non-financial wealth to the family enterprise. Each generation built upon the legacy values and success of their parents, as they took the family and its business in new directions. From sugar mills to business conglomerate, we see some themes that are shared by all the generations that may be the foundation for their success.

In the introduction we shared four principles they see as accounting for their success at continual development in each generation:

- A strong positive family culture of cooperation and common purpose starting in their first generation;
- Family members that know and deeply trust each other;
- The ability to anticipate and face new realities, make decisions that may depart from longstanding features of their business;
- Involving new leaders in each new generation and passing leadership across generations without losing the wisdom of the older generation.

These are continuities that lead back to the original vision of Arthur and Helena, that were internalised and remembered by each successive generation. But the world changed radically, many times, in their century of development. We end their story with four observations of what they did to thrive across generations.

Challenges never end. A family can never coast and relax very long before they must consider new ways. Every generation faces crises and must reconsider what has worked for many previous years. The family was able to anticipate and innovate continually, sometimes before a crisis. Each generation was able to reinvent the family enterprise in some radical ways.

To understand their success, we must look at their story as an evolution. Each business challenge and the emergence of a new generation led the family to make huge choices and enter new territory. They would not have succeeded if they were not resilient and continually rethinking what they did. We can see that the family office was an almost inevitable consequence of their business choices, as their success produced liquidity, diversification and increasing numbers of family owners. By choosing to have each family member to make choices about what to invest in, the family office, and its board of directors, became a family enterprise centre.

Their governance operated according to legacy values set in the first generation. But to evolve, these values had to be examined, updated and reaffirmed by each generation. The values continue but they must be implemented differently. The basic trust and cooperation of one generation must be actively learned by the next generation through a long period of apprenticeship and learning. Trust and cooperation arise from working together and each generation must learn that again. The family has invested time and energy in preparing and teaching the members of each new generation, and when their time comes the older generation has been ready and willing to step aside and make room for new leaders.

Governance must evolve with the family. Governance is the organisation of the family as a family and as a family enterprise. As the family grows in number and the business grows in size and complexity, in each generation governance has to be revised and developed further. From a few simple business principles and basic communication and family meetings the family has developed a complex and multi-faceted family governance organisation.

From the story of the Tavares de Melo family, other families who are not as far along can be inspired but also learn the enormity of the task that is faced by a family enterprise that seeks to thrive for many generations. We can look back at the cooperation and trust of the second generation of brothers, and how this was a model for development for their children and grandchildren.

Dennis T Jaffe, PhD, is senior research fellow at BanyanGlobal family business advisers, and author of Borrowed from your Grandchildren: The Evolution of 100-year Family Enterprises.

Carolina Cintra, based in Miami, is a senior wealth adviser at JP Morgan Private Bank, advising Brazilian families (alongside their legal counsel) in defining strategies and creating customised solutions of tax and succession planning, including multijurisdictional situations and family governance. Before joining JP Morgan, Carolina worked at Itaú Private Bank, Tozzini Freire Advogados and PricewaterhouseCoopers.

Maya Prabhu, based in London, leads JP Morgan Private Bank's Wealth Advisory practice for the EMEA region and the International Family Governance practice. She helps individuals and families articulate the goals for their wealth, and advises on family governance, philanthropy and on the establishment of family offices. Maya is experienced in working with families from a range of cultures including the UK, across Europe, Latin America, the Middle East and Asia.

Governance must evolve with the family. Governance is the organisation of the family as a family and as a family enterprise. As the family grows in number and the business grows in size and complexity, in each generation governance has to be revised and developed further.

Family office profile: VALUEworks AG, Zurich/Switzerland

Interview with Kecia Barkawi, CEO and founder of VALUEworks AG, by Barbara R Hauser

Tell me about your work experience before you founded VALUEworks?

After law school, I joined GAM (Global Asset Management) in Zurich as a private client lawyer to provide legal support to global families of wealth and manage trust structures to hold their diverse assets. It was a fascinating job that taught me a lot about the challenges associated with private wealth, as well as the different approaches to addressing them. After three years I transferred to GAM's Bermuda office where I structured and oversaw the trust operations. Despite living on a dream island, it was a challenging job. I was the youngest and the foreigner in the team yet I had to be a role model and train local staff twice my age.

Following GAM, I returned to Zurich to work for the private client business of STG-Coopers & Lybrand. I was responsible for a large client portfolio, mostly complex wealth-holding structures, for affluent multi-generational families from Northern Europe, Africa and South America. Like GAM, STG managed the bankable assets as well as the holding structures, so in addition to my work as a trust lawyer I became more involved in the investment side. Some families were engaged in philanthropic activities and I looked after their charitable trusts and foundations, a role that I found fulfilling and fascinating.

What led you to create VALUEworks?

I was brought up in an entrepreneurial family and had always enjoyed taking the initiative and engaging with people. When STG's sale was announced in 2003, I knew it was time to move on. It took me one long weekend to decide to set up on my own. After 10 years in the private client industry, I had a broad understanding of what global families were looking for and saw a growing demand for independent advice from a team which truly cares about and understands a family's hopes and fears. Passionate about multi-generational families, private wealth and international law, this is what I wanted to do.

How did you choose the name?

I was searching for a name that would be a wordplay on my ideas. One evening my husband and I listed all the words that could be part of that name and it ended up being a long list of ... values! That's how VALUEworks was born. Today, the values-based approach to working with families is part of our company DNA.

What were some of the early challenges?

Back in 2003 I knew that it would not be easy to start a trust company. Financial markets were unstable and there were regulatory and transparency pressures coming from the OECD's Financial Action Task Force. However, I realised this could be a real opportunity for a dynamic new player who did not have a 'legacy business'.

Another challenge was that I set up the company alone. I had two shareholders who supported me financially, but no sparring partner in the office. If I started over, I would not do it solo again.

So, you founded a trust company and turned it into a multi-family office?

Yes. We initially offered comprehensive and hands-on management services for family wealth-holding entities, many of which were trusts, and provided financial accounting and reporting. The main focus was on tax and estate planning for the global wealth owners. In addition, we managed our clients' charitable foundations and provided strategic philanthropic advice, using a distinctive values-based approach.

The more I worked with families, the more I came to understand that there was a need to go beyond tax and estate planning and the monitoring of financial assets. The bigger challenges for a family are the ones that place the family itself, rather than its assets, at risk. In those cases the question whether investments perform 2 or 6% rapidly moves down the priority list, and other critical issues emerge. When dealing with families for decades you realise that there are dynamics and patterns that can have a damaging impact on their well-being. Once internal family communication breaks down, it becomes difficult to find a solution and when a family loses touch with its values, no amount of wealth can bring the members back together.

Against this background we introduced our values-based approach across our offering, and to client onboarding, thus making the family members' values a core pillar of all the services we provide to them. At the same time, we added family governance advisory and next generation education. So today we are a fully independent multi-family office with a comprehensive tool set, providing families with strategic guidance and operational support in matters of wealth.

What about investment services, what do you outsource?

While we support clients in asset allocation, bank and asset manager selection, and performances and costs monitoring, I made the decision early on not to provide investment management in-house. We have an outstanding network of financial advisers from banks, asset management firms and family investment offices from which we can draw expertise for our clients. This is key for us to ensure there are no conflicts of interest and to maintain our independence.

Where do your families come from?

Most of the families we serve are global families with cross-border concerns. The majority come from Europe and an increasing number from Africa, South America and Asia. Many have a US connection, which is an area we focused on early in our wealth management services.

How big is your staff today?

We are currently a team of 11.

What makes VALUEworks different?

I would say it is our independence and the holistic approach to dealing with families and their wealth.

Being independent allows us to offer advice with impartiality and full transparency. We work solely in the best interests of our clients without any ties to other service providers.

Our holistic approach to family wealth focuses on three aspects: family values, family risks and family governance. We help our clients in developing a joint understanding of their core values as the foundation for their wealth management and governance decisions. Through a comprehensive risk-mapping tool, we support them in identifying, addressing and mitigating risks to the families and their individual members, their financial well-being and their reputation. Moreover, we support clients with family governance such as communication, conflict-management and decision-making by empowering family members and providing often-neglected moderation and implementation work. We believe that the responsibilities of wealth cannot be delegated and pay particular attention to the dialogue between the generations, providing tailored training, coaching and advisory to future wealth holders.

Increasingly, this holistic approach leads many of our clients to reflect their values in their investments and their philanthropic activities. We support them on their path with strategic advisory as well as with guidance in the growing field of sustainability and impact investing.

Our commitment is to go beyond traditional wealth and estate planning and to focus on preserving wealth alongside family values, and financial security alongside social responsibility.

What are some of the accomplishments that you value highly?

It is great to see the accomplishments we achieved together with our clients and seeing the positive impact they have through their wealth – whether it's through their entrepreneurial activities, their investments, or their philanthropic engagement. Being at their side, looking forward, and helping their next generation to step into what are often very large shoes is extremely rewarding. It was an honour to be recognised for our innovative approach and our

---

Our holistic approach to family wealth focuses on three aspects: family values, family risks and family governance. We help our clients in developing a joint understanding of their core values as the foundation for their wealth management and governance decisions.

---

holistic offering with the Multi-Family Office of the Year Award from STEP in London in 2012.

Personally, an important accomplishment was setting up the Swiss Women + Philanthropy Initiative in 2013. This peer network for female wealth owners of all age groups exchanges ideas on ways to give, grow and share. The aim is to motivate and inspire women to give more, and better. One of the highlights was for 40 of us to spend an afternoon with Nobel Peace Laureate Muhammad Yunus discussing new humanitarian ways of doing business.

Looking ahead, what are your goals for the next five years?

We are continuously working on strengthening our offering and reach in family advisory and creating greater awareness about the need for families to focus on their human capital.

In addition, we are currently expanding our investment advisory offering to include impact and sustainable investing and financial consolidation services. We also see a growing demand among our families in direct investments and aim to grow our capacity to support them better in this field.

Finally, I would like us to deepen our engagement with the next generation of wealth owners who are often advocates in their families for the type of values-based wealth management that is at the heart of what we do at VALUEworks. Supporting them in their aspirations and commitments to responsible wealth and sustainability is a key goal for us in the coming years.

It is important to recognise that the various family members might have a different culture, values, interests and aspirations. When analysing investment opportunities, they often have different objectives, competencies, time horizon and risk profile.

Family business, family office and next gen

Fabrizio Arengi Bentivoglio

Introduction

Starting in the Anglo-Saxon world, but rapidly spreading throughout the globe, many businessmen are wondering how to manage the family wealth, meaning the resources outside the core business that refer primarily to the family members. In that light, the family office has become a way to manage – with a professional and structured approach – the financial resources that were previously considered 'savings', more than active investments. Clearly, this trend is more relevant in certain countries than others since the family office culture presents various degrees of sophistication on a country-by-country basis.

Initially, the family office is in a sense residual in nature, the professional focus remains centred on the operating core business. The approach of this kind of family office is to concentrate in long-term, safe investments. The actual business, the one that generates financial returns, is something else.

As wealth grows and with it complexity, the family office becomes a true investment firm which requires professionalism and specialisation in portfolio management instead of individual investments.

In this context, it is important to consider some critical issues, such as:

- It is necessary to have a fair representation of the various family members of the family office and the different generations; this does not mean that everybody needs to be involved – actually, better if they are not – but the various members of the family and the various generations need to have, directly or indirectly, a seat at the table;
- It is important to make decisions that are clear, shared and agreed among stakeholders; additionally, there must be agreement about the decision-making process, the information flow, the reward system of the management as well as the family members with operating responsibilities;
- There must be a clear conflict-resolution process and a system to allow family members to exit the family office if they no longer wish to be a part of it.

It is important to recognise that the various family members might have different culture, values, interests and aspirations.

In fact, it is important to recognise that the various family members might have a different culture, values, interests and aspirations. When analysing investment opportunities, they often have different objectives, competencies, time horizon and risk profile. All of this is even more complicated when there are various generations involved as the implications could be very difficult to manage.

And so, we need to decide on the following:

- Where shall we establish the family office?
- How shall we set it up and manage it?
- How shall we preserve and protect it for the following generations?

Jurisdiction

The first and most critical decision is about the jurisdiction of the family office. Where the family office is incorporated will have important and long-lasting implications not only in terms of financial returns, but also for tax purposes. Moreover, the jurisdiction will impact the ability to attract and retain professional resources which may find the lifestyle offered by a particular location more or less attractive.

The choice about the jurisdiction has additional important implications. In fact, it not only has an impact on the geographic focus of the investments – unless the family office is large, the tendency is to be located in the region that represents the investment focus – but the related tax implications will impact the family office itself as well as its members, ie the family, not to mention the family desires in terms of lifestyle since certain locations might be ideal for managing the investment portfolio, but less desirable for the family lifestyle.

Size matters

"Size matters" is a commonly accepted slogan which applies in the context of a family office as well. In fact, size determines which functions will be kept in-house and which ones will be outsourced. Generally, tax and legal are managed through outsourcing so as to be able to access the most qualified competencies at a variable cost. However, large family offices may consider even these functions critical for achieving the best financial returns and therefore might decide to keep them in-house. Accounting is certainly a key support function and the decision to keep it in-house will depend on the reporting needs. Finally, compliance will be more or less critical depending on the number of family office members, their representation and involvement and therefore how much they are part of the operations and investment decisions. The larger the family office and the number of family members, the more likely that accounting and compliance are kept in-house as these functions become critical processes to share information, especially with the family members who are less or not at all involved with the operations.

Managing the investments, as opposed the family office, is a completely different issue. Regardless of the size, family offices take a mixed approach. Certain asset classes – those that are considered strategic, more long term, and/or part of an area of expertise – are managed internally, while professional asset managers are relied upon for other asset classes.

Finally, size will determine the ability to attract and retain professional competencies and will have a direct impact not only on the quality of the management team but also on the cost structure of the family office.

Governance

Governance is essential for an efficient management of the family office, but I would add it is even more important for managing the transition to the next generations. Governance drives the success of the family office for the following generation and the future of family members.

When talking about governance we need to separate the governance of the family office from the governance of the investments. In the latter, it is essential to delegate to professionals, especially so for large family offices. These professionals could be internal or external to the family office and, once again, it will be size that will drive this decision – size matters, remember? Whether these competencies are internal or outsourced, it is essential that the governance drives the definition of the investment strategy and supervision of the investment processes and activities.

On the other hand, with regard to family office governance, notwithstanding the importance of professional advisers, the involvement of the family members remains essential, not only for their competencies but also for a more objective and unbiased input.

Investments

With a clear objective of achieving the best performance while at the same time managing risk to preserve the wealth of the next generations, family offices tend to invest in a diversified portfolio, with a focus on liquid assets, private equity and real estate. Lately the industry has shown a growing trend towards co-investments, partially reducing the exposure to hedge funds.

Finally, family offices tend to invest alongside other family offices, regardless of each other's dimensions and ticket size, based on common values and similar investment strategy, approach and investment horizon.

Investment policies

Governance is extremely important as it defines the investment selection process which needs to be aligned with the long-term strategy of the family office. In fact, decisions about the various investments, asset classes, expected returns, risk profile, time horizon just to mention a few criteria, need to allow for the transition to the next generation at the appropriate time. There should also be mechanisms and processes to allow for family members to exit the family office should they decide to do so. If, for example, there is a transition to the next generation in the near future, then short-term, more liquid, less risky investments will be preferred to guarantee the availability of the cash required for the generational transition.

Branding

Another important decision is about the branding of the family office: shall we include the family name or not? While there are several pros and cons for either choice, it is clear that the decision has implications not only on the management of the family office,

---

Governance is extremely important as it defines the investment selection process which needs to be aligned with the long-term strategy of the family office.

---

but also with regard to the transition to the next generation. Not to mention that the successes (and failures, unfortunately) of the family office will be directly associated with the family should the family office be branded as such.

G3

All of this is critical because often the third generation is referred to as the 'generational drift', meaning that it bears the responsibility of coming after the 'pioneer', the first generation and the second that develops, expands and brings the business to a new global standing. Unfortunately, the third generation often suffers the increased complexity and the lack of processes and systems to manage the difficulties, especially in an environment that becomes more competitive. It is the governance, the processes and systems that support the family office and help navigate a complex environment in a timely and efficient manner.

Conclusions

Why is all of this important? It is because families grow and with them their assets grow (or at least they should), and one of the consequences is that managing the family office becomes more complex and therefore it requires new and improved capabilities, focus and vision. However, the beauty of a family office is that the business model, the strategy and its implementation can change more rapidly than for an operating business, sometimes multiple times even during the same generation.

Fabrizio Arengi Bentivoglio is a third-generation family member, chairman and CEO of Fidia Holding, the single-family office of the family who exited their pharmaceutical family business in 2007. Fabrizio draws on extensive professional experience having worked in the United States, Europe and emerging markets such as China, India and Latin America. Fabrizio is a member of the Council on Foreign Relations and the Council for the United States and Italy.

Single-family offices in the 21st century – remaining fit for purpose

Iraj Ispahani and Carl Sjöström

Often the comment is made glibly that no single-family office is the same because each is built around a single family and all families are inherently different. However, there are many things that owner families can learn from each other as they build, structure and manage family offices. Those contemplating setting up a dedicated single-family office today can also learn valuable lessons about issues and challenges, costs and benefits of privacy and control from precedent. With Covid-19 having changed the global socio-economic landscape, including reframing the dialogue around responsible wealth ownership, this is an opportune time to review one's family office operations and adapt its structure and remit as required to ensure it is resilient and fit for purpose for the remainder of the 21st century.

The linkage between business and society has been reinvigorated. Profit maximisation needs to be balanced with a corporate purpose; with businesses actively considering the needs of their wider stakeholders and not just their shareholders. Trust needs to be restored. With significant ownership of many listed entities now held through funds and passive vehicles, the ability of shareholders to influence corporate agenda change will be an important feature of this evolving landscape. While a heightened focus on sustainability by businesses is necessary, it raises many questions. Some of the changes that have taken place early in this century are positive and essential to our societies. Some of the changes are, and will be, destructive of family businesses and wealth. Disruption is likely to increase, partly driven by technological advances. Positive reputations for families and their businesses in this fast-evolving environment will likely be more difficult to maintain. What are the implications for family offices today?

The evolution of a family office

In the early days of a family business, the owner-operator typically uses the company's staff and his or her own personal advisers to manage all tax, legal and banking matters. This is the 'embedded family office' and it evolves using existing resources to address the family's needs. It often relies on the CFO and the company secretary who are already fully occupied with their corporate responsibilities. Little distinction is made between the family and the business at this stage until the capacity and skills to serve the family's interests clearly need to be added to. This leads to the adoption of a more proactive approach with which a host of pertinent questions arise: What do we need? How is it best delivered? What expertise should we bring in-house and what should we outsource? Who do we need to hire? How arm's length will it be? What oversight is required?

As families and their advisers come to understand the importance of separating the functions of the 'three circles'[1] – business, ownership and family – it becomes clear that while the business circle has a structure of management and support services and the owners have boards of directors, the family circle often has no organisational support.[2] Many families respond by creating, first, a family council to handle the interpersonal aspects of family ownership and, second, a family office to handle the financial and technical tasks. In these owner-investor family businesses the family council and the family office become the primary coordinating structures linking all aspects of the operation: wealth generation, wealth management, continuity, philanthropy and the family legacy. Where a family office has been created with no linkage to an operating business the role and structure will most likely be less complex.

A family office that serves a single family can be an integral part of family governance through which a decision-making framework is created encompassing leadership and family communication. The aim of the framework is to create cohesion in a family and support succession planning. Core to this is a family constitution[3] that captures the objectives and the essence of the family. The constitution formulates and formalises the family objectives into a strategy. Many families create a constitution as a good hygiene factor but don't implement it since embedding governance often requires behavioural change. Some constitutions also include a family office mission statement. Such a definition is a good starting point for a new family office as it helps align family members to the purpose which has been defined as well as providing the basis for its creation.

What can we learn today from families who are already dealing with scale and complexity in their family offices? With Ispahani Advisory's longstanding experience in the family arena and supplemented by a range of recent conversations held over lockdown with families of significant wealth, we want to share some perspectives which may be timely and helpful as we all look ahead.

The conversations

The conversations held were open-ended discussions with representative members from a dozen families and sought to highlight the issues around existing family offices and how families see them evolving in the future. Those we spoke to were members of a broad mix of families who carefully coordinate their affairs, including:

- Families based across Europe and Africa (we also had additional input from Asian and North American perspectives).
- Wealth created in the 18th, 19th, 20th and 21st centuries, represented by first through to eighth generation wealth owners.
- Wealth originating in manufacturing, distribution, retail and services businesses. Some families still own the original operating businesses, some have moved into different sectors and some have divested.
- Families using a single-family office structure (the majority of those we spoke to) and those using a shared multi-family office structure or no formal shared office structure.
- The number of family members whose affairs are coordinated range from six to over 1,000.
- The family offices have been in place in their current form between less than three years and more than 50 years.

What does the family office do?

A family office is an organisation, the main activity of which is to assist family members with their personal affairs in a coordinated manner, in particular around tax, legal and investment matters. For the families that we spoke to:

- A common feature is for the family office to provide advice on professional service providers, such as banks, insurance companies, law firms and accountants and to maintain relationships and negotiate rates with them.
- Many people think of family offices as private fund management firms and most of them do invest funds on behalf of the family and/or family members. However, there is a clear trend away from the family office providing discretionary investment services in traded securities, for example stock picking, towards providing advice on fund management services, acting as a fund of funds and/or advising on the selection and evaluation of third-party fund managers.
- Investment management remains a key activity in supporting the family in illiquid investments, in particular property and private equity investments. It is noteworthy that a number of families were explicit in favouring investments aligned with the family's values and fields of interest. If the family has deep expertise in a sector there is a tendency to double down with a less diversified portfolio and where a family has environmental or social objectives these tend to have a strong influence on investment choices too.
- Most of the families we spoke to no longer or never offered family members a concierge service coordinating travel, holidays or other personal matters. Most were strongly against such service coordination, with several having experienced it as divisive and conflict creating. Some family offices assist in the management of family properties, but again the potential for internal conflict was noted for those families too.

The Red family decided against a concierge service. "We don't want those tasked to make money to also be in charge of spending it. Cost control is difficult when you are also spending the money. If we want to travel or need something booked we do it ourselves."

Family inclusion and values

All the families we spoke to have a clear view of what the family is, but that view varies from case to case. For some the family is defined by the person who created the fortune and all subsequent generations are included, regardless of the financial situation. For others, only those who have a financial stake in the family business are included, perhaps extended to their heirs and possibly a further generation. Clear tensions arise when the family grows and dilution of wealth occurs. Sharing a name, blood and heritage becomes more difficult to coalesce around. The

A family office is an organisation, the main activity of which is to assist family members with their personal affairs in a coordinated manner, in particular around tax, legal and investment matters.

Most families found the definition and articulation of values to be quite difficult so they remain relevant from generation to generation.

definition of the family is therefore critical to how the family office operates and aligned with this are the values that the family espouses and adheres to.

How the family's wealth should be protected and grown depends on a multitude of factors but for many it is the core values of the family that are central. Most families found the definition and articulation of values to be quite difficult so they remain relevant from generation to generation. A common problem is that words may be adopted but are not clearly defined and so the values do not get embedded. For some families a dominant patriarch or matriarch have at times slowed work on developing common values, which need broad buy-in, but several of the families we spoke to have addressed this by tasking the next generation to deliver a solution.

The Purple family have agreed and adopted a set of statements over time that they see as the guiding values. "You can't say we all share the same fundamental values as people. However, we do have shared values for the assets we own together as a family."

Helping to hold the family together

Several family offices were originally set up at a point where two family members shared ownership of the operating business and many others were set up to protect the interests of the family when it grew. Avoidance of conflict within the family and conflict resolution are important considerations for most of the families we spoke to. Wealth suffers when conflicts arise and family cohesion is therefore paramount. Hence, one of the most important features of a family office is its role in facilitating education and communication as a neutral, trusted and confidential nexus. The family office is typically governed by a family board set up by the family council, with external trusted advisers providing input either directly or indirectly, and all family members meet with the family office representatives on a regular basis.

The White family addressed discontent within the family by overhauling the operations of the family office, increasing the frequency of contact with all family members, introducing a customer satisfaction survey and stressing the value of services being competitive by introducing an annual charge for membership of the family office.

Education is also critical in addressing a key concern raised by most families – to make sure that wealth does not become a disabler for the younger generations. Several families ensure that younger family members are educated in both understanding the key operating businesses but also, and more importantly, in financial matters to help them become 'better owners'. Most do not rely on the future generations' abilities to run operating businesses but they do need them to be able to make the right investment and divestment decisions to maintain and grow the family's wealth.

The natural tensions within a family of factors such as increased size, diverse interests, different risk appetites and geographic spread have also led most of the families to expect their family office structures to be relatively short-lived, even where they have a long history. All were very alert to the reality that even a large fortune can disappear quickly and that nothing can be taken for granted in an increasingly unpredictable world. All the families therefore wanted the family office to have a role in keeping the family's interests together but for it to be seen to earn its keep while being under constant review for continued relevance.

Single-family office or not?

A family office, in particular a single-family office, costs money to run and most of the families we spoke to had reviewed or were reviewing the costs and benefits as well as the services provided. Most hold that the family office must pay for itself but does so in different ways, such as through:

- Putting a value on owning and controlling the information.
- Closing down unprofitable areas, such as active stock picking and concierge services.
- Spinning off non-core services that have become less relevant for the family to maintain but that have a commercial future outside the family office.
- Charging participating family members fees for membership and/or services.
- Charging operating companies fees for services.
- Using family wealth as leverage to reduce third-party fees.
- A combination of the above, assessed against the external market on both quality and cost.

A significant majority of the families we spoke to have a single-family office in place to coordinate the affairs of a defined group of family members. When different family office structures were considered most elected not to share with other families in a multi-family office due to concerns over trust and privacy, wanting to own their own information, perceiving their needs to be sufficiently unique, in combination with funds being sizeable enough, to justify setting up their own family office. However, some of the families we spoke to had decided not to use the single-family office model for reasons other than costs, though they had the very same concerns.

The Orange family decided against a family office, concluding from the experience of surviving several geopolitical events where family members found themselves located in different countries that such a structure would not work for them over the long term. The family wanted each branch of the family to have independence and to use the operating company as the focal point for the extended family.

The Blue family knew a multi-family office well and decided against a single-family office model. To address the trust and privacy issues they set up a board of family members and trusted advisers to instruct the multi-family office as well as instructing other service providers and advisers, thus ensuring independence and confidentiality as well as competitive service levels and rates.

Using external advisers

All the families we spoke to make use of external trusted advisers to provide a combination of impartial views, technical expertise and outside perspective. Trust and discretion are paramount and advisers are often tested over long periods of time by either having been professional advisers to the family, such as lawyers, bankers and accountants, business associates of the older generations or former senior executives in either a family operating business or the family office. The trusted advisers typically sit on the family's operating company boards or the family office board but may have no formal role as such.

Attracting and rewarding talent

The people employed in family offices are typically recruited from professional services firms, banks or other family offices. The key attributes that families tend to look for are, first and foremost, trust and discretion, followed by technical competence. Many families are grappling with wanting trust, discretion and loyalty while also requiring a measure of staff turnover to ensure that competence and innovation keeps the family office prepared for future challenges.

Roles within family offices are distinctive from other similar roles. They tend to have more limited career trajectories but they also tend to have more autonomy and direct influence on the business. That said, family offices are often quite hierarchical in nature. The most senior employees, such as the chief executive and the chief investment officer, typically have personal interactions with and privileged access to the family, thereby separating them from the rest of the team to a greater extent than if they were at an independent firm of a similar size.

To attract and retain staff most families wish to pay well but don't always do so. As part of our research, we held a number of discussions with Botoff Consulting in the United States.[4] Botoff Consulting specialise in compensation studies of US family offices, where this is a relatively well-defined employment market. Interestingly, we found that when speaking to non-US families there was no consistent definition of the market for talent, the type of remuneration plans offered or what performance is most important to reward. Remuneration packages range from fixed salaries only to salary plus a discretionary bonus to salaries in combination with formal bonus, long-term incentive and a carried interest structure. Performance requirements similarly range from discretionary assessment of the quality of executing the family's wishes to value of funds under management to business strategy success.

Botoff Consulting has found that in the United States there is a clear correlation between family office AUM and the levels of compensation. There is also a lot of commonality in remuneration approaches. For larger family offices, with assets under management in excess of $1 billion, some 90% provide annual incentives, 95% review and adjust base salaries on an annual basis against peer benchmarks and approximately two-thirds use long-term incentive plans (deferred incentives, co-investment and carried interest being the most common).

All the families we spoke to make use of external trusted advisers to provide a combination of impartial views, technical expertise and outside perspective.

Most people were very alert to the real risk of the family's wealth being eroded within one or two generations, whether through the family growing, family ties weakening or wealth being poorly managed or spent.

The family office as part of the family governance

The families we spoke to all have family governance high on their agenda. They all have or are working on a family constitution and all have some sort of family board representing family members' interests. The position of the family office within the governance structure varies from sitting within, above or completely separate from the operating businesses. The role of the family office tends to be impacted by its position versus the operating businesses, in particular in terms of oversight role, separation of interests and how advice is used.

A key differentiator is whether the family is still involved in an operating business or not. The views on the importance of the operating business and the family office's involvement differ significantly. Some see the operating business as synonymous with the history and core of the family, others see it as a chapter in the history of the family. Some believe that the family office should have minimal links to the operating business, whereas others consider it difficult to draw exact lines between where the operating business ends and the family office begins. It appeared to us from our conversations, however, that the existence of an operating business created a stronger emphasis on family cohesion and that this often impacted the family's commercial decisions, in particular around very mature assets seen as iconic for the family. There is also some distinction in approach between entrepreneurs and longer-established business-owning families that have a family office. Entrepreneurs will typically create a family office after a liquidity event so have a greater focus on investment governance while business owners will also have ongoing business governance to factor into their thinking.

Protecting and growing wealth

Linked to the importance of the operating business is what a couple of families articulated as the need to differentiate between the part of their wealth which must be protected for longevity and the part that can be risked to create a new fortune. Most people were very alert to the real risk of the family's wealth being eroded within one or two generations, whether through the family growing, family ties weakening or wealth being poorly managed or spent. For some the operating business has the role of risking capital to create new wealth and the family office's role is to protect for longevity. For others the family office should do both and is seen as a natural source of investment capital when a member of the family is looking to set up or invest in a business. This can be described as the 'family bank'[5] though the families we spoke to differ in their approach to this, such as:

- Not allowing investments in family members' businesses, thus also avoiding conflicts of interest issues.
- Supporting investments only by helping the family member negotiate with banks and other advisers.
- Guaranteeing loans up to a capped value if the investment idea passes scrutiny.
- Making loans and investments at commercial rates with formal, planned exit strategies.
- Insisting on governance of a set standard, imposing family office chosen board members if performance is not meeting the business plan.

When acting as a family bank, the family values dilemma becomes even more critical for the family office. Where families have worked extensively on their common values, they typically translate these for investment purposes and give them a significant role in all investment evaluations. Most families recognise the growing importance of this, not only for internal reasons but also to navigate the increasingly complex areas of environmental, social and governance requirements and expectations from different stakeholders.

The Green family have evaluated all investments against ethical criteria for over 40 years. "We test investments against risk and moral appetite first, before we even consider the ROI, and we set KPIs accordingly for those who work in the family office."

The Brown family has two social and environmental areas that they want to prioritise and test all investment decisions and actions against. They see this as essential for the culture within the family office and the businesses they own. "Culture is essential – it is not bling."

One of the most unexpected findings from our conversations is the doubt many share as to the longevity of the family office.

Conclusions from our conversations

Single-family offices are built for different reasons, in different ways and the organisational structures that support a family will vary. These offices may be created purely to support one generational transition with a planned winding down of the organisation and distribution to beneficiaries after the founder's death. Other family offices are created specifically to support family longevity and cohesion across several generations. In some cases, family office capabilities are created which, while integral to family governance, do not require a dedicated standalone family office organisation. The success of any family office, however, starts with clarity on the family's objectives. These objectives are centred around the purpose of the family's wealth and need to be articulated clearly. This is important for the family now and for future generations, as well as for those employed by the family office.

Our conversations showed that there are many versions of a family office, indeed a few family representatives noted their dislike of the term as they associate it with something different to what they have created and wish to achieve. That said, there are a number of interesting points raised in our conversations indicating the general future of the family office and learning opportunities for those setting one up or reviewing their structures and choices.

To us there are three key take-aways for single-family offices. First, a core reason for having a single-family office is to retain control over information while benefiting from economies of scale in handling family members' affairs. Second, the success of a single-family office structure depends on how well it serves as a neutral nexus for communication and education to and between family members. Third, the family needs to keep the family office under constant review to ensure that it remains relevant and an enabler for future generations and further wealth creation.

Drawing on our experience and the experience of those we spoke to, other learning points can be summarised as:

- Family offices are mainly used to:
  - ensure best advice on technical services, such as legal, tax and investments;
  - identify and execute investments in illiquid assets; and
  - educate and communicate with family members.
- The key trends for single-family offices are:
  - investment in technology to support resilient family office infrastructure is likely to become increasingly important;
  - a move away from own discretionary investments in the trading markets towards the selection of third-party providers; and
  - as a consequence, a move away from hiring deep expertise, putting more emphasis on trust and confidentiality;
  - greater focus on formulating an effective risk management framework to identify risks, develop risk mitigation approach and proactive risk monitoring; and
  - paying more attention to the complexity of compliance around managing cross-border wealth.
- Key concerns are:
  - the need to develop explicit strategies for both protecting wealth and creating new fortunes by taking calculated risks;
  - that a family office can fuel the disabling aspect of wealth for the upcoming and future generations; and
  - how to articulate the family's values and make them implementable.
- Also worth noting is that:
  - investment strategies tend to follow a family bias;
  - the structure of the family office tends to follow purpose; but
  - the positioning of the family office versus operating businesses may have a significant impact on how those businesses evolve and how the family office works; and
  - family offices which embrace a learning and digitally enabled culture are more likely to survive and thrive.

The future of the single-family office

One of the most unexpected findings from our conversations is the doubt many share as to the longevity of the family office. If the family office is seen as a temporary solution to a changing situation it begs the question whether the exercise is worthwhile? We note that families have been generally pleased with the value to date, but if a family office is going to have a future one needs to define the direction of travel. To us there are three particular areas that should be considered, where we see opportunities to make family offices more 'evergreen' organisations.

From disabler to enabler

As we have noted, wealth becoming a disabler is a key concern that most of the families we spoke to share. Currently, family offices mainly address this through education and communication, providing younger generations with the tools to be owners and insights to make investment decisions. To do this and to recognise the need is very important but we also see a developing role for family offices through first redefining family wealth and then protecting and developing it as encompassing human, social and intellectual capital in addition to financial capital.

The family office as an organisation

To be sustainable and to be able to evolve the scope of its activities, a family office must be recognised as an organisation but without sacrificing its representation of the 'family circle'. Much of this is standard for an operating business but for a family office it is often overlooked due to size and control, with the family office seen as an extension of the family. However, since the family office is not staffed just by family members it is harder for it to survive the changes that the family more easily adapts to, such as geographic moves, political risk, management changes and new values. Family offices increasingly need to build their platforms with careful use of technology and digital data management to remain agile and relevant but also so that the family office can as part of contingency planning replicate itself in a fallback jurisdiction if circumstances require.

The family office as a business

One of the greatest risks we see with family offices is when they pursue areas that are better met by other providers or that are not relevant to the family. However, having broadened the scope and structured the organisation, there are opportunities for a family office to develop its own commercial value that should at least be considered. Family offices, as extensions of the family, can present interesting opportunities to disrupt and challenge established operating models. For example, one of the recent noteworthy developments is the emergence of the family office as a competitive force in private equity. Previously mainly a key source of capital, family offices increasingly do their own deals. What makes family offices interesting in this space is that they can compete with strengths that are difficult to match for private equity firms. Family offices can turn family ownership into competitive advantages by, for instance, working with much longer time horizons and drawing on deeper and more current expertise. Family offices can also trade financial returns for strategic advantages and draw on reputation in ways that private equity firms struggle to do as they are bound to the limited life of each fund.

If family offices are to remain relevant for the remainder of the 21st century they will have to stick to their knitting and remain cost-conscious but also be open-minded, agile and prepared to consider new ways of working. The question of what is best done in-house versus outsourced or via partnerships should be asked with increasing frequency in a business world facing disruption.

Iraj Ispahani is CEO of Ispahani Advisory Ltd and based in London. Ispahani Advisory advises family businesses on business strategy, governance, people and education. Iraj also serves as a Group Director and Board Member of the Ispahani Group, a family business headquartered in Bangladesh which marked 200 years in 2020. Prior to joining the family business, Iraj held global and regional leadership roles in banking at JP Morgan and organisational development at Korn/Ferry. He also co-founded Cantos, an online corporate communications business in 2001. Iraj is Chair of the Shakespeare's Globe Council and an independent trustee of the Standard Chartered Foundation. Iraj is an adviser to UNICEF in the United Kingdom and in Bangladesh and a member of the UK Development Board of the International Committee of the Red Cross (ICRC). For more information, please see: www.ispahaniadvisory.com.

Carl Sjöström is an independent senior adviser to company boards and management, working across Europe and with most industries and forms of ownership. With a focus on reward and performance, Carl is a frequent speaker and commentator on topics of strategy, executive pay and corporate governance issues from an international perspective. For more information, please see: www.vitisolutions.com.

1 R Taiguri and J Davies, "Bivalent Attributes of the Family Firm", *Family Business Review*, Volume 9, Issue 2, 1996.

2 B Murray, KE Gersick and I Lansberg, "From back office to executive suite: the evolving role of the family office", Lansberg Gersick, 25 January 2018.

3 Philip Marcovici, *The Destructive Power of Family Wealth – A Guide to Succession Planning, Asset Protection, Taxation and Wealth Management*, Wiley, 2016.

4 Botoff Consulting (www.botoffconsulting.com), Single Family Office Executive Compensation Survey, 2019.

5 E Lee, P Marcovici and S Liniger, "Family businesses and the increasing importance of the family bank", Institute for Family Business paper, August 2020.

There has to be a reality check on any vision or dream. For example, do the family members really have the capabilities to work together, the skills to lead the business, and the money to invest in the business (or in other joint family activities)? Furthermore, there should be active consideration of the obstacles that must be overcome in order to achieve the vision.

Essential Reads *on* Governance

Case study – design and set up of a family investment office[1]

Guillermo Barandalla

In 2019 we decided to reestablish the family (wealth) investment initiative, by designing what would be a fully professionalised investment office.

The initial focus was on creating a company that reflected how an institutional investor (asset owner) should act, from the profile of the team to its internal procedures.

To achieve this aim, we decided to tackle the project using an internal consultancy approach, which gave rise to six independent projects that, on completion, would produce the intended design of the office.

These projects were defined and developed internally in the following way:

- Tax issues project – which had a dual objective, (i) to construct the new company on a solid foundation of compliance and (ii) to take informed decisions, or in other words, to be fully aware of the existing investment formats, so that the path was chosen with the necessary criteria.
- Best practices project – its main objective was to identify investment companies (asset owners, specifically family investment offices) similar to ours, learn from their experiences (positive and negative) and find out, at first hand, about their approaches and corporate models. In addition, this work implicitly allowed us to establish interpersonal relationships that did not previously exist.
- Industrial knowledge project – this project would make it possible to exploit one of the competitive advantages of the business family, which is their specific business experience (compared to starting up an investment office with wealth but without this background). The fact that this initiative is led by a family with a history of business success would allow the investment office to be built on a foundation of knowledge about management, internationalisation, technology and more, potentially exportable to any of the investment areas.
- Technology project – understanding this term in its broadest sense, to include both technical financial calculation aspects and the technology systems used in investment activities. Regarding the former, and especially in the area of determining asset allocation, external suppliers with the appropriate quantitative models were selected. For the latter, software providers that allow both investment and monitoring and control tasks to be carried out were analysed.
- Organisational structure project – given (i) that decision making (in the investment area) had to be worked through, debated and, finally, contrasted and (ii) the intention was to use external specialist knowledge but without overloading the corporate structure, the proposal was to form two committees. The first was responsible for reflecting on the evolution of the office itself and the role of the business family. The second was tasked with specific aspects of the investment actually made and the economic and financial outlook.
- Corporate image project – finally, it was understood that the investment activity should have its own image as this would help with intangible aspects such as employees' sense of corporate belonging, corporate reputation, the talent recruitment and, in general, the scope of an independent entity.

From Table 1, three important aspects should be highlighted from the family perspective:

- the best practices project allowed the family to verify first-hand the lack of a single family wealth management or investment model, arriving at its own opinion on the basis of all the alternatives observed. This was an experience of testing (with qualified third parties) the internal initiatives we planned to carry out, reaching the necessary level of knowledge[2];
- the industrial knowledge project was one of the biggest challenges within the general approach taken. Far from focusing the business knowledge acquired on the sector in which the family business operates (the opposite was closer to the truth), it was a case of using ingenuity, hard work and intelligence to distil that added value so that it could then be applied to the investment office's activities[3]; and finally,
- the organisational structure project allowed us to complete the team with professionals of great value and experience who would not otherwise be involved.

Table 1: List of projects, questions they answer and some aspects they cover

In the regulatory field: What is the current situation? What paths should or should not be taken?	Tax issues project	✓ Tax analysis ✓ Impact by asset class and scenario ✓ Implementation
What are the others doing?	Best practices project	✓ Context of equals ✓ Understanding the situation ✓ Being aware of existing models ✓ Best practices versus set-ups to avoid ✓ Networking
What elements of our starting position can we use to support the office?	Industrial knowledge project	✓ Extracting knowledge from the family business (management, industrialisation, technology, internationalisation, etc) ✓ Additional collaboration with universities and consultants ✓ Networking with external professionals
How will we do the calculations regarding asset allocation and markets monitoring and investments?	Technology project	✓ Construction of the asset allocation and generation of scenarios ✓ Market monitoring ✓ Reporting
How can we organise the structure to enable reflection, contrasting and decision making?	Organisational structure project	✓ Advisory body ✓ Bodies as part of the investment process ✓ Activity map and procedure for investment monitoring and decision making ✓ Attracting external talent
How will the above produce an investment office with its own personality and characteristics?	Corporate image project	✓ Give the investment activity area its own image (family role as seen externally, attracting talent, belonging, etc)

With regard to the latter, in terms of the internal team, two professional profiles were initially included: (i) one in charge of internal tasks related to the areas of accounting, compliance, control, treasury and reporting; and (ii) another in charge of the investment activities and corporate strategy.

The above was supplemented with a team of outsourced professionals responsible for legal aspects in both the commercial and tax areas.

In general, within all of the above, each area was responsible for involving the best people and sources of knowledge possible, both nationally and internationally (taking them from professional associations, education, specialist reporting and experts). In addition, reputable suppliers were chosen in the area of information technology (investment, back office, governance, etc).

In addition, these tasks were supplemented by other specific ones, of which we can highlight three:

- the drafting of the investment policy statement and procedures regulating the activities of the investment office;
- the outsourcing to a specialist company of the integration of ESG aspects into the investment activity; and
- the specific tasks to define the strategic asset allocation (supported by the technology project).

On completion of both the six main initiatives and the supplementary ones, the outcome was:

- a team of internal and outsourced professionals heading up each of the defined positions, in charge of leading and performing the activities;
- an external team (advisory, via committees) of specialists from different areas, capable of

Figure 1: Areas of work to design and set up the investment office

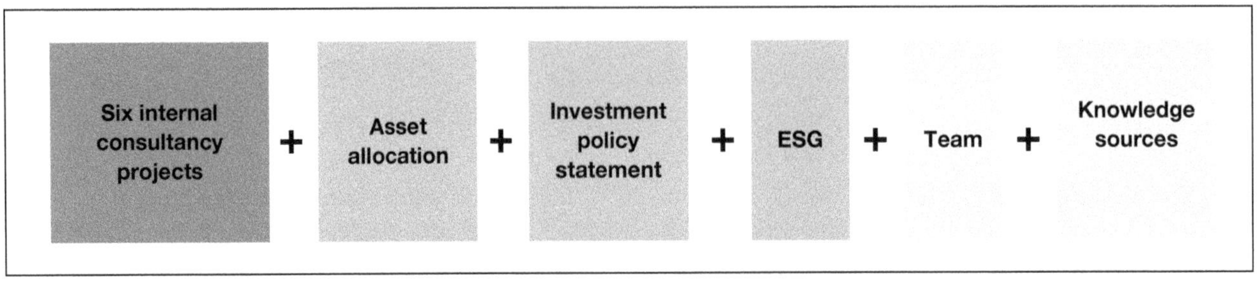

providing specific knowledge and checking the actions carried out by the office;
- control of all the office's activities through an investment policy statement;
- appropriate investment and reporting software;
- a business plan that follows a previously defined strategic asset allocation;
- a process for taking investment decisions;
- a code of conduct and ESG integration that reflect the highest quality standards;
- in short, a company with its own identity and an institutional investor (asset owner) profile, with a high degree of family buy-in to everything carried out, due to their first-hand involvement and participation in many of the initiatives.

Finally, it is worth mentioning that in this case all corporate governance issues had already been worked on and correctly implemented,[4] so this did not form part of the work to design the family investment office set out above. Otherwise, it would have been an important part of the projects listed.

Guillermo Barandalla, CFA, works as chief investment and operating officer for INJAT, the investment office of Jose Antolin Toledano, Honorary Chairman of Grupo Antolin. In 2019 he joined the project to perform the tasks of designing and setting up the family investment office.

1 Comments and recommendations stated in this article rely on the author's opinion. The author is not responsible for its suitability to another investment office set-up initiative.

2 "The aforementioned work allowed us, after thirteen visits to other family investment offices, to confirm that there were very different approaches. However, in all cases, their activities were designed to fulfill the purpose for which they were created.

In general, as with the family business since its foundation, the qualitative objective inherent to these offices was to promote family unity. In the investment area, they are usually focused on wealth preservation and contributing to the family's peace of mind.

The above was achieved by maintaining a consolidated family asset allocation with balanced risks. In many cases this went hand in hand with the acceptance that any business ambition had already been fulfilled with the family business (with capital preservation being more important than growth when it comes to the investment activity).

From the perspective of focus, being aware of its capabilities and defining what is not going to be done is very helpful; part of the success having been in knowing how to say 'no' to certain opportunities.

Similarly, the investment office, as the decision-making core, must be capable of internally maintaining control of all initiatives carried out, such as developing and maintaining its own investment criteria and culture.

Finally, but no less importantly of course, treating backoffice matters as important and providing the right level of information, transparency and enthusiasm in relation to the family were a guarantee of the future of the family investment office." (INJAT private research, "Spanish Family Investment Offices: Best Practices, 2019–2020", October 2020.)

3 On this point we must clarify that the existence of the family business affects the investment office, not only on the positive or constructive side but also by introducing reasonable restrictions on the scope of the investment (in the areas of concentration, asset profile, liquidity, asset class type, sector, geographic area, investment philosophy and emotional or behavioural finance).

4 The application of best corporate governance practices in family businesses plays a decisive role in professionalisation and favours the longevity of companies.

From this point of view, INJAT had already decided to incorporate governance procedures that would favour the involvement of the board of directors, transparency in decision making, access to information and debate; all of them focused on value maximisation and empowering the stakeholders' relationship.

The intangible value of corporate governance has an impact on the strategy and long-term view consensus in such a way that we could say that there is a virtuous circle of trust and profitability.

One of the responsibilities of the board of directors is to focus on the medium and long term, monitoring both market and inherent company risks. All of this generates enough control and stability to enable managers to focus on their own areas. This atmosphere creates the robustness needed to broaden market and financial alternatives for the company.

In conclusion, corporate governance provides stability and reduces conflict. It is an element of corporate culture that came to stay.

Family mission vision and values statements: the essential foundation of an effective family governance system or just another form that cannot function?

Christian Stewart

The family office might ask the family it supports for a family mission statement or a family vision statement or a values statement. Are these essential documents to form the foundation of an effective family governance system?

Will the family council be able to make better decisions on behalf of the family if it has a written family mission statement or family values statement to guide it? Does the culture of the family make a difference? Would these kinds of written documents be more expected and more helpful to family decision-making for a 'Western individualistic' family, as opposed to an Asian 'collective harmony' culture family where 'things are understood' and there is naturally a more collective orientation within the family?[1] How can a family office offer guidance to its family on this issue?

The term 'mission' seems to be most helpfully understood as referring to purpose or goals – a family mission statement therefore referring to the stated shared purposes or goals of a family. The term 'vision statement' refers to an ideal picture or image of how things should be in the future (ie, it has a future orientation). A 'values statement' refers to a statement of the core values of (in this context) a family.

Family values – how to capture them?

Dennis Jaffe, in his book *Stewardship in your Family Enterprise*, declares the following:

- Values are not created by a values statement; they are already there and just need to be highlighted and recognised.
- Values are about behaviour; and when a value is stated, it should be clear what sort of behaviour is expected – a values statement needs to specify what the values mean in action.
- There is always a gap between stated values and actual behaviour. We have to make a distinction between 'espoused values' and 'enacted values'.[2]

Dr Jaffe stresses the importance of starting with each individual looking at their own individual values, before moving on to developing a set of shared family values. This process helps to bring home to a family the point that there are always both individual values and shared family values and the two very naturally coexist. He writes:

> *The challenge is to take this work seriously – not to simply hold a half-day workshop and come up with a values statement that does nothing more than gather dust on the wall. The values that you define must be used as a yardstick for evaluation, as a basis for dialogue about what is right, and to help the family company respond to new realities without sacrificing what was special and important in the past.*

Mission and vision with a family business

In the context of a family that own a core operating business, experts consistently state that family enterprise continuity requires:

- a united family and capable owners;[3]
- family commitment to the business and a shared vision for the business and the family;[4] and
- commitment from the family to the collective enterprise, together with a 'shared dream', which is a collective vision for the future of the family enterprise.[5]

To get to the purpose or goals of the owning family, critical questions that the family should be discussing include:

- Why do we want to be in business together?[6]
- Why do we want to work together?[7]
- What does the family want to become by working together?[8]
- Why should we stay together as a family and as owners of this enterprise?[9]

- Should the family remain together as an entity?[10]
- Is the family there to serve the business or vice versa?[11]
- How much do we want to be connected and how much do we want to be independent?[12]

Randel Carlock and John Ward, in their book *When Family Businesses are Best*,[13] stress that an effective family business vision (FBV) has to lead to action. Specifically, it has to lead to the current generation of owners confirming their commitment to continue ownership of the business. 'Commitment' here refers to an active relationship between the family and the business and the contribution of talents and resources to the business.

To develop an FBV, the authors outline a very practical and grounded approach of including a consideration of family values, business potential, family expectations and family investment. They state that an FBV flows from a consideration of the values of the family and should in turn flow into a family commitment to the business that includes a decision as to what kind of investment the family is willing to put into the business. In short, is the family really willing to 'put its money where its mouth is'? Developing an FBV should point to the kind of dividend policy, for example, that the family wishes to adopt for the business.

Carlock and Ward have also written about an "enterprising family model" where the family decide that their goal is to grow a great family, and the business becomes viewed as a portfolio investment of the family. Ward writes:[14]

The Enterprising Family sees family as the central purpose. It sees innovation, quality and significance – how it conducts its affairs – as the core values. The Enterprising Family creates opportunities for most, or all, of the interested family members to participate and contribute to the collective good. The Enterprising Family focuses the challenge as personal family leadership of the family's priorities. The Enterprising Family has the privilege of supporting all members of the family, especially those with special needs. Special care for the match of talents and corporate needs is appreciated.

Ivan Lansberg, in his book *Succeeding Generations*,[15] says that developing a shared dream is the basis for successful family business succession. To develop a shared dream, one looks at the individual aspirations and goals of each stakeholder (in particular each owner), and then whether those individual aspirations connect and whether there is enough common ground to build a collective vision of a family enterprise. Therefore Lansberg is also stressing the need for this shared dream not only to be considered by each new generation of owners, but also for the aspirations of each individual to be counted in the process.[16] Lansberg has also written that a leader – especially one who does not personally have a controlling shareholding – is someone who is able to foster a shared vision. Lansberg writes:[17]

First, they must get in touch with their own deepest aspirations. Second, since leadership is fundamentally a relational process – an ongoing negotiation between the leader and his or her key constituents – leaders must actively engage their followers and get them to articulate their own deepest aspirations. Third, they must then weave a common vision from their own aspirations and those of their constituents. In so doing, they create conditions that foster and sustain collaboration over the long run.

Lansberg also takes care to stress the importance of reality-checking the shared dream, which must be viable in the real world.

When the family become a financial family with a family office

What about mission and vision in the context of a financial family where there is no longer a core operating business?

A purely financial family with its own single family office (SFO) should be in a different situation from a family that has ownership of, and perhaps manages, an operating business. When the family own a business, the family members are shareholders and the shares (if it is a private company) may be illiquid in nature. The shares can often represent the bulk of the wealth of the family at that stage, and the family shareholders all have common exposure (in proportion to their individual holdings) to the risks that their business faces. It is also easier to be emotionally attached to a business that has many stakeholders that go beyond the family, that provides jobs for employees and opportunities for customers, and that might provide support for the communities in which it operates. The values of the owning family can be reflected in the business and can become a competitive advantage for the business.

When the shares in the family business get sold and the family leaders set up a single family office, the family members are no longer shareholders but instead clients of the SFO. The SFO itself is an entity that provides services to the family; it does not represent an investment of the family.

Frequently the financial assets that the SFO has to help to manage will include some balance between pooled family investments and investments that are owned by (or held in trust for) individual family members or are held for a branch of the family (through a trust). This allows each individual client of the SFO to set their own asset allocation strategy and determine their own risk profile.[18] It also means that it is very easy for a client of the SFO – whether that is an individual family member or a branch of the family – to take their investment business elsewhere. They no longer have the shared asset of the operating business.

It seems harder to become emotionally committed to a pile of cash and other financial investments than to the continuity of a family business. Similarly, it seems hard to be emotionally committed to a service organisation, namely the SFO itself (unless you are one of the family members who has a significant role in the running of that office). It must logically follow then that once a family become a financial family, even more thought and effort need to be given to the questions of what the mission, vision and values of the family are. Without putting effort into these questions, without having a shared goal as a family, and without having organised processes to help achieve or sustain the family mission, vision and values, it is quite predictable that family unity and cohesion will dissipate.

Thus if the family office asks the family to develop a formal written mission, vision and values statement, logically this is a very important task for the family to attend to – and again, logically this is something that the SFO should be initiating as soon as possible. However, contrary to the foregoing logic, there are a number of strong and experienced voices from the family advisory field who are saying that, for the financial family in the real world, this might not be the right way to start – nor may it actually be that important after all.

The power of telling stories may be more effective

Family adviser Matthew Wesley has written a piece with the intentionally provocative title of "Burn all the Mission Statements",[19] in which he explains that mission statements are really a tool taken from the corporate consulting environment that consultants coming from that environment are wishing to apply to families. Wesley says that families are not corporations, they are tribal. He explains:

> *Our friends in the world of anthropology would tell us that families function organizationally as tribes – not corporations. Tribes are what are known in their parlance as "kinship systems". This means that they are bound together by ties of blood and marriage. They function not so much because of organizational structure but because of cultural values, roles of individuals, and complex systems of norms and expectations. In tribes, all of this is carried in stories. ... At the end of the day, families are tribes, not corporations. Mission statements are a business solution for a family problem. After doing work with families, I have become convinced that telling stories is the way to go. If a family can change the story it tells about itself, it is able to slowly shift its destiny.*

A mission statement can only emerge out of the joint decision-making experiences of the family.

Wesley says that, in his practice, what he has found to work effectively is to guide family groups through a process of creating stories together about the possible futures of the family. Wesley also makes a distinction between governance documents and agreements that have been made 'from the neck up' (ie, as a purely intellectual exercise) as opposed to a process where family members have been moved or touched emotionally.

Another mission statement sceptic is Barbara Hauser, author of the book *International Family Governance*.[20] She too points out that mission statements might make sense in the corporate world where you have a group of strangers who are voluntarily associating.[21] In a family, Hauser says there is already a group and it is an involuntary group. Taking a simple and practical approach, Hauser stresses the importance of an adviser having one on one conversations with each family member and drawing out of them what their individual goals are and what they want from the family: its financial capital or its business. She then feeds this information back to the family on a consolidated, no-names basis. The goals and objectives of the family group can be developed organically from this process.

Hauser notes that she would avoid referring to the family goals and objectives as a mission statement. If a family came to her and asked her to help them prepare a mission statement, she would ask them to explain why they wanted one. She is particularly wary of anything that even looks like a standard mission statement. However, she advocates that families create their own family constitution (their own written joint decision-making framework) and that this document should commence with a preamble.

Hauser states:

> *The family needs to explain to its members why this seems important to do. This is extremely important, as it contains the reasons for engaging in family governance. To be successful, in my experience, the beginning of the project must have the full support of all of the "key" family members and they must agree about why they are doing this.*

James E Hughes Jr, author of *Family Wealth: Keeping it in the Family*,[22] notes that: "the problem with the mission statement is that most of the families who have them don't use them". Hughes offers the following points:[23]

The original wealth creator has a powerful dream – a dream that they cause to materialise. However, the more powerful the original dream, the more likely that it will in time change, from being a bright sun that has provided so much for the family of the founder into a powerful black hole that has the effect of silencing the dreams of the later generations of the family.

- A mission statement that is handed down from the wealth creator is not really a mission statement of the second and later generations of the family; rather, it is the founder's own legacy statement – essentially an ethical will.
- It has to be voluntary and it has to come from the second, third or later generations of the family.
- Families do not have an obvious common purpose; they have to discover it.
- A mission statement can only emerge out of the joint decision-making experiences of the family. You cannot have a mission statement that is effective and 'real' unless it is a reflection of, or consequence of, a shared journey of the family.
- If there is a family committee formed to work on developing a mission statement, the best people on that committee will be the family's 'leaders from behind' – ie, those interested in the bigger picture, not the transactional or business leaders of the family.
- The ideal kind of consultant/facilitator to help a family to develop its mission statement is one who says: "I'm going to find out whether your family is at a point that it has a common purpose that can be reflected in a mission statement". It is very possible that the consultant might in the end report back and say: "Sorry, you don't actually seem to have a common purpose."
- The mission statement has to be about doing something.

Writing in *Family: The Compact Among Generations*,[24] Hughes says with families, "form should follow function". This means that written forms such as governance documents, legal agreements, trust structures and mission statements need to be designed to reflect the way that the specific family actually functions. In answer to the question of how to respond when the family office asks for the family to develop a mission statement, Hughes answers as follows:

> *When a family first decides to have a family office and needs a mission statement and hasn't had significant experiences together and wants to make decisions together, I would say wait on that. Get your office going, make decisions together. See what your experience is over three to five years [and] then begin the process. First you must have a sense of what your common purpose is. You don't do these things at the beginning or what seems to be the beginning of a family's decision to govern themselves.*

The family mission statement and the black hole of the founder's dream

Hughes is also the co-author of *The Voice of the Rising Generation*,[25] along with Keith Whitaker and Susan Massenzio. When a family decides that it wants to develop a mission statement, it would be well advised to reflect on the metaphor of the 'black hole' as described in this book and to understand how this black hole can have the effect of silencing the voice of members of the second and later generations of the family.

The original wealth creator has a powerful dream – a dream that they cause to materialise. However, the more powerful the original dream, the more likely that it will in time change, from being a bright sun that has provided so much for the family of the founder into a powerful black hole that has the effect of silencing the dreams of the later generations of the family.

The authors counsel each member of the rising generation of a family to reflect on whether they personally are within the gravitational pull of the black hole of the founder's dream and to ask the question: "Who stands for me and who is helping me to be free from the gravity of the black hole?" They write of the importance of coaching each member of the rising generation of the family to identify their own dreams and voices and to 'test the boundary' of the black hole – as opposed to automatically rejecting it and running away from it (or falling into it). They need help to understand where their own dreams might intersect with or diverge from the founder's dream.

The family office mission statement

An SFO is a company formed by a single family (which can also include several branches of the original family) to help provide administrative and organisational support for the family.

Does an SFO need a mission statement – a statement of its purpose? Here, Hauser says:[26]

If it is an SFO I think it's odd for the office to have a mission statement because in my view the SFO is reactive to whatever the needs are [for] the family. So the family could have its goals and those would be carried out with the help of the family office administration.

A family that forms an SFO can set its own unique mission and purpose for the SFO. This mission and purpose can evolve over time. Logically it would make sense that the mission or purpose of a SFO is described as being to support the mission or purpose of the family.[27] Interestingly, it is suggested that one point of differentiation between the SFO and the multi-family office (MFO) is that the family can set the mission of the SFO, but not so with an MFO.

In practice the relationship between the family and the SFO should be a two-way street. The family council can make decisions and set direction for the family, which the SFO would then help to administer and implement. Likewise, the SFO can help ensure that there are regular family meetings being held and give suggestions as to the next steps that the family might take to evolve its family governance.

The cultural framework makes a difference

As a consultant working with families in Asia of a collective harmony culture, I have never had a family come to me and ask for help with the preparation of a mission or vision statement. But being asked to document the family values as set down by the founder generation (ie, really the founder's values) happens a lot.

The idea that there will be a representative family council that refers to a written articulation of the family mission, vision and values to guide its decision-making reflects a Western, formal, legalistic cultural approach (which is not to say that I don't advocate the creation of family councils for Asian families). I am often reminded that, in Asian families, things are 'simply understood' and don't need to be written down on paper (although, as noted, a desire to entrench the founder's values is a frequent exception to this sentiment).

Given that Asian families (or at least the older generation) tend not to be legalistic in approach and given that there is a risk that among the family members any written family mission, vision or even values statements tend to be forms with no capacity to be made to function, it might be more useful to focus on ensuring that the right forums are created so that there will be an ongoing process of the family members developing a shared understanding together of their common goals and reasons for remaining together as a family. Let's not put too much weight on the form but instead focus on ensuring there is an ongoing process of thoughtful and respectful family conversations. Additionally, my own personal experience in exploring Wesley's recommendation to use storytelling with family groups in an Asian context is that the story is indeed a powerful tool to build family cohesion, as well as to explore possible futures for the family.

In a collective harmony culture, the family unit is more important than the individual, family members have their roles to play in the family (which continues in their adult lives), there is respect for elders, for family hierarchy and for ancestors. Asia's Confucian wealth creators attribute their success to having lived their lives in accordance with traditional Asian values, which they want to pass on to future generations. It is a hierarchical, patriarchal culture (though there are also matriarchs).

My impression, however, is that where formal written mission, vision and/or values statements are being prepared on the instruction of Asia's wealth creators, and notwithstanding the strong pull of tradition and respect for elders, in most cases these are still just paper exercises (or at least with respect to the family members[28]).

The paradox of Asian families is that while family togetherness and family harmony and traditional values of the older generation are all important, Asian families are just as prone to the proverb "Wealth does not survive three generations" as families are elsewhere. Another Chinese saying I find to be telling is: "Parents in heaven, children in court". Carlock's observation that in too many Asian families the family harmony is an espoused, rather than an enacted, value has already been referred to.[29] Carlock's prescription is for Asian (business) families to adopt the practice of holding regular family meetings, with a focus on ensuring that there is honest communication, and that each family member has a voice and gets listened to.

In a 2015 report by the Business Families Institute at Singapore Management University, entitled "Asian Business Families Governance: Crossing the Chasm for Intergenerational Change", which was based on a survey of 102 Asian families, Professor Annie Koh concluded that Asian families take family glue for granted – with the predictable consequence that by the third generation it has all but faded away. The report showed that Asian families state that they are committed to business continuity but are not doing anywhere near enough to address succession planning, family governance, and engagement to preserve the family's harmony, values and culture.

As an adviser working with collective harmony families, my own personal conclusion is that it is critical to strengthen the importance of the individual family member and their own personal aspirations, goals and purposes and their individual values. I believe that by highlighting or promoting the importance of the individual in the Asian family (as well as ensuring equal 'air time' for family members who are going to be in ownership – but not management – roles) this will help to strengthen and preserve the family glue, which research shows is otherwise not going to last.

This is also a theme explored in *Cross Cultures: How Global Families Negotiate Change Across Generations*, by Dennis Jaffe and James Grubman,[30] who explain:

> *Rather than seeing the dimension of individualism versus collectivism as a single axis with two poles, it may be more useful to view individualism and collectivism as two independent qualities present to greater or lesser degrees in various cultures. Family enterprises can be low or high on each of these dimensions, depending on their orientation and the effort they put into developing their skills and core values.*
>
> *... We propose that a necessary adaptation of all successful family enterprises is to grow toward healthy support of both the individual and the family, capturing that crucial balance between Independence and Interdependence.*

Mission vision and values – drawing some conclusions

There are eight conclusions that can sensibly be drawn from the foregoing analysis and the work by other authors that is quoted from, as follows:

- We should distinguish between documents that are statements of the founder's vision values and goals from the 'family mission and vision' statement developed by second and later generations.
- We should always be aware of statements that are espoused rather than being enacted. These statements should lead to some action, to some doing.
- The process is critical, starting with each individual on their own before moving to the collective discussion. With each individual there is the question to be answered of where does that individual stand in relation to the 'black hole' of the founder's dream? Each individual in the process should be respected as an adult – ie, as entitled to have their own view respected as any other member of the family.
- The process should include education, hearing examples and considering alternatives and possibilities.
- The process is much more important than the product; and perhaps rather than be concerned about having a product at all, it might be more productive to see the questions of family purposes, goals and values being incorporated into ever-ongoing respectful family discussions.
- Remember the rule that "form should follow function". Don't launch into a mission statement project for the rising generation of the family. It would be far more effective to start providing opportunities for family members to make joint decisions together and to have collaborative experiences together.
- There has to be a reality check on any vision or dream. For example, do the family members really have the capabilities to work together, the skills to lead the business, and the money to invest in the business (or in other joint family activities)? Furthermore, there should be active consideration of the obstacles that must be overcome in order to achieve the vision.[31]
- The role of the SFO and how the SFO might support the goals and purposes of the family is something the family should be considering and communicating, as part of an ongoing dialogue between the family and the SFO.

So mission, vision and values can be helpful. For the family with a core operating business, the family business vision will be an essential tool. For the pure financial family with its own SFO, the need for a formal written statement of mission, vision and values is less clear – the ongoing experiences of working together jointly and the ongoing dialogue within the family is more critical. Families and family offices need to keep in mind that the best products will come from the best process, with the common goals of the family at the core.

Christian Stewart is the managing director of Family Legacy Asia (HK) Limited, a process consulting firm based in Hong Kong. He is also an associate of the Boston-based think tank and consultancy Wise Counsel Research Associates. Mr Stewart assists families around Asia with family governance and succession.

1 The characterisation of the dominant ethnic cultures in the world as being 'Western individualistic', 'collective harmony' or 'honour' is taken from the 2016 book entitled *Cross Cultures; How Global Families Negotiate Change Across Generations*, by Dennis T Jaffe and James Grubman.

2 INSEAD Professor Randel Carlock has written of how many Asian families have an espoused value of family harmony – yet it is often not an enacted value, and hence the prevalence of family feuds in Asia despite the cultural importance, in theory, of preserving family harmony. See "Solutions for infighting among Asian business families", Randel Carlock and Loh Keng Fun, *South China Morning Post*, 5 June 2015.

3 John Davis, *Next Generation Success* (Cambridge Family Enterprise Press, 2014).

4 Randel Carlock and John Ward, *When Family Businesses Are Best* (Palgrave Macmillan, 2010).

5 Ivan Lansberg, *Succeeding Generations* (Harvard Business Press, 1999).

6 Ken McCracken, "STEP Advanced Certificate in Family Business Advising" (course brochure).

7 Carlock and Ward, note 4 above.

8 Carlock and Ward, note 4 above.

9 Lansberg, note 5 above.

10 DT Jaffe, *Stewardship in Your Family Enterprise* (2014).

11 Jaffe, note 10 above.

12 Jaffe, note 10 above.

13 Palgrave Macmillan, 2010.

14 Ward, "The ultimate vision for continuity?", *Families in Business*, Sept/Oct 2003.

15 Harvard Business School Press, 1999.

16 Jaffe also writes: "Each generation of the family must get together and ask, 'What is our purpose relative to the business and to each other?'" – see *Stewardship in Your Family Enterprise* (2014).

17 "The Dreams that Drive Business Success", *Families in Business Magazine*, Spring 1999.

18 Professor Roger King, Hong Kong University of Science and Technology.

19 See www.thewesleygroup.com/blog/?p=348, posted 21 March 2013.

20 Mesatop Press, 2009.

21 Hauser's comments are from a Family Office Association Q&A paper entitled "When Mission Statements do more than collect dust".

22 Wiley, 2nd edn, 2004.

23 Hughes' comments are also drawn from the Family Office Association Q&A Paper "When Mission Statements do more than collect dust".

24 Bloomberg Press, Wiley, 2007.

25 Wiley, 2014.

26 See Family Office Association Q&A Paper "When Mission Statements do more than collect dust".

27 Professor Roger King, Hong Kong University of Science and Technology.

28 Unfortunately for the members of the rising generation of the family, if these paper exercises have been incorporated into the terms of family trust structures, perhaps through the letter of wishes, there can be non-family trustees and advisers who may be very happy to enforce their terms literally on the family.

29 See footnote 4 above.

30 A primary focus of *Cross Cultures* is on how to help the members of the rising generation of a family from a collective harmony or an honour culture, who have been exposed to Western individualistic culture, negotiate across cultures with their elders.

31 Hartley Goldstone of Wise Counsel Research Associates stresses this last point and points to the book *Rethinking Positive Thinking* by Gabriele Oettingen (Penguin Random House, 2015).

The concept of creating a formalised written family constitution has become generally accepted as representing a key best practice for family enterprises.

The three family constitution archetypes[1] and a wise alternative

Christian Stewart

If you are an adviser helping a family to consider the creation of a family constitution, or if you are involved in helping a family through the process of creating one, an important question to ask yourself and your client family is "what kind of family constitution are you going to create?"

The concept of creating a formalised written family constitution has become generally accepted as representing a key best practice for family enterprises. As such we should now be at the stage where we can move past the question of "what are the benefits of developing a constitution?", to a more detailed analysis of common family constitution 'archetypes' – basic models or patterns that can often be recognised.

The following framework assumes there are three basic family constitution archetypes:

- the first is the constitution that is a 'Monument to the Founder'[2];
- the second is the 'Family First Constitution'; and
- the third is the 'Expert Structure'.

Each of these three main archetypes has its strengths and advantages, but each also has its shadow side. It will be a helpful process to name and explore these archetypes with a family that are developing or reviewing a constitution – or to identify if one of these archetypes seems to fit the path the family are taking – to help them to be more conscious of the choice they are making so that they will carefully reflect on both the positive aspects as well as the potentially negative aspects.

In addition to these three archetypes, there is a fourth kind of family constitution which is the 'Wise Constitution'. To create a Wise Constitution, a balancing act is required. A Wise Constitution will represent the right combination of the virtues of Will, Love and Intelligence.

What is a family constitution?

Before going into the specifics of the three archetypes, it is worth briefly reflecting on the term 'family constitution' (or 'family charter') in general, with respect to which there is no standard definition.

- A family constitution establishes a framework for how a family will make joint decisions together, in other words it is concerned with how the family is governed. It will typically address the mission, vision and values of the family and how conflicts are to be managed. It might have a section on the values and principles of the wealth creator. It will likely involve a clarification of roles and responsibilities, an examination of the boundaries between family, ownership and business, and it might create or define communication forums and decision-making bodies. It is advisable when creating a family constitution to consider making provision for the role of family elders.
- A family constitution is often thought of as being a single document that covers all of the matters described above, but a family does not have to adopt that approach. An alternative is for the governance documentation for a family to comprise a collection of separate documents such as a family mission statement and values statement, and separate charters for family institutions, eg the family council, family assembly, family elders. In addition, a charter for the board or boards of family companies will be important documents, as well as charters defining any committees created under the terms of any family trusts. This later approach could allow for a more organic and iterative approach towards developing the family and corporate governance documentation.
- Often families will draw a contrast between a constitution – which expresses the spirit of the family – and its agreements and policies, which are its 'laws'. The constitution is the framework or the foundation of the laws. Laws will change from time to time, depending on circumstances. A constitution is much more enduring and less likely to change. If the 'laws' are not in accord with the constitution (written or unwritten) it is much more likely that the laws will be ignored or voided than that the constitution will be overturned. That's why coming up with agreements or 'laws' in the absence of doing the work around the constitution is so often fruitless.
- It is assumed that a constitution will be a written document (or collection of documents including family policies), but then there is the observation that "every family has its own natural family constitution – it is just not in writing". Therefore, when talking about a

The focus will often only be on family financial capital – the most important thing is to protect the business or to protect the money – ignoring family human and intellectual capital.

formal family constitution perhaps it is better to think in terms of a joint decision-making model that has been discussed and articulated so that everyone in the family is on the same page together. Of course, having it in writing would be a significant benefit.

- The process of creating a family constitution is to be emphasised. "It is the process that counts rather than the product." According to family wealth expert Jay Hughes, it is a process of creating a generational, voluntary horizontal social compact together, as a family of mature adults who have individuated and differentiated. The process should be a 'Fair Process'.[3] The individual family members involved need to have the capacity to listen to each other 'with empathy' in order to be able to create an effective constitution.
- Finally, it is usually assumed that a family constitution is not a legally binding document, but this need not always be the case[4] and in any event it would be normal to expect that there will be supporting legal agreements, such as a shareholders' agreement, or the terms of a family trust deed, that are intended to provide support for the terms of the constitution. The constitution might include a section that summarises the legal agreements and explains their intended purpose in plain language. It is important to make sure that the legal agreements and the terms of the constitution are in alignment.

The first archetype: the Monument to the Founder

The Monument to the Founder is a monument created to honour the extraordinary achievements of the heroic wealth creator, so that his or her legacy will last 'for generations'. The Monument to the Founder can be created by the Founder, but it can also be created by the sibling generation in honour of the Founder.

Characteristics

What is the defining characteristic of such Monuments and of wealth-creating Founders in general? It is strength of will power, determination and resolve; they embody the virtue of Will. This is what you expect from a successful patriarch, one who is used to being the sole decision maker; one who is used to 'centralised control' of family, ownership and business; one who is able to get things done.

The positive side

The constitution that is a Monument to the Founder has its benefits. The defining, strong will power can bring family members to the table to work on the constitution together, and can ensure that the project gets done. The Founder might be careful to take steps to protect the business from the family. The Founder might be very 'business first' in his philosophy. Being familiar with patriarchal control, the constitution might seek to perpetuate this model by ensuring (with the help of the supporting legal structure and/or agreements) that there is a clear mechanism for the Founder's designated successors to continue to exercise the voting control over the family business or wealth. Indeed, rather than a family-wide process, the task force that creates the constitution might be limited to these family business leaders. The constitution will go into detail as to the values the Founder wishes to perpetuate and the principles that he wants his business to follow. With the Monument, the designer(s) of the constitution are often willing to spend time and effort to think very carefully about its terms and conditions and they will likely be thinking far into the future – there will be a clear vision, and a clear structure.

The shadow side

However, the bigger the Monument to the Founder, the bigger the shadow it can cast. Typically, the creation of such a Monument does not call for and does not take into account the importance of family emotional commitment or engagement. It might be created in a top-down fashion without any real participation from the members of the rising generation of the family. The focus will often only be on family financial capital – the most important thing is to protect the business or to protect the money – ignoring family human and intellectual capital. The Founder is often able to operate without having to be accountable to either family or owners and so the Monument created may seek to entrench a similar autocratic style of governance system, one where those who take on decision-making authorities are not (or do not see themselves as being) accountable to the rest of the family members. Often Monuments are restrictive and don't provide for easy or fair exit mechanisms. A key characteristic of the Monument to the Founder is an unwillingness to have to deal with the 'messiness' of divergent voices and opinions. Another problem with Monuments is that founders typically do not like transparency – they prefer secrecy in order to maximise their control.

As an example of the shadow side of the Monument, it is easy to imagine a complex, restrictive and long-term trust structure and constitution being designed that limits the ability to exit, that limits the ability to have a voice, and that was designed without any real input from the beneficiaries. However, nothing lasts forever.

The second archetype: the Family First Constitution

The second common archetype is the Family First Constitution, the positive characteristics of which can be summarised in a single word: love, and more specifically, love for family. The Family First Constitution is a reflection of the virtue of Love.

Characteristics

The Family First Constitution will put an emphasis on the intangibles of family mission, vision, values and family principles, but might not go into the specifics of forums, roles, responsibilities, exit and conflicts. It is a constitution that puts a premium on the family values of togetherness, equality and harmony. An example of a policy that would fit with this archetype would be that "every sibling receives the same salary". Another example might be "every family member is entitled to the benefit of the doubt when it comes to jobs in the business". Composition of the corporate board might be based on branch representation rather than required skill set.

The positive side

The kind of family that create this kind of constitution might themselves be inwardly focused and self-reliant. In extreme cases the family might be enmeshed. Even in that scenario there are benefits to the Family First Constitution. First it has been said that there are no right or wrong answers when it comes to designing a constitution – the only answers that matter are those that the family devise for themselves. Therefore, the Family First Constitution can be beneficial to the family that created it where the 'rules of the road' have been articulated, are understood and are consistently applied. This second kind of constitution can also be expected to encourage a sense of belonging, a supportive emotional environment, a focus on finding roles for family members to play. It won't have the problems with emotional commitment or disengagement that lie at the foot of the Monument to the Founder.

The shadow side

The Family First Constitution also has its shadow side. An insistence on family harmony as a value can quickly translate into conflict avoidance and the avoidance of difficult conversations. An insistence on togetherness at all costs can stifle diversity within the family and send the message that individual values do not count. Enmeshment is not healthy. It can also send the message that if you are not a part of the business then you are not a part of the family. A focus on equality of family members can lead to 'too many cooks in the kitchen' and 'no structure chart' for the business. Remember that in family firms, fairness does not always mean equality. Conflicts can also arise with the Family First Constitution over issues such as birth order versus competency, and where different family members contribute to the business to different extents. Family system rules will apply in the management system. The Family First Constitution can often work for some sibling partnerships, especially where all of the siblings are in management, but is hard to maintain into the third generation and beyond.

Investing in trust and communication

If a family are really serious about putting family first they will invest in trust and communication. Just because a family see themselves as being committed to working together and having a shared vision and values, and a commitment to their legacy, this does not mean that they have the relationship skills to make it work. A necessary precondition for a family to form a family council and work on their constitution

A focus on equality of family members can lead to 'too many cooks in the kitchen' and 'no structure chart' for the business. Remember that in family firms, fairness does not always mean equality.

and policies together is the ability to listen with empathy. How does a family invest in trust and communication? The family could do a programme together on learning how to have difficult conversations or non-violent communication. The family council could engage coaches or counsellors to work with individual family members on relationship issues. The family meeting agenda would include time for listening skills, active constructive responding, and to teach family members other relationship skills and tools.

Investing in the dreams of the rising generation

There is another way of thinking about putting family first. Jay Hughes says that if a family want to beat the shirt sleeves to shirt sleeves proverb and flourish, the most important place to focus on is the family circle, and see that as being more important than the ownership circle, with the least important being the management circle. (Those who design Monuments to the Founder will tend to reverse this order of priority and put all of their focus on the management circle, and practically none on the family circle.) This means using financial capital to invest in the growth of the individual family members. A practical way to start to put this philosophy into practice is to help each individual family member to 'know themselves' using an assessment process[5] and working with experienced coaches and counsellors. Hughes is essentially saying that the strongest foundation that a family can provide for their family governance system is a group of mature adults who have differentiated and individuated and who know themselves including knowing their own vocation or calling. Hughes summarises by saying that the mission of a family that want to postpone the proverb is simply to invest in the dreams of the rising generation.

The third archetype: the Expert Structure

The third common kind of constitution is the Expert Structure. The Expert Structure reflects a good model based on all of the latest best practices in terms of both family and business governance. The Expert Structure is the embodiment of the virtue of Intelligence.

Characteristics of the Expert Structure

As the first part of the name implies, with the Expert Structure, there is likely to be one or more expert advisers involved helping to design the family constitution. An 'expert' adviser is a subject matter expert, though this does not preclude such an adviser from having deep experience and wisdom. Traditional professional advice is typically provided as expert advice. Expert advice and advisers can be contrasted with a 'helping relationship' or with advice on process. At the extreme an expert adviser is one who relies more on his or her own expert answers to provide to the family, than on a process of helping the family develop their own answers.

As the second part of the name implies, with this third archetype there can also be an emphasis put on 'the structure' which can refer to either the use of trusts and vehicles like private trustee companies and other ownership vehicles to 'bring structure' to the governance arrangements; or sophisticated governance structures, or both of these.

The positive side

The Expert Structure is intelligent. It can reflect an effort by the family to seek out the best possible advice to guide them through the constitution process and to achieve their mission and vision. It can also reflect an inclination to making sure that the smartest, most competent people are appointed to decision-making roles within the Expert Structure. Intelligence includes thinking about appropriate checks and balances, and addressing the relevant tax, legal, matrimonial and succession issues. It could mean bringing a 'prevention focus' mindset to the planning process,[6] which is a valid and critical mindset. It can also mean having a well-thought through philosophy, guiding principles, processes and practices that are intended to help the family to achieve its mission and to flourish as a family. The best aspect of this archetype is if in making the constitution the family members get to thoughtfully consider all of the appropriate options and relevant best practices and to debate and make an informed decision. Intelligence is also manifested through a commitment to learning. Jay Hughes stresses that with the advent of the new Fourth Industrial economy, for a family to build resilience and adapt to an ever-increasing rate of change, it is critical that it view itself as a learning organisation.

The shadow side

When faced with an Expert Structure, the questions to reflect on, and which point to its shadow side, will be 'will they' and 'can they' implement it? Will the family members be able to make this structure work? Will the family members be able to integrate this structure into their family system? Or will it just end up being put in the bottom drawer and forgotten about? Will they understand it and will they put in the effort required to learn how the governance system and the structure works? When helping a family with a family constitution, it is critically important to pay attention to the implementation stage.

The Expert Structure might be strong in terms of good theory, but it might get put into the bottom drawer because it fails to take into account family dynamics[7] and the capacity of the family members to

It is helpful to remember that with a family constitution there is an inverse relationship between the time spent developing a constitution and agreeing its terms, and the success of the family implementing the constitution.

learn and evolve. A successful guiding principle is always that 'evolution is better than revolution'.

It is also important to reflect on the composition of the advisers and non-family professionals working with the family. Are all of the advisers traditional expert advisers? How many members of the professional team are professionally qualified to work with the qualitative issues involved with growing family human, intellectual, social and spiritual capital? If the technical advisers and non-family professionals are not balanced out with those with skills and experience in addressing the qualitative capitals of the family, then don't expect family qualitative capitals, and the capacity of the family members, to grow.

The intelligently designed Expert Structure can sometimes also fail (like the Monument to the Founder) in the area where the Family First Constitution is strong, which is by overlooking the importance of cultivating family emotional commitment. Where there is a lack of emotional commitment the basic problem is one of engagement.

The Family Constitution Product

There is a variation on the Expert Structure archetype which is the 'Product' – the 'off-the-shelf constitution'. As its name implies, the Product is all product and no process and predictably will not be something that the family can integrate and implement. Avoid constitutions that are merely products.

When studying constitutions, it is common for families to ask to see examples and templates. It is a major mistake, however, for a family to simply take a template or someone else's constitution, and adopt it as its own. Sometimes family leaders have the mentality that they need a family constitution and it becomes one more task on their task list that they want to complete as quickly and efficiently as possible, so they can get back to business as usual. As mentioned, it's the process not the product that matters. It is helpful to remember that with a family constitution there is an inverse relationship between the time spent developing a constitution and agreeing its terms, and the success of the family implementing the constitution. One of the families in Hong Kong that have successfully crafted their own family constitution tell their peers that it is always an ongoing process, it never ends. Rather than the family business leader being responsible for the family constitution, identify a family champion who has the time and temperament to engage the whole family in a fair process.

Pathways to balance

The three family constitution archetypes each embody Will, Love and Intelligence respectively. As highlighted, each of these archetypes has both a positive side and a shadow side to it. How can a family avoid the potential shadow side of their family constitution? Following are a total of 12 suggested pathways to finding balance for each of the three archetypes.

The *Monument to the Founder* is characterised by clear decisive strong leadership; the importance of protecting the business and respecting the experience and wisdom of the family wealth creator. To avoid the shadow side of the Monument:

- Ensure there is a family champion or family leader from behind who is committed to family engagement and involvement in the governance process.
- Give growing the qualitative capitals of the family at least equal priority to the focus on the business or financial capital.
- Differentiate between vote and voice in the decision-making processes. This is an aspect of Fair Process. Giving family members who are not involved in decision-making roles a communication forum and a voice, is not the same thing as allowing them to insist on their ideas being implemented.
- Ensure there are family elders who are respected by both the older generation as well as the rising generation. Family elders can help to build a bridge between generations.
- Make sure the constitution includes a mechanism to make amendments and addresses the question of the rights of family members as citizens under the constitution.[8] An effective family governance structure is one that is based on a voluntary decision to be a participant.

The *Family First Constitution* might be characterised by engagement and a commitment to invest in family human capital. To avoid the shadow side of the Family First Constitution:

- Build strong boundaries between the family and its enterprises; have a commitment towards professionalism, and again following the principles of Fair Process in decision making. Family voice supports family engagement, but it does not mean the boundary between ownership and management is ignored. A family can adopt an Enterprising Family Philosophy and invest heavily in the development of its human intellectual and social capital and still insist on professional qualifications for all roles, whether family, corporate governance or business roles. As a rule of thumb, Jay Hughes advises that you should only put family members into roles for which they have a demonstrated commitment and calling.
- When the family invests in developing the qualitative skills and capacities of its individual family members they become mature contributors to both the family and corporate governance roles.
- Invest in increasing the skill set of the family members to have difficult conversations, in working together collaboratively, in effective decision making and to resolve conflicts.
- Adopt the philosophy of 'both together and apart'. Encourage family members to go on their own path, to stand on their own feet independently of the family.

The Expert Structure might be characterised by best practices, complexity and reliance on professional advisers. To avoid the shadow side of the Expert Structure:

- Create a multi-disciplinary team of advisers that includes a mix of both expert technical and quantitative advisers, as well as experienced qualitative advisers, including individuals from the helping professions, and process consultants.
- Commit to family learning and development, create a family learning committee and develop a curriculum for family learning experiences. The family members have to learn about the governance and ownership structures.
- Remember and apply the maxims:
  - "Evolution is better than revolution";
  - "Family culture eats structure for breakfast"; and
  - "With family governance, there are no right or wrong answers, the best answers are the ones that the family members come up with on their own after thoughtful consideration of the pros and cons".

In all, 12 Pathways are important for each of the archetypes, though families and their advisers should focus first on the ones suggested for each particular archetype, before they review and work on the rest of the Pathways.

The Wise Constitution

So what is the best kind of family constitution? The best kind is one that embodies wisdom, and hence it can be called the Wise Constitution. The Wise Constitution is one that seeks to balance Will, Love and Intelligence.

First, wisdom implies taking the time to be aware of the bigger picture and to be aware of the culture and capacity and skills of the client family, as well as the transitions the family are facing.

Second, the wise approach to developing a family constitution will include considering whether there is any one of the three archetypes at play; to consider which direction it looks like the family are going in, to help the family to be conscious of that direction, to get the family to reflect on the negative or shadow side of that approach, and to consider how to avoid or to compensate for those possible downsides.

A Wise Constitution will involve an effort to integrate the best features of the three archetypes that have been discussed, the positive sides, recognising that there will need to be some trade-offs and compromises and perhaps paradoxical solutions to be developed to achieve a balance. To achieve balance first work with the Pathways to Balance recommended for the specific archetype then consider adopting as many of the remaining 12 Pathways to Balance identified above as possible.

Remember the process of creating the constitution is more important than the product. More than that, the focus should be on what are the ongoing processes that the family will need to implement to bring the constitution to life.

The Wise Constitution will have elements of will power and decisiveness and the ability to make hard judgment calls that the Monument to the Founder embodies. It will also take into account the critical importance of family values and of family emotional commitment and support and of finding roles for family members that the Family First Constitution offers. Finally, it will be made intelligently after thoughtful study of good models and best practices, it will consider how to put the smartest, most competent people into the right places, but it will be tempered with realism of the dynamics and skills and culture of the family.

Archetype	Virtue	Positive aspect	Shadow	Pathways to balance
The Monument to the Founder	Will	• Clear structure • Clear leadership • A clear legacy • Business principles that have worked	• Patriarchal control • Lack of engagement • Lack of voice • Lack of flexibility • Lack of exit rights	• A family champion • Invest in qualitative capitals • Differentiate between voice and vote • Family elders • Make sure there is an amendment power • Consider a sunset clause. • Outline the rights of citizens
The Family First Constitution	Love	• Engagement • Stewardship • Investment in human capital • A foundation of trust and communication	• Enmeshed family • Poor boundaries • Exploitation of business resources • Lack of professionalisation • Lack of credibility, lack of competence	• Clear boundaries • Fair process in decision making • Enterprising family philosophy • A commitment to professionalism • Invest in skills including relationship skills • Together and apart
The Expert Structure	Intelligence	• Best thinking • Best practices • A clear philosophy • Good set of checks and balances • A learning organisation • After action review of decisions	• A formation • A structure the family is unable to integrate • Lack of engagement • Advisers working on the family not working with the family • Family reliant on advisers	• Create a multidisciplinary team of advisers also including qualitative advisers • A commitment to family learning and development • Evolution better than revolution • Help the family create their own unique answers
The Wise Constitution	Wisdom	All of the above	The family must be willing to support and invest time and effort in maintaining the structure	All of the above

Christian Stewart is the founder of Family Legacy Asia (HK) Limited, a process consulting firm based in Hong Kong. He assists family enterprises around Asia with family governance, succession, learning and development.

1 The author would like to thank the following individuals for their contribution to this article and for freely sharing their ideas on family constitutions: Jeremy Cheng, Barbara Hauser, Jay Hughes, Hartley Goldstone, Dennis Jaffe, Ian Marsh, Matthew Wesley and Keith Whitaker.

2 The term 'Monument to the Founder' was coined by Jay Hughes in relation to a trust structure the sole purpose of which is to create a monument to the founder, ie creator of the family financial wealth.

3 The five principles of Fair Process are explained in *When Family Businesses Are Best*, by Randel S Carlock and John L Ward, Palgrave Macmillan, 2010.

4 Barbara Hauser, "Family Ties", *The STEP Journal*, April 2012.

5 The assessment process recommended by Hughes can be found in chapter 19, *Educational Assessment Tools of Family, The Compact Among Generations*, Bloomberg Press, 2007.

6 Hartley Goldstone observes that the prevention focused mindset is a common one for fiduciaries but it needs to be balanced with a 'promotion focused mindset'.

7 See the article "Culture does indeed eat structure for breakfast" by Matthew Wesley, available at www.thewesleygroup.com/blog.

8 "Is My Family Constitution Unconstitutional?" by Allison Anna Tait, May 2019, *Law & Inequality: A Journal of Theory and Practice*.

Family constitutions, the rule of law and happiness

Barbara R Hauser

Family constitutions have become a hot topic in many parts of the world. A family that is organised enough to have a family office is likely to have, or to be considering, a family constitution.

This article will cover:

- What is meant by a family constitution?
- What issues does it address?
- What is the process to create one?
- Is it binding on a family?
- What strength is added by a focus on the rule of law?
- How does this result in fairness and happiness in a family?

1. Constitutions in general

"Imagine that your family is a small country", I often begin, "What rules would you want to have?" In comparing families to countries, I have been told that for those who come from the United States there is an advantage: the country was new, with an opportunity to create its original rules of governance.[1] Governance of a group was not invented then, of course, but has been part of forming groups, and countries, during all of history.

Going back to perhaps the earliest set of group rules, the Code of Hammurabi,[2] there was a lot of attention on the laws of inheritance. Perhaps even then it was inheritance issues that caused the most disruption. In the Code, written during the Babylonian era, inheritance rules were spelled out in some detail, and everyone was expected to abide by them as a condition of being part of the community. It may be that the ability to rely on inheritance 'expectations' is a core element of the human condition. We know that some of the most widely known disputes revolve around inheritance issues – see King Lear and others. In the modern era it has also been the differences in inheritance laws that have made it impossible for England and the rest of the European Union[3] to agree on a unified set of inheritance rules. English common law allows freedom of disposition; the civil law has automatic entitlements for children.

The constitution of India is an instructive model of embracing such contrary rules of inheritance – it defers to personal and religious law on those issues. As the longest constitution in the world, it had a history of many legal and religious systems to coordinate, with some 395 Articles. Its inclusive approach has been praised by Professor Menski, who wrote: "The future of the world lies evidently not in simplistic legal uniformity, but in considered, carefully weighed respect for diversity."[4] The same respect would be admired in family groups.

The word 'constitution' also refers to the actual make-up of a group.[5] So whether called a 'code', a 'charter', a 'compact' or a 'constitution', the basic idea is the same. Each individual makes a decision to give up some personal freedom to be part of a group, in exchange for protection by the group and possible other benefits, as discussed below. Chaos and uncertainty are traded for an ability to rely on certain common rules. The family members constitute the group.

Following contract law we can compare the agreement in a group setting to a compact. John Locke wrote in 1690 about why a group would make a 'social compact' when they came together.[6] The individuals would see a benefit to agreeing to be in a group. The same is true of families.

2. Family constitutions

The first issue is to examine the reasons that individuals agree to be subject to family rules, or compacts, to use the word chosen by John Locke. His explanation, written in 1690, of coming together as a group in society can be read to apply just the same to families today. He writes:

> *Sec. 95. MEN being, as has been said, by nature, all free, equal, and independent, no one can be put out of this estate, and subjected to the political power of another, without his own consent. The only way whereby any one divests himself of his natural liberty, and puts on the bonds of civil society, is by agreeing with other men to join and unite into a community for their comfortable, safe, and peaceable living one amongst another, in a secure enjoyment of their properties, and a greater security against any, that are not of it.*[7]

In a family setting then, the members come together and agree to be bound by certain rules, for the benefit of being part of the family group. The nature of particular rules may differ significantly from family to family. Differences come from many sources: cultures, external environments and economies, personalities, religious beliefs, experiences with wealth, resentments and jealousies, family history, and family goals for the future, to name a few.

In helping families create their own constitutions, I have found that the process is extremely important. Indeed, in many ways the process itself can teach families about what fair governance is. Professor John Ward, a recognised authority in this field, has always said that the process is very important. He has even concluded that the process is the most important aspect. He has written "We believe the *process* of developing the family agreement is *more* important than its contents [emphasis added]."[8]

This practical value of a good and fair process is a very important point, although one that families do not always see at the beginning. Advisers to wealthy families tend to focus on structures, and families become accustomed to having tangible elements in their plans: trusts, private trust companies, family limited partnerships, holding companies, special purpose offshore vehicles, etc. With a family constitution project, they often are more interested in the final product than in the process. That attitude changes as the process takes shape and the family can appreciate the results.

What is the process to follow?

In my experience it works best to have an independent outside adviser to assist and facilitate the process. This is because the family members already have a way a making decisions, expressed or implicit. Often there is some dissatisfaction with the existing system, which motivates someone in the family to make a change. Often it is a restless member of the second generation who raises the idea. Its reception will depend on the status of that person within the family. The first hurdle is to have the family agree to hire the adviser.

It is quite common to meet with an initial and definite rejection by a successful wealth-creator patriarch whose official position is that "everything is just fine as it is". What seems to be changing that view is the increase of distressing and very public family litigation, in many countries and cultures. Families who want to avoid that public disgrace and family dissolution are turning to the relatively new field of 'family governance'.[9] This leads to an interest in family constitutions.

If the family agrees to hire the adviser, the next step in my opinion is for the adviser to write a tailored engagement letter. My letters, for example, include the statement that although I am a lawyer I will not be giving any legal advice. I also make a point of saying that I will be working on behalf of the entire family, regardless of who pays my fees. The letters are usually no more than a page long.

I have seen other agreements that include a list of obligations the family will have – to provide requested information and to participate in an inclusive and timely basis. I have hesitated to spell out the duties of the family, especially as this can change over time. In any event, these clear short and friendly letters I find to be a welcome change from the formalised, intimidating, lengthy engagement letters I was familiar with in law firms.

The next step is to have a series of private interviews with each family member.[10] These are critical and provide the content for that family's constitution. I explain that I will keep any information confidential when they express that wish. In the United States, a lawyer is not likely to be able to have those multiple confidential interviews: there is a professional duty to zealously represent the [one] client.[11] I often think of the patriarch who hired me with the assurance that it should be a simple project because "there are no issues in our family". In that case I proceeded with the individual interviews. After those private interviews I wrote a 10-page report of the issues I had heard. Those feedback reports are essential, both to show each person that they have been heard, and to record the issues that family members for a variety of reasons have been reluctant to raise.

Those feedback reports list the issues that have come up and which could be improved by family discussion and resolution.[12] Here the adviser comes back in to facilitate the meetings. These work best if they are treated as important formal meetings: written agendas in advance and written minutes afterwards.

Who is included in the drafting meetings varies by family. In most of the families I have worked with it is the younger generation who have the initial motivation and the senior generation who must approve the project. Going forward it is important to have both generations participate. In some other cases it was the senior generation who needed to meet first, to sort out some of their own issues, and then invite the younger generation in for comments and even drafting. In another family it was the younger generation who did all the work, but then they reviewed it with the senior generation for approval and changes.

The one process I do not see as very effective is for the traditional patriarch to be in charge of the writing – often done by an adviser – and then ask the younger family members to sign. When the younger members have not participated in the process they have no real commitment to the document. To start the process it is even important to change the family's habitual seating at the table – the facilitator should take the seat at the head of the table.

On reflection I think that this motivation, to create a family constitution, may go beyond the practical current one of avoiding conflict. On a deeper level, it may well be an important part of documenting a family legacy.

The meetings are usually slow going. In addition to grappling with difficult issues, the inclusive new process might need some time for the family members to adjust to having all of the voices heard, not just the traditionally dominant voices. Again it is the process in these meetings that is so important. Everyone needs to participate and all opinions need to be respected. By following this process they are in fact learning how to manage the governance of the family.

I have heard of advisers who can hurry and complete the whole process for the family. I have also heard of advisers who promise to complete a family constitution in one weekend. Unfortunately the result is not very meaningful to the family, as they had limited participation. In many ways I think the family in that case is actually worse off – they feel they have completed their governance, and will not pay more attention to it. The document sits in a drawer somewhere.

The best feedback of all is to hear a family say: "this constitution is starting to feel like it is ours".

A sample of subjects in a family constitution

Every family constitution is unique for that particular family. Many families and advisers ask to see samples though, so below is a description of many of the subjects I have seen included in family constitutions. Particular families may include some of these, and may add their own additional ones. If the family has already created several agreements on specific issues – such as a dynasty trust – those can be referred to or even incorporated in a family constitution. The goal is to have the family constitution be the framework for all of the issues.

Preamble

The Preamble is a section I view as a 'required' section, to be included at the beginning of the constitution. It sets out the family's reasons for creating a constitution – what they hope to accomplish, and what the family and the family history mean to them. It is a place to honour ancestors, if desired, and a place to describe important family values and their hopes for future generations.

On reflection I think that this motivation, to create a family constitution, may go beyond the practical current one of avoiding conflict. On a deeper level, it may well be an important part of documenting a family legacy. This in turn could be driven by an instinctive desire to achieve immortality. When I looked into the history of societies allowing inheritances in general, I saw this as part of creating family continuity – from early Roman times:

> *[t]his continuation of the dead man in his heres or heredes probably had its roots in social and religious rather than in economic considerations. It manifested the continuity of the patriarchal family and ensured that there should be someone on whom the duty of maintaining the family sacra would devolve....*
>
> *It is the sui heredes who are primarily entitled ... They are 'heirs to themselves,'... Even in the lifetime of their father they are in some way already owners of the family property ... There was no gap in the ownership of the family property... 'the King is dead, long live the King' expresses the same principle ... The continuity of the family is more important than the interests of the individual.*[13]

This awareness of the desire for immortality infuses the lasting constitutions. The original Roman concept of the *paterfamilias* was seen as "the transitory head of a self-perpetuating organism, as the trustee of the family property rather than the absolute owner".[14] These families tend to think of themselves as a self-perpetuating organism – a 'multi-generational family' in today's language. We still use the word 'patrimony' and in India the 'undivided' family property concept continues.[15]

A family board or a family council

Perhaps the next most important provision is the creation of a family board or family council. The earliest form of a family representative group is probably the family council. Particularly when there is still a family controlled operating business, forming a family council creates a place for the family to come together as a family. A family council has the ability to act as a liaison between the entire family on the one hand and the company management on the other. The council could, for example, express to management a wish by the family to change the company strategy, or to dispose of, or acquire, certain assets. In the other direction the council can share company information with the larger family group.

When the family's holdings are more diverse, it may be appropriate to create a family board. Prior to working with family constitutions, in my legal practice I often suggested to a patriarch that he restructure his assets to be controlled by a holding company. I was thinking of coordination, tax advantages and simplified inheritance.

Today, when the holdings are complex, I usually recommend a family board to oversee and govern all the family holdings. Many families may already have a family council, as discussed above, which can function in many of the same ways.

The main advantage I see of referring to a board is the ability to transfer many of the global corporate board governance aspects to the family board.[16] For example, Principle 5 of the OECD Principles of Corporate Governance applies quite well to families:

The corporate governance framework should ensure that timely and accurate disclosure is made on all material matters regarding the corporation, including the financial situation, performance, ownership, and governance of the company.[17]

So often it is a lack of information that causes distrust and dissension among family members. There are also local laws regulating the operation of traditional corporate boards, and many of these can be adapted to apply in the family board setting. Finally, in my opinion the use of a family board denotes a more active and formal engagement by the family.[18] The family board would act as the holding company in a similar role as the supervisory board functions in Europe.[19]

The family board, very similar to a family holding company, would be described in the constitution. Issues would include:

- What is the responsibility and/or authority of the family board?
- Who are the initial family board members, and how are they chosen?
- Are spouses eligible to serve? Are children – at what age?
- Could non-family advisers be included?
- How are successors chosen?
- Is the board required to have equal representation from the primary branches?
- Are there positions for the next generation? Are those on a voting basis or non-voting?
- Is there a chairman and how is he/she selected?
- Are members paid to be on the board, paid to attend meetings, including travel reimbursements? Is the chairman paid a larger amount?
- How often does the board meet? Must the meetings be in person?
- Is there a penalty for not attending?
- Is a written agenda distributed prior to the meeting?
- What is a quorum – a minimum number – for a meeting?
- Can absent members give someone their proxy?
- How and why can someone be discharged from the board?
- Are there term limits? Age limits?

Committees of the family board

I have found committees to be an excellent way to engage a larger number of family members, with the extra advantage of having them work together in small groups. They are also a great way to include multiple generations. The types and numbers of committees will vary by the size of the family and their interests. They might include the following:

- investment committee;
- education committee;
- philanthropy committee;
- art/collections committee;
- trust oversight committee;
- family gatherings committee;
- family celebrations committee;
- family history committee;
- homes/yacht/jet usage committee;
- family office oversight committee – which might include how the costs are allocated.

For each committee the membership selection and procedural questions listed for the family board should also be addressed.

Many families are concerned about their ability to grow the family wealth, inside or outside of a family business. As part of encouraging a spirit of entrepreneurship they might create a family venture fund which would be available to family members.

Family council
If there is an existing family council, what is its functions, how is membership determined and how does it interact with the family board?

Family business issues
If there is a family owned business, all of those separate issues could be included in the constitution. Those issues, often addressed in a shareholders' agreement, could include the following:

- restrictions on the transfer of stock;
- disposition on death;
- right of first refusal;
- valuation of stock;
- voting agreements;
- qualifications for a family member to work in the business.

Additional subjects that might be included

Junior board
Some families like to have a way to train younger members to become knowledgeable board members, of their own family board, or company board, or outside boards. I have seen a very effective use of a junior board to provide this training.

Family venture fund
Many families are concerned about their ability to grow the family wealth, inside or outside of a family business. As part of encouraging a spirit of entrepreneurship they might create a family venture fund which would be available to family members. Usually there are a number of requirements: a solid business plan, a pay-back schedule, approval by industry experts, and close monitoring and reporting. These have been especially popular in the Gulf Region.

Family bank
Some families create an informal bank that is available for family members, to take out loans and provide other traditional banking services. As the family wealth becomes divided among later generations, some of the resulting unevenness can be ameliorated by having access to the private family bank.

Regular risk audits
One of the key concerns in the management of a family office is to monitor and evaluate all of the possible risks that are likely. These range from property damage to kidnapping to adequate life insurance. Several providers are focusing on a very holistic view that includes all family members. Another area of increasing risk is reputational risk, which can be devastating to a family. Today there are also ever-increasing risks associated with cyber security.

Head of family
In some cultures it is common to have one person known to be the head of the family. The successor, and the related responsibilities, might be set out in the constitution. This is one of those areas that is very personal to the particular family.

Social media policy
Modern concerns include having a clear and safe policy on the use of social media by family members. This includes having a strong cyber-security policy.

General principles and values
Some families like to include a list of their agreed-upon family principles and values. The more specific they are the more meaning they have for the family. If they have worked on a family mission statement, this could also be included or referred to. This would be coordinated with any description of values in the preamble.

Conflict resolution
It seems inevitable that conflicts will arise. It can be very helpful to provide a process to handle them. Often that would involve sending the conflict to the family board, but other procedures are also available. Again, whatever would work best for a particular family will be good to consider.[20]

Exit provisions
This is a tricky one, much like working on a prenuptial agreement before the marriage and agreeing on divorce provisions. Some families, however, credit the existence of an exit provision with the reaction by family members that they all want to stay in. Knowing that it is possible to leave makes remaining in seem a free choice – to participate in the social compact. Some exit provisions are very brief – the request could be made to the family board, which would have the authority to take care of the details. Other exit provisions can be quite detailed, as to procedures, timing and possible valuation discounts.

Amendment procedure
The second provision I require[21] is to have a procedure for amendments. Particularly if the constitution is meant to apply to future generations there needs to be a method for making changes.

Finally, if we step back and analyse what happens when a family creates its own constitution we can see that they have agreed among themselves to create a 'rule of law' with written policies and procedures. This is similar to countries following the rule of law.

3. The rule of law
What happens when a family creates its own family constitution is that they have agreed to honour

In a family setting it is just as important as it was with the Magna Carta that the 'ruler' of the family agrees to be bound by the law. Being able to rely on a set of rules is critical to planning a life.

certain rules. One of the key benefits is an assurance that the difficult issues will be decided in accordance with policies, not by arbitrary decisions. Decisions will be made by rules, not by persons.[22] Again, if we compare the family group to a country – we can now say that they are following the rule of law, a highly valued global practice.

What is the rule of law, and why is it so important? As I wrote recently in "Constitutions, Cultures and the Rule of Law"[23]:

> *I have seen that despite strong cultural differences successful families generally end up following principles of the rule of law. I believe that justice – following the rule of law – is linked with happiness in families, the same as it is with countries. Living in a just system allows one to plan more reliably for the future; there is stability and predictability. Those families are more secure, more resilient, and just happier. In creating their own constitution, they have created their own 'rule of law'.*

As much as the rule of law is talked about, it can be difficult to spell out its meaning. One meaning is that a country does have a developed legal infrastructure – with laws, lawyers and courts. In my opinion, having that infrastructure is not enough – we need to add that the system is just and fair. A succinct definition by an Australian jurist that I find quite helpful is:

> *... most of the content of the rule of law can be summed up in two points: (1) that the people (including, one should add, the government) should be ruled by the law and obey it and (2) that the law should be such that people will be able (and, one should add, willing) to be guided by it.*[24]

The first point is about the process; the second is about the content. In working to create a family constitution, the family is in fact agreeing to be ruled by those rules, and at the same time is creating the rules that they would want to be ruled by. This is why the enforceability of the constitution is never raised when the constitution has been created in a fair and participatory process.[25] Meaningful participation is vital. So is the ability to change those rules, but only by following an agreed-upon process. Adopting the rule of law is to reject arbitrary and capricious decisions.

In a family setting it is just as important as it was with the Magna Carta that the 'ruler' of the family agrees to be bound by the law. Being able to rely on a set of rules is critical to planning a life. One needs to know what can be relied upon. It is reassuring for each family member to know that their agreed-upon rules will be followed and honored by all family members.[26]

In the common law legal system *stare decisis* means that settled cases will be followed. Promises need to be kept – in a society and in a family. Even the common law legal system developed a way to enforce promises that did not fit squarely in the required legal format. The concept of *promissory estoppel* applies when someone makes a promise that he knows the other person is relying on, but he also knows the promise would not be legally enforceable.[27] This principle of fairness was developed in the courts of equity, and is still followed today.

The ability to rely on promises is an essential part of fairness. As John Rawls wrote: "The most fundamental idea in this conception of justice is the idea of society as a fair system of social cooperation over time from one generation to the next."[28] Because of the global impact Rawls has had,[29] it is worth quoting in full these precepts of his, and translating them to a family setting:

> *2.2. The central organizing idea of social cooperation has at least three essential features: (a) Social cooperation is distinct from merely socially coordinated activity – for example, activity coordinated by orders issued by an absolute central authority. Rather, social cooperation is guided by publicly recognized rules and procedures which those cooperating accept as appropriate to regulate their conduct. (b) The idea of cooperation includes the idea of fair terms of cooperation: these are terms each participant may reasonably accept, and sometimes should accept, provided that everyone else likewise accepts them. Fair terms of cooperation specify an idea of reciprocity, or mutuality: all who do their part as the recognized rules require are to benefit as specified by a public and agreed-upon standard. (c) The idea of cooperation also includes the idea of each participant's rational advantage, or good. The idea of rational advantage specifies what it is that those engaged in cooperation are seeking to advance from the standpoint of their own good.*[30]

The rule of law is also an integral part of 'justice'.

The World Justice Project, founded in 2006 under the leadership of the American Bar Association and 21 strategic partners,[31] is dedicated to promoting the rule of law on a global basis. Its premise is that the rule of law equates to justice. It states that the rule of law exists when four universal principles are included – again think of families in each of these principles:

- all are accountable under the law;
- the laws are clear, stable, just and honour basic human rights;
- the process by which the laws are made is accessible, fair and efficient; and
- justice is delivered timely and ethically by neutral persons from those communities.[32]

The Project ranks countries according to how well they follow the rule of law, and accordingly how just they are. In its 2015 rankings, the top five countries, in this order, are: Denmark, Norway, Sweden, Finland and the Netherlands, with the United Kingdom ranked 12th and the United States ranked 19th.[33]

For families, a focus on the rule of law should lead to a just set of written principles – the family's own 'civil code' – which they can document in a family constitution. If done well, they will be living in a just system, one they created for themselves, and they will also be happy, as discussed in the following section.

4. Happiness

When the 13 colonies of the United States agreed upon their "Declaration of Independence" from England, they did so with a prefatory statement that all men are endowed with certain unalienable rights: "that among these are Life, Liberty and the pursuit of Happiness" and that it is to secure these rights that governments are created "deriving their just powers from the consent of the governed".[34] Again, the same could apply to a family group. The powers of, say, the family board, are regarded as 'just' when they are given with the consent of the rest of the family.

At least two global organisations are studying, and ranking, the extent of 'happiness' in various countries. The World Happiness Report was first published in 2012. In its 2016 report, which includes some 156 countries, it notes the increasing interest in 'happiness' and comments that the growing global interest uses "happiness and subjective well-being as primary indicators of the quality of human development". The 2016 Report lists the following five countries at the top of the list, in this order: Denmark, Switzerland, Iceland, Norway and Finland, with the United Kingdom ranked 23rd and the United States 13th.[35]

This study of happiness is a serious business.[36] The Report stresses its importance:

Because of this growing interest, many governments, communities and organizations are using happiness data, and the results of subjective well-being research, to enable policies that support better lives.[37]

In the family setting the support of better lives is usually a primary goal. We could add a slight modification to the teaching of Confucius that "The strength of a nation [family] derives from the integrity [happiness] of the home."

Conclusion

Families who work together to agree on the rules they choose to be governed by, will be happier families – with the common culture of the family binding them together, one hopes for generations to come.

Note: I thank very helpful readers of prior drafts including: Susan Schoenfeld, Dennis Jaffe, Jim Grubman, Raimund Kamp, Marijke Kuijpers, Bonny Landers and Gene Lipitz.

Barbara R Hauser is an independent adviser based in Minnesota in the United States. She is a leading author on global family office issues and family governance. She was the advisory editor for Family Offices: The STEP Handbook for Advisers (http://www.globelawandbusiness.com/FOS).

1 I am reminded of the Pakistani patriarch, for example, who told me that he spent an entire summer in Philadelphia to study how the US constitution was created. He then applied those lessons to his own family.

2 Referred to as "The Oldest Code of Laws", it was written during the reign of Hammurabi, 2285 BC–2242 BC. A large number of the rules concern inheritance. For example, Section 179: "If a lady ... whose father has granted her a marriage portion, has written her a deed, in the deed he wrote her has written her 'after her wherever is good to her to give' ... she shall give, her brothers have no claim on her" (at p39).

3 During such time as England was part of the European Union.

4 Werner Menski, "The Uniform Civil Code Debate in Indian Law: New Developments and Changing Agenda," 9 German LJ (1 March 2008), p212.

5 See www.oxforddictionaries.com/us/definition/american_english/constitution.

6 See John Locke, *Civil Government*, Book II, 1690.

7 John Locke, *7 Works* (Kindle Locations 2681–2685).

8 Professor Daniela Montemerlo and Professor John L Ward, *The Family Constitution: Agreements to Secure and Perpetuate Your Family and Your Business*, Palgrave Macmillan 2011, p2.

9 Families searching for solutions were often referred to my book, *International Family Governance: A Guide for Families and their Advisors*, Mesatop Press, 2009, which seemed of special interest to families in the Gulf Region facing a generational transition – it is now also available in Arabic.

10 Deciding who is included is often a difficult issue in families, especially as to whether spouses should be included. I limit my role to sharing information on these and other issues but look to them to provide their answers.

11 See, for example, the District of Columbia rules of professional responsibility, at https://www.dcbar.org/bar-resources/legal-ethics/amended-rules/rule1-03.cfm.

12 Excluded are issues that are quite personal and not part of the group's concern or those that would not benefit by group discussion. This is not 'therapy' and it is not a revisit of past grievances – it is proactive agreement on issues that could become disruptive.

13 See generally, Barbara R Hauser, "Death Duties and Immortality:

Why Civilization Needs Inheritances", *Real Property, Probate and Trust Journal*, volume 34, number 2 at 400–401, and Barry Nicholas, *An Introduction to Roman Law*, Clarendon Law, 1962, pp237–238.

14 *Id.*

15 Known as the 'Hindu undivided family' (HUF) property, there are often tax advantages due to the lack of single ownership. See, for example, http://www.incometaxindia.gov.in/Pages/i-am/huf.aspx.

16 See, for example, the OECD Principles of Corporate Governance, updated in 2015, at http://www.oecd.org/corporate.

17 See https://www.oecd.org/daf/ca/Corporate-Governance-Principles-ENG.pdf.

18 Also, the term 'Family Council' has been used in a variety of ways. See the call for more research on Family Councils in "Do Family Councils Really Work? The Need for Empirical Study", by Carmen Bianchi and Keanon J Alderson (2012).

19 In the European Two-Tier Board system one Board is the management Board and one is the Supervisory Board. See, for example, https://www.researchgate.net/publication/228285393_Choosing_between_the_US_Single_Board_or_the_European_Two-Tier_Board_A_Brief_Comparative_Corporate_Governance_Analysis.

20 I remember Professor John Ward's advice to me many years ago that if a family chooses to roll dice to settle disputes, and they agree on that approach, that will work just fine.

21 The first is the Preamble, as discussed above.

22 I thank Jim Grubman for pushing for this explicit connection to the rule of law.

23 Barbara R Hauser, "Constitutions, Cultures and the Rule of Law", STEP Journal, September 2016.

24 Geoffrey de Q Walker, *The Rule of Law: Foundation of Constitutional Democracy* (1st edn, 1988), http://www.ruleoflaw.org.au/principles/. See also Brian Z Tamanaha, *On the Rule of Law*, Cambridge University Press, 2004.

25 See Barbara R Hauser, "Family Constitutions: Are They or Should They be Legally Binding?" *STEP Journal*, April 2012.

26 One family I worked with was at an impasse with the rules that would apply to the use of vacation homes, which rules the patriarch did not like. They reported their solution: "Those rules will not apply to him." Even that will work because the whole family agreed on it.

27 See also John Goldsworth, "Lexicon of Trust and Foundation Practice," at https://books.google.com/books?id=yf6-CwAAQBAJ&pg=PA278&dq=promissory+estoppel+origin&hl=en&sa=X&ved=0ahUKEwijt5HUtPbOAhWjAJoKHXI4DHgQ6AEILDAD#v=onepage&q=promissory%20estoppel%20origin&f=false.

28 John Rawls, "Justice As Fairness", p5, available at http://www.willbrehm.com/wp-content/uploads/2016/02/Rawls-Reading.pdf.

29 See, for example, http://www.academia.edu/1974076/Political_Philosophy_in_Italy_the_Influence_of_John_Rawls.

30 *Id* at p6.

31 See http://worldjusticeproject.org/who-we-are-0.

32 See http://worldjusticeproject.org/what-rule-law.

33 See http://worldjusticeproject.org/sites/default/files/roli_2015_0.pdf.

34 For the full, official text, see http://www.archives.gov/exhibits/charters/declaration_transcript.html.

35 See http://worldhappiness.report/wp-content/uploads/sites/2/2016/03/HR-V1_web.pdf.

36 Interestingly, Richard Layard, the author of the seminal *Happiness: Lessons from a New Science*, has an active role in the World Happiness Report.

37 See http://worldhappiness.report/.

Stress tests – building resilience in the face of a crisis

David Werdiger

I get knocked down, but I get up again
You are never gonna keep me down
Tubthumping (Chumbawamba, 1997)

Abstract

The international hit song Tubthumping *is about "the resilience of ordinary people"*[1] *and helped bring the working-class band back together after a period where they "had become directionless and disparate", according to vocalist Dunstan Bruce. Its catchy lyrics embody the essence of what resilience is about irrespective of class or social status, and are as relevant as ever during the Covid-19 pandemic.*

The pandemic has knocked us all down in various ways – for some families and individuals, it has been a significant 'jolt' to their sense of self and created doubts in the minds of family business owners and the leaders of family offices, as to their capacity to lead, and their trust in others they have appointed to do so.

At the same time, many have quickly been able to get back up again. Their family system has withstood the incidence of the risk and the investment they made, in good times, to develop values and a sense of shared purpose which has been the basis upon which they have not only survived but thrived. For many the crisis has reaffirmed the strength and benefit of their good governance.

A great deal of this is attributable to how deeply embedded the family's values were within the family system and, in particular, an appreciation of what it was possible for them to control – primarily their own reaction, personally and as a family, to the crisis.

This article, using case studies, will explore how family systems have reacted – for better or worse – to the Covid-19 health risk and how their ability to respond has been reflected in their foundations of good governance and shared values.

Approach

The impact of Covid-19 affects entire family systems, but specifically is felt by individuals in various positions of authority and/or leadership within the family enterprise. The resilience of those individuals is a function of both their personal resilience and that of the family system. They typically draw upon both wells to respond.

I have chosen to illustrate the response with three case studies that illustrate examples of the types of stresses that impact families:

- the weight of expectations (two examples);
- the actions of the non-family CEO; and
- a personal crisis (eg, divorce/illness/isolation).

These case studies are taken from real-world cases, and suitably de-identified and adapted to illustrate the impact and the response.

Case study 1 – weight of expectations

Everybody has a plan until they get punched in the mouth.
Mike Tyson, 2012

It has been many decades since the world has experienced an event of this magnitude, with an impact that is both broad and deep. Many businesses will not have seen anything like it in the business lifetimes of owners and managers. Western society has, in the main, enjoyed peace and prosperity for decades.

The popular 'generation wars' narrative has Baby Boomers calling Millennials 'soft' because they have never experienced war, extreme poverty or economic depression. At least now, no-one is gloating.

Consider two families that have followed similar paths: in each, third generation members Alan and Barry – aged in their 40s – are now responsible for the management of family A's operating business (Alan as CEO) and family B's pool of capital (Barry as CIO). Each did their required apprenticeship – spending at least five years working in external businesses, and completing MBAs – before joining the family enterprise. Each reported to the family board and have been working in these roles for over 10 years. These look like textbook models of good family leadership succession plans.

But in the face of Covid-19, both families were hit hard financially: family A's operating business – in retail fashion – was seriously disrupted, and family B's passive investments took an initial hit of over 20%. Nothing in the experience or education of these two rising generation leaders prepared them for this, and they each took it hard.

Alan went to see his grandfather, the founder with whom he always had a close relationship, and broke down in tears. "I don't know what to do next. I can't sleep. The burden of managing this responsibility on behalf of the family is just too much for me." His grandfather talked about his experience during wartime, and how the business nearly folded. "More than my bank manager keeping faith in my ability to trade through the crisis, it was your grandmother who stood by my side and was so supportive. It will be tough for everyone – financially and emotionally – but we will get through it."

Barry was similarly distraught and felt totally out of his depth in stewarding the family's investment portfolio through this. He took a couple of 'mental health days' where he was almost unable to get out of bed and questioned whether he had fallen into depression. After his return to work, he felt awkward raising the issue with his uncle ahead of preparing the quarterly reports, but knew he couldn't keep it to himself. His uncle offered support and encouragement, and they worked through the figures together, which included recommendations for a pause in family dividends.

This is where the stories of the two families diverge.

At family A's next family meeting, Alan's grandfather made an opening statement – speaking of his own experience overcoming adversity, and the family's series of meetings five years prior that had helped establish their shared vision. It set the context for the bad news that Alan had to deliver, and that portion of the meeting went extremely well. Afterwards, Alan hugged his grandfather: "Of all the ways you've helped me over the years, that would be up there with the best. I really feel everyone is behind me now, and that we can get through this".

Family B's meeting didn't go so well. There were already rumblings prior to the meeting of the investment losses and the planned dividend cut. Barry put on a good face, and his report was clinical and brutal. He didn't make excuses – the family had only marginally underperformed the market, and he remarked that there was little he would have done different with the benefit of hindsight. It was just a bitter pill the family had to swallow, and he remained stoic. But the demeanour around the board table was flat and unsupportive.

Both families took a punch to the face. In family A, Alan's grandfather gave Alan the support he needed at the time by drawing on the family's own experience. That was good old-fashioned parental empathy. But the preparation for the family meeting was a masterstroke of family leadership and strategy. They knew it was going to be tough. By drawing on the family's shared values, Alan's grandfather reframed how the bad news would be taken, and it had the desired effect. It gave both the family members the strength to accept what was happening, and Alan the mandate to steward the family assets through the crisis.

For family B, the punch to the face was felt like a punch to the gut that shook the family's foundations. While Barry's uncle was a strong personal support, there were clearly cracks in the unity of the family and their sense of common purpose that led to recriminations rather than support for the leadership. This acted as a vicious cycle – the family's despondence and lack of confidence in Barry spread to Barry, and made his job that much harder.

Case study 2 – family values under pressure

It's tough to be strategic when your pants are on fire
Ron Kifer, VP of Global IT, Hewlett-Packard, 2013

In response to Covid-19, the non-family member CEO took the necessary actions to ensure the family business's survival. In practice, that meant cutting staff, closing stores, or putting harsh terms on suppliers/customers. The business was stabilised and able to return to a steady footing through the crisis.

But something was amiss – there was a discomfort among family members about some of the specific steps the CEO took. It started as small talk – "I'm sure Grandpa wouldn't have done that when he was in charge" and slowly percolated around various family members. Eventually, it reached the stage where the family members who sit on the board of the operating business recognised there was significant discomfort within the family regarding the actions of the CEO.

At the next board meeting, they raised the issue with him, and naturally he felt a little under fire. "You employed me to run this business, and that's what I'm doing. We needed a very firm response to the pandemic, and as you can see, we will pull through OK." The CEO makes a strong case – the board has given him the authority to run the business. Equally, the family also have a point – the business bears their name, and the actions the business takes are a reflection on the family and their reputation.

There are lots of questions: Did the CEO do the right thing? Do the family have reasonable grounds

As families grow, it can be helpful to have a process (which engages a wide group of family members) where those values are discussed and clearly spelled out.

Organisational culture is driven top down, so the starting point for cultural change is always the board. How deep the board and the family want the values to permeate within the business is up to them.

to be upset? With a professionalised family business, could this have been done differently or better? If so, how?

This is a case of family operating business professionalisation half-done, or done in the wrong direction. The process was driven by a consensus succession decision by the founders and their children that they should appoint a non-family CEO. This was done with an operational focus: recruiting the role, and ensuring accountability to the owners via a board composed of family members plus independents. Most of the time that might be enough, but when put under stress the deficiencies became apparent.

The core issue here was a clash between the family's values and the behaviour of the professional, non-family CEO. In the past, the family values would have had a more direct link to management decisions made by family members in the operating business. With the professionalisation of the business, that link appears to have been broken. But how to re-establish the link?

The process starts with understanding the family values. While all families have a set of values, not all families are aware of them. They may have a sense of what they are, but can't necessarily articulate them. As families grow, it can be helpful to have a process (which engages a wide group of family members) where those values are discussed and clearly spelled out.

A family business, while created for the purpose of wealth generation, often embodies the values of the founders in some way. Because the family members are deeply engaged in the business, their personal values drive business behaviour and practice. Hence "how Grandpa would do it" becomes both the unwritten operations guide for the business, and part of the family story. Values and organisational culture become embedded in the business, and transmitted to employees – family members and otherwise – who join.

The professionalisation of a family business – addition of external management, a board with independent directors, and the departure of some family members from executive roles – can lead to a loss of both corporate memory and some of the cultural/values underpinnings of the business. That is where the family's process fell short. To resolve this, two steps are required.

The first is for the family to have those facilitated discussions about their values. Family values are not transmitted generationally like Moses coming down from the mountain with two tablets of stone – they evolve over time. Accordingly, it is important to involve family members from multiple generations in the discussions. The result of the values discussions may be a document like a family charter or constitution, but that is not a necessary outcome. Indeed, the discussions themselves and the journey of discovery are as important as the destination.

Once the family has a clear understanding of its values, they can gain insight into how those values have or have not been honoured by the actions of the CEO.

The second step is to formally embody those values in the family business. Usually, we think of non-profits as values-driven organisations, and for-profits being about 'maximising shareholder value'. But, as explained, values are an important part of the family business, and indeed one of the things that makes the family business special and more enduring. It is possible for those businesses to be both profit-seeking and true to their values.

The values can be articulated in board documents to give them the authority and gravitas to drive management behaviour. Organisational culture is driven top down, so the starting point for cultural change is always the board. How deep the board and the family want the values to permeate within the business is up to them. It can be expressed in the delegation to management, or go further through the human resources side of the business.

This example showed the weakness in the family's governance structure, and the lack of articulation of the shared values. The CEO did everything that was asked of him. But the family didn't realise the additional things they needed to ask of him. Knowing or even articulating family values is not enough; those values need to permeate the family enterprise, up to and including non-family member employees. Only then can they be an effective support structure in times of stress.

Further, we see that setting the values and governance framework is not something that can be done in a hurry, and certainly not when the operating business is under severe stress. The lack of well-articulated values (in stable times) poses a risk to the family enterprise's ability to respond in unstable times.

Case Study 3 – personal crisis

A problem shared is a problem halved.
proverb

In this family, the impact of Covid-19 was as direct as it gets: Frank, the 58-year-old second-generation CEO of the family enterprise fell ill with the virus, and was hospitalised. His condition rapidly declined and he was moved to intensive care and put on a ventilator.

There were several layers to the impact on the family. His parents, both in their mid-80s and in reasonable health, were devastated and took the extra precaution of moving to their holiday residence, safe and away from the rest of the family who remained in the city. His immediate family members were equally distraught, the situation compounded by restrictions on visiting times. Two other family members developed milder symptoms, but did not require hospitalisation.

The family operating business board convened an emergency meeting (via zoom, of course) when Frank fell ill. When Frank turned 50, he had a full panel of health checks and initiated a review of key person risk in the business, with a special emphasis on family members. The risk discussion focused both on health and lifestyle – family members who worked in the business expressed the desire not to be bound to the business (as the founder was) and have the option to take regular extended vacations with their families without a material impact on operations. That aspect made the risk review more comfortable, as it helped avoid unpleasant discussions about mortality. The operating business employed Frank's brother-in-law, and four members of the third generation.

The COO (Mary, a non-family member) stepped up as acting CEO, and two others from middle management were seconded to support her on a part-time basis. The board also switched to meeting twice per month, with weekly updates from the acting CEO. Frank's father had retired nearly 15 years earlier and had not attended a board meeting for 10 years. While neither he nor any of the family had any interest in him returning to an operating role, he did catch up with Mary every two to three weeks to provide general support and guidance.

The operating business struggled with the dual hits of Covid and Frank's absence. Mary was initially uncomfortable about some of the decisions that were required of her, and regularly consulted with the board and Frank's father. Everyone around her stepped up and ensured she was aware that they were prepared to help.

The family council also convened an emergency meeting to discuss the physical and emotional support needs of the whole family. Additional resources were procured to ensure everyone stayed healthy in both body and mind. The council initiated weekly zoom check-ins for the entire family (which numbered nearly 30) – done at an agreed dinner time so it felt like everyone was having dinner together. There was a regular update on everyone's health, and a chance for everyone to talk about their challenges and feel supported. Frank's parents took the opportunity to tell stories of their own adversity challenges. The dinners were a very effective family bonding exercise, at a time when regular social contact was suspended.

After several tense weeks, Frank's condition started to improve, and eventually after nearly three months, he returned home – weakened but alive. As of July, he remained at home and maintained a part-time role supporting Mary as acting CEO.

This is a model of a strong family governance response to a crisis. In hindsight, the family considered itself neither underprepared nor overprepared. In a crisis, people often overcompensate, which is not sustainable. It is impossible to plan for all possible scenarios. There are many points at which this still could have turned bad (and still could). Equally, the structures were there to support the family and its operating business in a crisis, and they went into effect like a well-oiled machine.

Analysis

Strategy without tactics is the slowest route to victory. Tactics without strategy is the noise before defeat.
Sun Tzu

Through these case studies, we have seen several examples of the impact of Covid-19 and the family's response. In the boxing metaphor, the impact is felt in specific places (a punch in the face), but the body's ability to respond is a function of the boxer's core

In a crisis, people often overcompensate, which is not sustainable. It is impossible to plan for all possible scenarios.

strength. In family systems, the impact is felt by specific family members in specific roles. Depending on their role within the family, that impact can reverberate throughout the family system. Accordingly, the response requires the support of various other aspects of the family system, and for families, this means their governance and values.

We can think of this using the diagram below, which positions resilience at the top of a pyramid, which has good governance and shared values as its foundation. The family's resilience is tested during the stress of Covid-19 at the top of the pyramid, but can only be remedied through those elements at the bottom of the triangle.

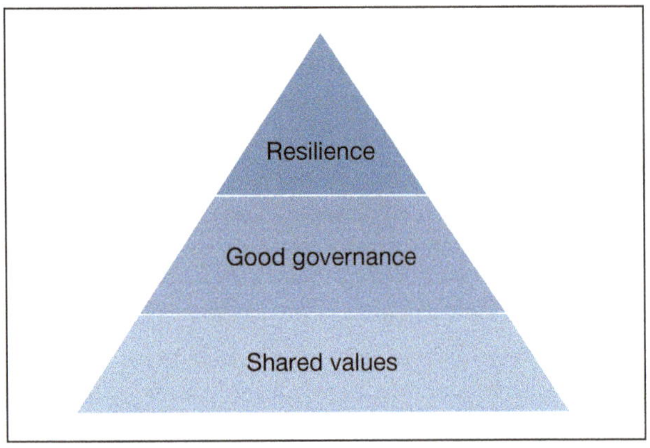

We can similarly view resilience (both impact and response) as tactical, and the foundations of governance and values as strategic. As Sun Tzu points out, a family response to a crisis that is only tactical is just noise before defeat. The succession response of the families in our case studies are built upon the strategic work completed earlier in discovering – usually through facilitated discussions – their shared values and articulating them clearly, and using that as a foundation to build the governance structure by which the family operates.

We can further illustrate this through a summary of the case studies in the table below, which shows the state of their shared values and governance at the time of the crisis, and noting their response.

Conclusion

The importance of shared values and governance is well known, yet families often push the activity required to establish these to the back burner. Why? Because operational issues tend to take a higher priority, and because of the amount of effort required to explore and articulate family values and establish governance. It gives rise to unpleasant feelings about mortality, and can bring latent conflict to the surface. The easy path is to kick the can down the road, and push it out to the next family meeting for consideration.

Its value only becomes evident during a time of crisis, by which time it's too late to quickly cobble together the foundation. Inadequately articulated values and lack of governance are therefore a risk to families, and accordingly need to be part of the broader risk discussion, which often only focuses on financial and operational risk.

In Case Study 3, the family had key person contingency plans. Family enterprises more than others have significant key person risk, and being aware of these risks and planning for them is certainly not being overprepared.

No family can avoid the punch in the face. Every family can build a strong core so that they can bounce back.

	Case Study 1A	**Case Study 1B**	**Case Study 2**	**Case Study 3**
Shared values	Articulated and deeply embedded; expressed by leaders in times of crisis	Unknown or lacking	Known, but not articulated, and not reflected in policy	Well articulated
Governance	Good	Good	Good	Excellent: included contingency plans
Resilience	Held up well	Cracks in the castle	Under pressure	Strong and robust response

Based in Melbourne Australia, David Werdiger works with high-net-worth families and their businesses with a focus on succession planning, family/business shared vision and governance, managing family conflict, and general strategic advice. David's diverse background gives him a powerful mix of skills: second generation family member, tech entrepreneur, Adjunct Professor at Swinburne University, best-selling author on wealth transition and a dynamic conference speaker and educator.

1 Homa Khaleeli, "How we made Chumbawamba's Tubthumping", *The Guardian*, 5 April 2016, www.theguardian.com/culture/2016/apr/05/how-we-made-chumbawumba-tubthumping.

Why is family governance important? For the same reasons that good governance at a country level or a corporate level is also important.

The benefits of applying the rule of law in family governance

Barbara R Hauser

Overview

This is a shortened version of my PhD thesis at the University of Zurich Law School approved in October 2021. After a career as an international private client lawyer, I began paying attention to how families make decisions – a field known as 'family governance'. This field gradually supplanted the tax and legal advice with which I was so familiar. I concluded that more important than the sophisticated legal structures put in place were the underlying decision-making patterns, explicit or implicit, in a family. A poor governance system too often results in family conflict and family litigation. This seems particularly true when inheritance is the issue. If, however, a family group can be compared to a country and general governance principles can be applied in a similar manner, why not begin with the rule of law? If a country is better governed when it is committed to the rule of law is not a family better governed if it also follows the rule of law? To go one step further, if a country has benefits from following the rule of law would not a family have similar benefits?

What is family governance and why is it important?

Governance in general is the process by which decisions are made. Family governance then is the process by which a family unit makes decisions. Why is family governance important? For the same reasons that good governance at a country level or a corporate level is also important. As stated by the Canadian Institute on Governance,[1] governance is extremely important because good governance builds citizen trust in the democratic institutions, builds social cohesion, and is the foundation for economic growth and stability. At the corporate level we can also benefit from the work done by the Organisation for Economic Cooperation and Development (OECD) at the corporate (listed) company level. The two key principles promulgated by the OECD for corporate governance are transparency[2] and accountability.[3] I ague that those are also two key principles that should be applied in family governance. In addition to those two key principles, I have developed a third principle which I have found to be quite important in a family context – the principle of participation.

Looking at the value of those three principles, applied in a family setting, we would have the following. First, the transparency principle would mean that the secrets so many families harbour would be coaxed to come out for public discussion and thereby lose their negative strength. Second, the accountability principle would mean that family members would be expected to keep their promises. Keeping one's promises is the very foundation of justice.[4] Third, in all governance systems, but especially in family systems in my experience, it is critical that each family member has been able to express themselves and to have their views heard. In studies of countries in which the citizens rate themselves as high in subjective well-being, one of the distinguishing factors is that they feel they participate in their governance.[5]

Let's look briefly at family decision-making, which is how I translate family governance at a practical level. When do families actually make decisions as a family? As I have written previously,[6] there are two categories of decisions. The first category, which is one that estate planners face most often, is when the family members have joint interests of some kind. It could be that there are a series of family trusts; it could be that they actually own an operating business together; or there could be properties or assets – compounds, yachts, villas, aircraft, etc – that are considered jointly owned in some respect. In terms of decision-making, some of the classic systems revert to the primal issue of control. Control over family decisions is also akin to having power in the family.[7] A second, and more nuanced, category of family decision-making is when they do not necessarily own assets jointly but they have an emotional desire to stay as a family group, committed to each other, for several generations.[8] These groups also encounter issues of power and control. They have the daunting challenge of developing a way in which and a compelling rationale for the younger family members[9] to opt in to the family culture, legends and commitments. The field of family governance includes these efforts.

In my dissertation I review an inventory of the current tools that are used in family governance. There are many, including: family meetings, pooled investments, family balance sheets, family councils, family boards, junior boards, mission statements, values statements, family trusts, shareholder agreements, partnership agreements, marital agreements, holding companies, family offices, family constitutions, family venture funds, philanthropic entities, etc.

These are all helpful tools. What they seem to lack, in my opinion, is a basic common foundation. This *ad hoc* collection of family governance tools would benefit immensely from having a strong base so that the governance system could be founded upon principles of justice and fairness. The framework would then have woven into it the three critical principles: transparency, accountability and participation. This search leads us directly to the rule of law.

What is the rule of law and why is it important?
The rule of law is referred to often, but is not easy to define. As stated in *Democracy and the Rule of Law*: "The relationship between the rule of law and democracy is asymmetrical: the rule of law can exist without democracy, but democracy needs the rule of law".[10]

The simplest definition of the rule of law is that it refers to a system of ruling by laws, not by men.[11] This refers to the prevention of individual treatment that could be implemented in an arbitrary, capricious and unfair manner.

The phrase 'the rule of law' is often contrasted with 'the rule by men' as an explanation of why it is better to have non-discretionary laws and not to give power to men who can be arbitrary and unpredictable.[12] This sense reflects a choice "which extends as far back as Aristotle, to prefer the rule of law to unrestrained rule by another".[13] Brian Tamanaha, author of *On the Rule of Law*, argues that the rule of law has three distinct meanings.[14] The first meaning is that even the government is limited by laws, as in the Magna Carta where even the king agrees to be bound by the law.[15] Professor Tamanaha argues that despite the riddle of how the person who made the law could be bound by the law, it did work because "everyone in society shared in the belief that officials were bound by the law, which insured that this attitude remained constant through changes in regimes and officials".[16]

The second meaning that Professor Tamanaha describes is the existence of legal rules that are promulgated and followed, making predictability possible.[17] Although the existence of formal rules may look like a positive, Professor Tamanaha makes the point that the legally formal and clear rules may nonetheless be unjust rules, predictable though they may be.[18] He comments that a limitation of the rule of law is that "it is compatible with a regime of laws with inequitable or evil content ... An unjust set of laws is not made just by adherence to formal requirements".[19]

The third and final meaning of the rule of law that he presents is a return to the original basic concept that it is "better to have a rule by laws and not by men".[20] The underlying weakness in this basic meaning, however, is that it does not provide for an enforcement mechanism.[21] In a government this enforcement role would fall to the judiciary.[22]

How would a family apply the rule of law?
The central criticism of the panoply of available tools in the family governance field, described above, is that it is a random *ad hoc* collection. There is no overall structure or framework.

My proposition is to design a framework and then fit the various tools into that framework. That framework can be a version of the rule of law. In an earlier section we described several meanings of the rule of law. For family decision-making we will use a combination of those meanings: the central tenet that the rules will apply to all family members; that the rules will be arrived at through a process that appears to be a just one, incorporating the principles of transparency, accountability and participation; and that a method to raise disputed issues is included.

In a family setting, the members come together and agree to be bound by certain rules for the benefit of being part of the family group.[23] An experienced adviser, Ian Marsh, writes that "we feel safer being part of the group than if we are left out".[24] As Marsh describes the importance of belonging to a group, just as with Locke's social contract there is a trade-off. Marsh comments that "to keep our membership current, we may need to forgo some of our own particular wants and needs".[25] The nature of particular rules may differ significantly from family to family. Differences come from many sources: cultures, external environments and economies, personalities, religious beliefs, experiences with wealth, resentments and jealousies, family history, and family goals for the future, to name a few.

The issue is whether the rule of law can be applied to family governance, and, if so, then how it would be

The phrase 'the rule of law' is often contrasted with 'the rule by men' as an explanation of why it is better to have non-discretionary laws and not to give power to men who can be arbitrary and unpredictable.

The most crucial element of the rule of law is the kernel of procedural justice – the principle that the rules that are developed, whatever they may turn out to be, will apply to everyone in the family unit.

applied in a practical manner. Finally, it needs to be determined whether similar benefits as those that accrue at the country level would also accrue at the family level. This critically important proposition has not received any attention in the field of family governance.

The most crucial element of the rule of law is the kernel of procedural justice – the principle that the rules that are developed, whatever they may turn out to be, will apply to everyone in the family unit. That will ensure that the family will have agreed to be "ruled by laws and not by men" as stated by Aristotle.[26] Additional features of the rule of law that will apply to a family unit include the key three features of good governance, discussed above, transparency, accountability and participation.

Advisers to wealthy families tend to focus on structures, and families become accustomed to having tangible elements in their plans: trusts, private trust companies, family limited partnerships, holding companies, special-purpose offshore vehicles, etc. With a family constitution project, the families and their advisers are likely to be more interested in the final product than in the process.[27] That attitude changes as the process takes shape and the family can appreciate the results. For many families, this will be the first time they have worked together to communicate their wishes for a decision in any number of sensitive areas. As Professors Montemerlo and Ward explain, it is the process of developing the Family Agreement that builds family decision-making and problem-solving skills.[28] The process "educates family members about their own histories and their business as it functions today. The process motivates family members to consider the collective good and an overarching sense of purpose for business ownership and for family as family".[29]

Two case examples – applying the rule of law in family governance

The clean slate

In the first case, the family, of ethnic Chinese heritage, had become quite separated from each other as each adult child moved to a different part of the country, even in one case to another country. The parents who had created the wealth had kept the family together for social purposes. When the parents both passed away the four adult children continued with increasingly separate lives, without the parents to call them together from time to time. As time went on, the four children had their own children, who when they grew up also moved to different locations, even different countries. Gradually the family members seemed to have very little in common.

Then one day the privately held company they had inherited from their parents issued a successful public offering, which generated a large amount of cash together with an obligation to serve on the board of the company. One brother had been involved in the company operations; the other siblings had not been involved and did not in fact have much information about what the company operations were, although they could check the value of their stock at any time. After a few years, clear tensions had developed. The sister and brothers who did not know much about the company began to ask questions and want more information. In addition to the company shares, there were a number of complicated trusts that had been created by the parents, and the children also had very little information about those trusts.

The oldest brother who was active in the company took over – without discussion or agreement – much of the investment function of the new liquid portfolio, seeing himself as the representative of the company and of the family wealth. The members of the third generation knew very little about the company or the family wealth and were busy creating their own professional lives and starting families of their own.

Their financial adviser could see the likely conflicts that would arise. There was no transparency, no accountability and no participation (other than by the one brother.) The money manager conducted a search for a consultant, without having a clear idea of what was needed by the family. The chosen adviser began by getting to know each of the second generation. It was clear that they had not developed successful methods of discussing issues among themselves. One went too fast, another did not understand the business jargon, another was just not very interested in trying to work together. They had not developed any system of family decision-making. What they needed to create was a comprehensive method of good decision-making. This was more than a single issue, this would be a new experience – they could commit to following the rule of law.

One of the first recommendations by the consultant was to hire a specialist human resources adviser who administered a variety of personality tests to help each family member better understand the others and the various communication and learning styles they had. This enabled the family to begin to have successful conversations and to take into account their varying communication style preferences. They could discuss how they would want to make decisions as a family. Note that this incorporated the principle of transparency. For the first time all the family members received the same information and reviewed it in a group setting. They agreed to honour their decisions. This agreement, which included making written reports on the decisions that had been made, included the principle of accountability.

The method of building their interest was done gradually. With an awareness that there had not been much education on the family trusts and wealth for the younger generation, the second generation agreed to include the younger generation at the beginning of a new project – the establishment of a family office.

The third generation was offered the opportunity to choose the name for their new family office. That project had the third generation working together for the first time. The second generation assured them that the name they chose would be the final name. This created an immediate interest by the third generation.

For the first time, they were actually invited to participate in building an entity for the entire family, including future generations. Note that this incorporated the crucial principle of participation. The third generation continued to be interested as the family decision-making process was developed.

Both generations decided to work together to create a family constitution. They liked the idea of putting all of their governance rules and decisions into one master document. They started drafting a comprehensive family constitution. In it they included a number of oversight committees to provide for more participation.

A new family office would interact directly with each family member and provide quarterly reports. Now all the family members had a source of information about all of their investments and interests. This reinforced the concepts of transparency and accountability. They also created a Family Council, providing for representation by each branch. This provided a means for the continuing participation by the third generation.

Finally, they created a number of committees and filled them with volunteer members from both generations, allowing even more participation. One committee that undertook immediate action was the investment committee, which was admittedly one of the more urgent needs. By involving the new committee, both generations had an opportunity to organise the information about their many holdings in a manner that was understandable to each of them. As they became familiar with the holdings, they were able to begin evaluating the various managers.

For the first time the family was in a position to give true oversight to their own investments. They had transformed themselves from disinterested and uninformed wealth owners to active and competent owners, with transparent information and accountability to each other. They worked closely together and found an enjoyment in the process itself.

In sum, this was a situation where the family did not begin with a developed system of decision-making. Instead, their decisions had been *ad hoc* and often unilateral, often without informing other family members of those decisions. This family was able to start its governance work with a clean slate.

They agreed they wanted to work together as a family and also to do so for the benefit of future generations. They agreed to adopt the rule of law in creating their decision-making and to follow the three key principles: transparency, accountability and participation. This included a commitment by the entire family to abide by the outcome of the fair process, even though it is not known at the beginning of the process.

The second case, discussed in some detail in the book, is one in which the family-owned operating company had been in existence for nearly 40 years and employed some 5,000 people in three main branches. The senior branches fostered numerous conflicts and

They had transformed themselves from disinterested and uninformed wealth owners to active and competent owners, with transparent information and accountability to each other.

disagreements about the future of the business conglomerates. Their younger generation worried that the company would be split apart, due to the conflict, and they wanted to keep the company together. They persuaded the elders to hire a governance consultant.

The challenge in this case was to change the governance process while continuing to operate the company. It would be quite a challenge to propose management changes while continuing to operate. Because the company had grown without much strategic planning, there was a lot of ambiguity about the roles of each position. There was a lack of clarity about the qualifications needed for a specific function. There were multiple overlaps in the reporting lines. There were more than 100 separate balance sheets for the multiple divisions.

It was decided that the organisation would benefit from a fresh restructuring. A human resources consultant was hired. He helped the owners prepare new organisational charts that described the nature of each position and its corresponding capabilities – without reference to the existing occupant.

Special off-site management sessions helped reach agreement on the structure of the company from the ground level up. When the focus eventually moved up to the senior management level it was much easier to justify the placement of the various managers.

Throughout the process there had been a commitment to transparency, accountability and participation, which made all the difference. Going forward, the management added an independent board for the first time. The result was that the company increased its financial success while pleasing the younger family members who now had clear roles. It was a great outcome.

Additional benefits of applying the rule of law

The original thesis – that following the rule of law would result in better governance – has led to the appearance of a number of additional benefits. The first, and primary motivating principle is to lessen family conflict.

An additional and valuable benefit, referred to earlier, is the feeling of subjective well-being or to use the original term 'happiness'. If following the rule of law leads to happiness in the family unit, that spreads among the neighboring society. On a country level, studies show a correlation between countries that follow the rule of law and those that rank high on subjective well-being.[30]

These and additional experiences have convinced the author that when the rule of law is followed those in the group – whether it is a country or a family – are able to plan with confidence that there will be transparency, accountability and participation. In other words, there will be a sense of fairness and justice.

Conclusion

Family groups engage in governance all the time. Good governance can strengthen a family and increase family harmony. The best approach is to begin with a commitment to follow the rule of law. This means that they will follow procedural justice as they make decisions, being careful to demonstrate transparency, accountability and participation.

Dr Barbara R Hauser, PhD, JD, is the Founding Editor of The International Family Offices Journal. *She began her career as a private client lawyer and gradually moved into the area of family governance. Barbara has worked with a diverse group of families and has written extensively about the principles of family governance.*

1 The Canadian Institute on Governance, www.iog.ca.
2 The Organisation for Economic Cooperation and Development's Principles of Corporate Governance, www.oecd.org/corporate/principles-corporate-governance.
3 *Ibid.*
4 See John Rawls, *A Theory of Justice* (1971).
5 See Richard Layard, *Happiness: Lessons from a New Science* (2005).
6 Barbara R Hauser, "Family Governance: Who, What and How", *Journal of Wealth Management* (2002).
7 This power is similar to the ancient Greek theory that the family's wealth was under the legal control of the *paterfamilias*.
8 See Dennis T Jaffe, *Borrowed from your Grandchildren: The Evolution of 100-Year Family Enterprises* (2020).
9 Now referred to as the "rising generation" by Jay Hughes.
10 John Ferejohn and Pasquale Pasquino, *Rule of Democracy and Rule of Law* (2003), pp242–60 and Jean Hampton, "Democracy and the Rule of Law", *Nomos* 36: 113–44 (1994), www.jstor.org/stable/24219503. See also Brian Z Tamanaha, *On the Rule of Law: History, Politics, Theory* (2004), p37 and Jose Maria Maravall, "Democracy and the Rule of Law" in *Cambridge Studies in the Theory of Democracy* (Kindle location 943–944).
11 See, eg, "The rule of law, at its most basic, means that the law applies to everyone equally. It means that no one is above the law". It is also popularly understood as "a government of law, not of men", Judge Rowena Nievesa A Tan, "A Government of Law, not of Men", *The Manila Times*, Philippines, www.ipsnews.net/2016/09.
12 Brian Z Tamanaha, *On the Rule of Law: History, Politics, Theory* (2008), p122.
13 *Ibid.*
14 Brian Z Tamanaha, *On the Rule of Law: History, Politics, Theory* (2004), pp114–23.
15 "By declaring the sovereign to be subject to the rule of law and documenting the liberties held by 'free men,' the Magna Carta provided the foundation for individual rights in Anglo-American jurisprudence", Britannica, www.britannica.com/topic/Magna-Carta.
16 Brian Z Tamanaha, *On the Rule of Law: History, Politics, Theory* (2004), p116.
17 *Id*, p119.
18 *Id*, p120.
19 *Ibid.*
20 *Id*, p122.
21 *Ibid.*
22 In a family this role may be filled by selected elders.
23 *Ibid.*
24 Ian A Marsh, *If it is So Good to Talk Why is it So Hard?* (2018), p230.
25 *Ibid.*
26 Brian Z Tamanaha, *On the Rule of Law: History, Politics, Theory* (2008), p122.
27 In the author's experience.
28 Daniela Montemerlo and John L Ward, *The Family Constitution: Agreements to Secure and Perpetuate Your Family and Your Business* (2011), p2.
29 *Id*, p5.
30 See www.worldjusticeproject.org and www.worldhappiness.report.

The great man fallacy and family governance

Franklin J Parker

The great man ...

When Philip II of Macedon rose to power in 359 BCE, his kingdom was a mess. Macedon had been defeated by the Illyrians, and his eastern flank had been invaded and sacked by the Paeonians and Thracians. Worse, the Athenians had landed on the coast with a would-be usurper to his throne. Over the course of decades, Phillip II secured his reign and pushed back Macedon's enemies through clever manoeuvring, diplomacy and a complete reorganisation of the Macedonian army. The now-famous Greek phalanx was the brainchild of Philip II.

Today, Philip II is better known as the father of Alexander the Great. Looking to give his son every possible advantage, Alexander was educated by no less than Aristotle himself, and his father also encouraged his education in more practical matters, sending him on military campaigns throughout the Balkan region at the age of 16. At 20 years old, upon the untimely death of his father, Alexander inherited the throne of Macedon. For a over a decade, he expanded the borders of his kingdom on what is now considered the most successful military campaign in history, subjugating over 5 million square kilometres with a 'mere' 50,000-man army (by comparison, Darius III of Persia is estimated to have fielded anywhere from 100,000 to 250,000 men). Philip II and Alexander, by any definition, accomplished great things and left their inheritance in better shape than they found it.

... fallacy

Yet, even the most famous rulers in human history are subject to the tired cliché, "from shirtsleeves to shirtsleeves in three generations". Alexander died at age 32 with no heir. This lack of clear succession plunged the expansive Macedonian territory into chaos. His generals and their descendants fought over fragments of the kingdom for at least a generation, and not until the Roman empire some 350 years later would another political body control so wide a territory.

By contrast, Rome grew steadily and prosperously (by ancient standards, at least) generation after generation. Even in the imperial period, the loss of an emperor was not a cataclysmic political event. The chain of command remained relatively intact and social order was generally kept (civil wars aside, of course).

Rome and Macedon have more to teach us than just history. Contrasting them is an object lesson in family governance, believe it or not. What was it that made Rome successful, generation after generation, while the kings of Macedon lasted just two? Of course, there are many variables at play, but I would suggest that Rome had one critical thing which Macedon did not: governance.

While Philip or Alexander were in power, the state held itself together through the will and competence of one man. However, as soon as that powerful man was no longer occupying the kingship, the state fell apart – along with the peace of the empire. Rome, by contrast, had the Senate, a system of jurisprudence, and a well-defined hierarchy of leadership that lent a stability to the transition of power. Sure, there were arguments about who was in charge between those near the top, but the whole apparatus did not generally fall apart when such arguments occurred.

One wonders what might have happened if Alexander had spent time overhauling Macedon's governance structure rather than pushing further east? Maybe 3 million square kilometres would have been enough if it could have been held for generations to come? Maybe a generation of war between Alexander's generals – as close as brothers when Alexander was alive – could have been avoided?[1]

At work in families

Wealthy families are not too dissimilar in this contrast between Rome and Macedon. In her 2002 article, "Family Governance", Barbara Hauser[2] draws a similar analogy between family governance and a political governance. The reliance on one great man is essentially a family dictatorship. As Hauser points out, at its best this governance structure offers the philosopher king, as envisaged by Plato, but the low probability of this outcome and the corrupting influence of power lend considerable weight to the argument against such an approach.

In my own practice, I have occasionally seen families stuck on the great man fallacy – the idea that the family must continue to produce and train great leaders to operate the enterprise or handle the family wealth. There is an air of tradition, pride and legacy in such an idea. To be fair, it is often a great man or woman who created the family's wealth in the first place, so there is some justification drawn from the family narrative. If it isn't broken, why fix it?

This is, however, a Macedonian attitude. While it

may work for a generation or two, it will not be long before a great leader is hard to come by and the family is left to scrabble over the territory that is left, like Alexander's generals. Such an approach also tends to crush competent family members under the weight of generational legacy, silently thrusting would-be leaders to seek other paths – paths that offer places to fail safely and quietly. Also, the data seems to show that a family business that goes through a leadership transition does worse than its peers when the successor is a family member.[3] It is rare, as it happens, that a family has someone in the next generation who can lead, wants to lead, and builds the requisite skill set to do so.

The insidious thing about the great man fallacy is that most families are entirely unaware that they've adopted it as an ideology. None of it is conscious, of course, it tends to seep silently into the family's culture, the family narrative. There are, however, a few tell-tale signs:

- The family's history is one of direct heirs from one line in the dominant position of influence or control;
- Non-controlling shareholders are unengaged;
- Next gens are unengaged and/or actively looking for ways out of the business of the family;
- Shareholder decisions are all unanimous; and
- There is little to no formal governance structure, or if there is it exists on paper only.

The first point is obvious. If the family leader comes from one line of the family, typically the firstborn from a long line of firstborns, then this is a strong signal that the great leader fallacy is at play. Again, this is very likely unnoticed by the family – this is the way it has always been done, so no one thinks to question it – but it should be questioned. If nothing else, we can make a statistical argument: what are the odds that the very best leader for the family is always descended from that side of the family? What are the odds the best leader is drawn from the family at all? As referenced earlier, the data seems to indicate that this approach is inferior.

The next two points might be counterintuitive. How are unengaged shareholders a signal for the great man fallacy being at work? Isn't entitlement, especially among the younger generation, a more plausible answer? Perhaps entitlement cannot always be ruled out. However, in my experience, entitlement is rarer than we might think, at least among family shareholders older than 25 or so. At play here, in my view, is a subtler dynamic of which disengagement is a symptom. Characteristic of the great man fallacy is a concentration of power, often outright voting power but sometimes less overt power – a power of influence and expectation.

Here is the telltale question: can the family leader be fired by shareholders? If the answer to that is 'no', then unengaged shareholders are probably a symptom of the great man fallacy at work in the family. Think about it: why should shareholders bother with the hard work of staying engaged? Why learn to read financial statements? Why lean in and ask the difficult questions at shareholder meetings? Why vote against the recommendation of the leader? Shareholders know when their voice matters, and when it does not. Which is also why unanimous shareholder decisions can be another signal of this problem. That is, if there are shareholder decisions.

Often, in such scenarios, there is no formalised governance structure. Rather, there is one person as the decision maker with an unspoken structure of influence and proximity to him or her. In other cases, some form of shareholder council exists but it is just a rubber-stamp organisation, mindlessly approving the decisions of the family leader.

A deeper problem

Setting this right is a critically important task.

Concentration of governance in the hands of one individual leads to the same problem Macedon experienced with Alexander the Great: generational transitions are fraught. Other problems can arise, too, such as the corrupting influence of power. The real necessity, however, is deeper and subtler than that.

Shareholders have an important job. They are the last line of defence against a failing business. Because it is their capital at risk – and often their livelihood in the case of a wealthy family – it is assumed that shareholders are properly motivated to uncover and solve problems as they arise. The great man fallacy removes that motivation, however, for many of the reasons just mentioned. Unengaged shareholders who do not develop the necessary skill set, who do not ask the difficult questions of their executive, who become a rubber-stamp function are in no position to find problems, much less solve them.

This abdication of responsibility puts the shareholders, the business, all of the employee's

Shareholders have an important job. They are the last line of defence against a failing business.

Turning a ship is not an easy task – larger ships require larger rudders. So, too, with the human aspects of an organisation.

families and even the business' vendors at risk. Just to put the broader picture into context: some 80% of global GDP is produced by family businesses.[4] The decisions (or indecisions) of family shareholders ripple far beyond the family – they ripple through your local community and out into the global economy.

It is the ultimate responsibility of the *shareholders*, and no one else, to ensure that their business remains a going concern. When the great man fallacy is at work, however, shareholders abdicate their sacred responsibility with the assumption that it will get taken care of. That works until it doesn't.

Powerless (or toothless) shareholders are a recipe for chaos when trouble does finally hit. Once shareholders have to forego quarterly checks or, worse yet, put cash into the business, engagement will not be an issue. By then, however, it may be too late and the constructive dynamics needed to solve the problem are unlikely to be developed amidst a crisis. Even worse, the family itself risks being torn apart.

We can again draw an analogy from the political sphere: revolutions tend to occur when the basic needs of the populace are no longer met. The contract between citizen and leader – even in a dictatorship – is my wellbeing for your power. When my wellbeing is compromised, so is your power.

The same dynamic is at play in family governance. When the great man has broken the implicit contract (my wellbeing for your power), a revolution is very likely to occur in the family, and revolutions are notoriously ferocious. Revolutions may give rise to new forms of governance, but familial relations are almost certainly the first casualty, with wealth not far behind.

Governance allows wealthy families to navigate a crisis without sacrificing their wealth or their family. Governance builds the dynamics for productive crisis management before the crisis. Governance empowers family shareholders to do their sacred duty as overseers of organisations that feed more people than just the family. Governance even allows for 'bloodless revolutions' when power changes are required.

To be fair, the reliance on a strong family leader *is* an approach to governance. Rather than spreading responsibility and authority among many individuals, this approach vests it all in one. As experience, data and the long attrition of human history has taught us, however, this is an extremely dangerous approach to governance in the long term. Better, by far, for the family to conduct a peaceful revolution today and restructure their approach to governance from the ground up.

A bloodless revolution

Turning a ship is not an easy task – larger ships require larger rudders. So, too, with the human aspects of an organisation. Family size and wealth size hint at the size of the effort required to implement changes in influence, power and the dynamic between individuals. How then can great man families turn their ship?

Most importantly, family members vested with the most power and influence must lead the way. This is a big ask, to be sure. For one, rarely does the leader of the family realise the need for change. A realisation may arise from a disconnect from deep-seated family assumptions (eg, "my son will take over one day") or from a groundswell in interest and pressure from other family shareholders (eg, "we have all decided that something has to change"). Absent such a realisation, however, I would dare to say that a move away from one-man rule (or few-man rule) in family governance is nigh impossible without the support and ongoing effort of the one man (or few men). It is possible, but that is almost certainly not a bloodless revolution.

Manoeuvring can push families closer to an alternate governance path. Some traction might be gained through pleading or legacy concerns, but, ultimately, family members must wage a proxy fight – voting shares in a common way to counterbalance the heavy voting power of the one. Of course, if majority voting power is vested in one person, then even that is not a viable road. It might be possible to chip away at that voting power over time through small changes, but without sufficient influence or voting power, concerned family members must simply lay plans for the next generation in the hope that they might persuade the powerful to lay down that power for the greater good.

That is not to say there are no influential arguments to make. Indeed, a family leader can become a family legend by giving the family the gift of self-governance. This is an argument for legacy. An argument for business is even simpler (though less emotionally powerful): this business is unlikely to remain a going concern without sustainable family governance. Morally, an argument might run like this: people should have at least some power over their own destiny; robbing them of that power robs them,

Change is hard and painful. Overthrowing what came before is difficult and emotional, but its a small price to pay to hold wealth and – most importantly – a family together for the long haul.

at least a little, of their humanity. And so on. I, for one, am not above cajoling powerful family members to effect changes of this import.

Counterintuitively, for families with the privilege to undertake big changes in their governance, it is fellow family members who tend to resist the most – especially the old guard. That resistance is often not to the path itself but overcoming the very human mental and emotional response to change. More difficult: changes in deep-seated family assumptions tend to clash with deep-seated family values such as duty, honour, loyalty and respect. Duty to the family, honour to those who came before, loyalty to the family and respect for the family's shepherds. Replacing what came before with something new is likely to sting all of these perfectly human responses to important change. Allowance for those responses is key to maintaining (or building) support. Mourning, for example, is entirely reasonable, as are angst and anger. Family leaders (and their advisors) must be prepared to hold space for these responses, validate them and listen to fellow family members.

Change is hard and painful. Overthrowing what came before is difficult and emotional, but its a small price to pay to hold wealth and – most importantly – a family together for the long haul. Surely it is better to change than to keep "pushing further east", as Alexander did.

The role of governance

Suffering significant word-count might lead one to conclude that family governance is important. It is, but it is not the final destination. Family governance is important only because it is the foundation upon which the family can build everything else. Foundations are required, of course, but we cannot live in a house with no walls. Governance offers a strong foundation to build and secure the family's vision through time. But what is the family's vision? And it is here that we reach the end of governance and the start of everything else.

"Everything else" begins with leadership, at least in my view.

Leadership cannot be outsourced to governance. Rather, leadership can only occur within the context of governance. Someone ultimately has to cast a family vision, and then execute it. Vision construction ideally incorporates the views and values of many, communicated through an effective governance structure. However, we quickly face a mathematical hurdle when amalgamating disparate views.

Arrow's impossibility theorem tells us that there is no voting system that can convert the ranked preferences of individuals into a community-wide preference without making compromises.[5] While this is an important line of social research with all sorts of interesting consequences, I take it is as an admonition for the importance of leadership. Leadership is listening to the voices of those whom you lead, taking in the operational environment, then making decisions with as much wisdom and discernment as can be mustered. There is a reason why good governance structures require a leader.

Leadership differs from dictatorship in its oversight. Leaders submit to the will of those they lead when that will is clearly expressed – up to and including exiting their post. Dictators impose their will on those they lead. The spirit of this distinction was summed up nicely by Georges Pompidou, former Prime Minister of France, "A statesman is a politician who places himself at the service of the nation. A politician is a statesman who places the nation at his service." Do you serve the family, or does the family serve you? If the former, then lead boldly until you are called aside.

This also speaks to those whose role is oversight. Family boards – indeed any boards – can easily drift from their purpose. Recall, it is the role of family shareholders to oversee and advise, not to execute. Board members are there as a check on their executive. Of course, they have ultimate power to replace the executive, but that power should really be confined to high-level and previously agreed to performance indicators. Board members can and should lean in and ask difficult questions of their executive, then square those answers with the story being told in the financial statements (meaning, obviously, board members need to develop the skill set to do both). However, board members should not be micromanaging their executive. If the executive is meeting her performance expectations, then she is a good executive. Questioning why invoices are sent on the 10th of the month instead of the 1st is not proper conversation in a board meeting, to use one (very real) example. Rather, board members should communicate clearly the will of the family, debate the merits of a given direction, then empower someone to execute that vision. Once empowered, board members are to hold that executive to account for progress toward that vision. It really is that simple.

Yet profundity hides within this simplicity. Simple structures give room for great leadership, for family statesmanship, for creativity and serendipity, for passion. What's more, there is room for risk and failure, for new family members to learn the ropes without catastrophic consequences to themselves or the family. Such structures also lend themselves to geater continuity.

Rome survived because governance allowed continuity across geographies and time, but it is wrong to say that great leadership was absent. Indeed, one might argue that absent her great leaders, Rome, while enduring, might never have grown beyond a small regional hegemon on the Tiber. Leadership has much to offer families, but only families secured with the foundation of effective governance.

Change is hard

Most wealthy families are wealthy because someone in their past built something meaningful. Indeed, great people are an asset to those around them, pulling up themselves, their families and their communities. Alexander was not 'the Great' for nothing. We can praise the accomplishments and celebrate the vision of those who came before while also working to maintain what they built.

Yet, breaking the hold of the great man fallacy is difficult for many families. In some cases, it is the resistance of the family leader. In other instances, it is the ingrained assumptions and values of the family. Recognising and acknowledging that the fallacy is at work is often difficult on its own.

David Foster Wallace relates this idea in a pithy story. Two young fish swimming along together one day pass an older fish swimming the other way. The older fish greets the younger fish jovially and asks, "how's the water today, boys?" They mumble a polite reply and swim on. After a minute the first young fish says to the second, "what the hell is water?"[6] Much of changing family culture and structure starts by asking "how's the water?" We humans, generally, fail to notice our own assumptions, much less question them, so this is not a problem unique to wealthy families. A problem unique to wealthy families, however, is when those unquestioned assumptions become catastrophic to their business, wealth and the family itself. Ensuring every assumption is built on a solid foundation is the job of wealthy families and their advisors.

Change is hard. Family empires falling apart is harder, and families falling apart is harder still. Governance is the foundation of all that families build together. Without a firm foundation, the house falls sooner or later.

Governance also offers opportunities for the next generation to learn safely. It offers buy-in from family members who would otherwise be checked-out (or entitled). It offers opportunities for fresh ideas, creativity, leadership and family statesmanship. Great people are important, but rare. Proper governance allows families to recognise, train and gain from visionaries when they appear. Then it preserves their hard-won progress for current and future generations.

Families are a microcosm of the world as a whole. To build a generational family is to build a society of sorts. We can, therefore, draw many lessons from the sieve of ideas that is human history, of which proper governance is but one. Families would do well to begin building the foundation that is proper governance. Though the effort seems great, and the road seems long, we can take comfort knowing that Rome was not built in a day.

Franklin J Parker, CFA has advised wealthy families internationally for over a decade. He is author of the book Goals-Based Portfolio Theory, *and the founder of Directional Advisors, a Texas-based registered investment advisor.*

1 The wars of the Diadochi were fought between Alexander's generals from 322 to 281 BCE, who each took a portion of the kingdom for himself.

2 B Hauser, "Family Governance", *The Journal of Wealth Management*, 2002, 5(2), 10–16, DOI: https://doi.org/10.3905/jwm.2002.320439.

3 F Perez-Gonzalez, "Inherited Control and Firm Performance", *The American Economic Review*, 2006, 96(5), 1559–88.

4 "Family Firm Facts" published by: Grand Valley State University, Family Owned Business Institute, accessed 16 January 2023, www.gvsu.edu/fobi/family-firm-facts-5.htm#:~:text=Global%20Impact&text=New%20business%20is%20fueled%20by,(FFI%20Global%20Data%20Points).

5 K Arrow, "A Difficult Concept in Social Welfare", *Journal of Political Economy*, 1950, 58(4), 328–46, DOI: 10.1086/256963.

6 DF Wallace, "This is Water", 2005 Commencement Speech at Kenyon College, 2005, transcript: https://jamesclear.com/great-speeches/this-is-water-by-david-foster-wallace#:~:text=There%20are%20these%20two%20young,What%20the%20hell%20is%20water%3F%E2%80%9D.

A carefully orchestrated transition planned well in advance may suffice to avoid many pitfalls of family office leadership succession. The existing leaders should select a successor well in advance, organise and plan for a detailed process to groom that successor, and be sure to communicate with all the stakeholders to ensure a smooth transition.

Essential Reads *on* NextGen

Family office succession planning[1]

Susan R Schoenfeld

A number of years ago, John and Ann Williams[2] sold their successful family-owned business and established a single family office to invest the sales proceeds and support their family's investment, reporting, tax and other needs. They had professionalised the office with strategic investments in staff, including a senior level COO and CFO who reported directly to John. Over the years, the office took on more responsibility, not only for John and Ann's affairs, but for those of their children and their children's families as well.

Now that John and Ann are getting ready to retire they ask for advice on succession planning for leadership of the family office. As a significant portion of the Williams' family wealth is managed by their single family office, this decision takes on great importance for their family. This article will cover three important considerations to prepare them for this all-important transition.

Selecting the successor

Ideally, the identification of a successor leader should happen years before the anticipated transition, but this step is often the most emotionally difficult for a successful patriarch and matriarch, who often don't believe that their children are 'ready' or that they possess the right combination of skills necessary to assume the leadership role. Successful entrepreneurs often reach their level of success by hard work and long hours in the extreme, the vision to see beyond what exists to what might be, and exceptional business acumen, with or without formal education. These traits are not as commonly found in second generation inheritors, who don't face the same level of economic adversity, though being the child of wealthy parents certainly brings its own challenges. It is difficult for many parents to recognise and appreciate the value, unique skills and experiences of their children.

John and Ann provided their offspring with the best of everything, and encouraged them to follow their own passions. As a result, their children did not grow up with the 'hard knocks' life experience or the fire in the belly that their parents have, and John and Ann have come to believe, perhaps too late, that none of their children are suited to take over the leadership reins when the time comes.

This view cannot, by definition, be entirely objective. Many parents never fully believe that their children are ready, no matter how old or accomplished they may be. John and Ann might ask their advisers for a more objective perspective on the readiness of the children to take on a greater leadership role, and for suggested interim steps to help them get there. John and Ann may need help coming to terms with the fact that, while they may never believe that their children are ready to take over, it is important for them to plan ahead. As an ageing patriarch and matriarch, they need to take steps to plan their retirement, and identify and train new leaders to take over.

In some cases, it makes sense to skip a generation, and select a grandchild to groom for this critical role. Depending on relative ages, interests and capabilities, it could prove to be the best solution for the family. One family that I advised several years ago, the Watts family, had three children, each of whom had three children of their own, or nine grandchildren in total, all in their mid-to-late twenties. As the patriarch contemplated his impending retirement, I encouraged him to initiate exploratory conversations about who in the family was best suited to succeed him as family head with each of his children and their spouses.

As a result of those conversations, he learned that they were each busy with their own lives and businesses, and it would be an imposition to ask any one of them to sacrifice their professional time to take on the successor mantle. Instead, we set up meetings followed by formal interviews with the grandchildren. In conducting the interviews we looked for who was most ready, willing and able to take on the leader role. I asked the retiring patriarch to list and rank the qualities and characteristics that he thought would be most beneficial, and then we asked the family's attorney, financial adviser and other trusted advisers to add to the list. The final job description included such traits as intellectual curiosity, financial acumen and the willingness to embrace change, including openness to new technologies.

After the interviews were completed, we identified a promising and willing successor among the grandchild generation, and began to develop her for future leadership roles. Instructive in this example is that the patriarch did not make these decisions in a vacuum – he sought out input from each of the stakeholders involved, and took into account their points of view. It is often true that self-made wealth creators are not accustomed to seeking or considering the opinions of others; this is one decision that requires the input of all concerned.

The new leadership should be selected with an eye towards the future. The new family office head will have to face very different challenges than did John and Ann, due to changing external socio-economic factors, ever-shifting global, political and economic realities, as well as the internal family challenges presented by an expanding diversity as family members marry and have children of their own. We have only to witness the recent Brexit vote in the United Kingdom, and the US presidential election to realise that the world is changing quickly, and the global political landscape is much less predictable than it used to be.

In the Watts family described above, as each of the nine grandchildren married, they dispersed and lived in many different countries, all of which have different tax and securities laws. The family office had to consider the expanding universe of the tax impact of its distribution and investment decisions. It also had to evaluate how the shifting political landscape might impact the regulatory and reporting rules in the various countries involved. The family office took on a critical role for the overall sustainability of the family enterprise; they coordinated and assumed responsibility for anticipating the impact of monumental global events on the family.

The spouses of all the grandchildren also brought another kind of diversity to the family office. They brought their own expertise, some of them investment, legal or tax professionals themselves. No longer could the family office operate in a vacuum, subject to the oversight of only the patriarch. Now many different sets of eyes would be watching and evaluating the performance of the office. This brought a heightened level of accountability and oversight to which the professional staff were not previously accustomed, which further enhanced the value of the family office to the various branches of the family.

While many families are tied to the idea of a bloodline-only succession line of leadership, increasing numbers of open-minded families are willing to consider naming an in-law for this important role. If neither of John and Ann's children are interested in or qualified for the role of heading the family office, perhaps a spouse might be appropriate. One family I know has been grooming their son-in-law for leadership for quite a few years, starting by including him on various governance committees, which led to his being named head of the family council, with the longer-term plan to name him as head of the family office. Not only did this provide needed diversity and expertise, but it also made a significant statement to the entire extended family about trust and inclusiveness. This individual was not just their son-in-law, he was the parent of their grandchildren and, as such, had just as much to say in passing along the family's stories and culture to the next generation as anyone.

Increasingly common in today's society is the blended family, produced by second marriages – or third – with children from previous marriages. The Watts family had such a situation. Two of the nine grandchildren were not of the family bloodline; one of the children had married someone with two adult children from a previous marriage. This child considered her husband's children as her own, though she did not legally adopt them, and wanted them treated equally with all the rest of the grandchildren. Other family members disagreed, and there was animosity among the family branches as a result. The patriarch did meet with them as part of the grandchild interview process, but ultimately selected a different grandchild whom he determined had broader education and experience, and therefore was more qualified. Each family must decide for itself how they will handle family members who are not of the bloodline, whether they are stepchildren or in-laws.

Not only might John and Ann think that their children are not prepared to assume the mantle of leadership, but another significant hurdle is their own readiness to give up that mantle. They have gotten accustomed to the financial and psychological trappings of leadership, including the literal and figurative seat at the head of the table, running the

We have only to witness the recent Brexit vote in the United Kingdom, and the US presidential election to realise that the world is changing quickly, and the global political landscape is much less predictable than it used to be.

family meetings, and having the ultimate decision-making authority. They might not be comfortable relinquishing this power role to someone else, even as they realise the necessity of doing so. A possible solution might be to develop a longer-range governance process whereby John and Ann can maintain the titular leadership position of their family office, though not necessarily day-to-day management which they would transition over time to their successor.

In addition, John and Ann must bear in mind that planning for one's retirement has frequently been compared to planning one's own funeral, and often brings up deep-seated fears about mortality. Estate planners know too well how clients postpone critical planning out of reluctance to discuss thoughts of their own mortality. This common phenomenon is even more prevalent among strong-willed, successful, self-made entrepreneurs, who are convinced that only they are qualified to hold the keys to the kingdom. It is hard for them to imagine the day when they will not be at the helm to make all the important decisions.

I have often found it a useful exercise to ask them to imagine what would happen if they stepped out onto Fifth Avenue in New York City and got hit by a passing bus. Who would make the necessary decisions the very next day to carry on all the family's extended business and investment interests? Who would be prepared with the necessary authority, information, experience and education to do so? Was it fair to his wife and children, just at the moment when they would be dealing with personal grief over the loss of their husband and father, to also have to wrestle with unfamiliarity with the family's widespread holdings and business interests? Wouldn't it make more sense to begin sharing details now, in case of an untimely accident?

In some unfortunate cases, John and/or Ann have gotten on in years and may no longer have the requisite mental capacity to continue as leader of the family office. They have become increasingly forgetful and disoriented, and it appears that they should no longer be in control of the family's financial affairs. In such a case, their children might need advice on a course of action to relieve their parents of their decision-making roles while still providing them with respect and dignity.

In the United States, the Health Insurance Portability and Accountability Act of 1996 (HIPAA) provides privacy and security requirements for safeguarding medical information. While the intent and spirit of this law is to afford privacy to patients about their health care and medical conditions, it can present a serious impediment to families who need to plan for the orderly transition of their assets and who will be in control of those assets.

Many trusts and other estate planning documents have in their 'boilerplate' that two physicians must certify when someone no longer has the requisite mental capacity to continue to serve as a trustee. HIPAA restrictions may well prevent physicians from discussing the condition of a patient whom they have examined, creating a Catch-22 for the family. They can't remove their family member who is suffering from an evident mental incapacity, because they can't get physicians to violate HIPAA by certifying to that incapacity. How does a family resolve this without going to court?

One example of creative drafting to circumvent this obstacle that I have seen is to require that, if demanded by a majority of the co-trustees, the trustee must choose to either submit to a mental capacity evaluation and waive their HIPAA rights or else resign as trustee. This clause, or something like it, would provide John with a graceful way out instead of engaging in a potentially embarrassing competency hearing.

If none of the children, grandchildren or their spouses, has a real desire or ability to assume the leadership role, John and Ann might have to consider a non-family member successor. The long-time COO and CFO of the family office have served the family faithfully for many years, watched the children grow up, and likely know more about the family wealth enterprise than even the family members themselves.

In such a case, it might be very appropriate to name one or the other of these long-time employees as successor. This person would likely bring on more professional management of the family's investment and tax functions, providing a greater level of accountability and service to the family at large than the founder generation would have.

As the family office takes on increasing numbers of professional managers, it will become increasingly more expensive for the family to maintain its family office. Who will bear the expense for funding the family office, and how will the expenses be allocated? Some families elect to share the cost equally among the branches, while other families address the inequality in how much they respectively use the family office resources by strict time allocations among the family branches. It is recommended to consider these potential trouble areas long before they become problematic.

Appropriate new policies would need to be established, not only for a compensation structure to incentivise the employee to continue on, but also a structure to groom a successor for this long-time employee who would continue the family's goals and values. The family is making a significant investment of trust in its future with this employee, and they wouldn't want him to leave for a better offer, or suffer a lapse in judgment that would put the family at risk. In addition, the senior-level employee not chosen might decide to take early retirement or seek other employment, rather than report to a long-time colleague, and the office will have to replace this talent in short order.

John and Ann may be confident that their COO, Charles, is trustworthy beyond reproach, but is this confidence justified? What checks and balances have been put in place to assure that the family's assets remain secure and that private information remains private? How well is Charles vetting and supervising the staff he hires to work under him? And what safeguards are in place to cultivate and retain talent that he may come to view as a threat to his own position and wrongfully terminate? And who is supervising Charles so that when he makes inappropriate remarks to female subordinates at the office holiday party, the family has a confidential reporting mechanism in place to learn about it and take corrective action so that they are not subject to a lawsuit?

Grooming the designated successor

Once John and Ann have selected their designated successor, the next step is a process to groom and develop that successor to eventually lead the family enterprise.

Many years ago, when John and Ann's children were young, they began to teach the children basic financial literacy skills in age appropriate ways. They kept this up over the years, established bank accounts for their children and encouraged them to save a portion of their weekly allowance. The children learned about interest compounding, and the basic principles of investing. They were also encouraged to donate a portion of their allowance in order to teach them about their responsibility to their greater community.

As the children got older, John and Ann would bring them to the family office, informally educating them on much of the day-to-day operations of the office. The children spent increasingly more time at the family office over time, taking on summer internship positions to learn about all the different accounting, investment and tax functions. Because all of this groundwork was laid over the years, the children have more than a passing familiarity with how the family office operates.

This continuing pattern of education is important for all children, not just the designated successor. I recently facilitated a family meeting with the King family: the mother and father and all three of their college-age children. The parents realised that their children were at an important crossroads in their lives; they were about to select and declare their major courses of study at university, and the parents wanted their children to have a basic understanding of their expectations for inheritance before they each made this important decision.

Their plan was to provide each child with a sum of money substantial enough that they could pursue a less remunerative career which might be more personally satisfying to them – one of the children was talented in the arts, for example – but not so much that it could be squandered indefinitely, if they were inclined to do so. In the course of the family meeting, these plans were discussed, questions were asked, and meaningful education and communication resulted. Each of the children was then able to think about their passions and future career path with a better understanding of what economic impact might be involved.

Now that John and Ann have officially designated a successor, a formal educational programme can be put in place to prepare the successor to take control. More intensive training about the inner workings of the office, and in-depth discussions about overall business vision and investment philosophy should become the priority. A detailed discussion about family office policies and procedures should be undertaken, with particular emphasis paid to the distribution policies for the family members.

The transition process should be a gradual one, in order for the new leader to develop the necessary knowledge base. The designated successor will have much to learn even as he or she may have already been exposed to the inner workings of the family office. The process might start with a shadow programme, where the successor may watch and learn from the retiring leader, not only the operational and management issues, but also the values and the vision that led to the success of the family enterprise.

The next step might be an interim power-sharing arrangement between the current leader and the designated successor. This step can last for varying time periods – in some families it is a mere matter of months; in others, it can last for years. It is important for all concerned to become accustomed to the new face at the head of the table.

In the Watts family with the nine grandchildren described above, we undertook a comprehensive training and development programme for Elizabeth, the designated successor. We started with a review of the family history, including the detailed inner workings and growth of the family business, even though it had been sold about 10 years before, so that Elizabeth could understand not only the source of the family's wealth but also its values and culture. We then moved on to extensive sessions with the investment personnel so she could understand the investment philosophy behind the family's holdings. As Elizabeth grew more comfortable with the existing positions, she was given increasing input over new investments, so that eventually the resulting portfolio was her own responsibility and reflected her own, more global, philosophy. Similarly, she was given

The non-management family members may have a more passive interest in the management of the family office, but will undoubtedly care very much about their continued financial interest in the ongoing family enterprise.

ultimate hiring authority over all new personnel, so that she had their loyalty and respect, and had responsibility for their performance.

We also reviewed all of the office's policies and procedures with her, paying special attention to the policies impacting the family, especially the distribution policy. The current policies had been established by the retiring family patriarch on his own over the years, and reflected his own needs and point of view. While he always had tried to consider his family members' concerns, the family rarely ventured to contradict him or offer any input and viewed him as a benevolent dictator.

The incoming successor, by contrast, sought out and encouraged differing points of view, and recognised that the family's needs had expanded over the years, as indeed the family itself had expanded, and that there were new distribution needs voiced, new careers to be launched, homes to be purchased and educations to be financed. Over time, she implemented changes to the family office policies that were more reflective of the current needs and concerns of the whole family, not just those of the senior generation.

Power-sharing can be tricky for many reasons. John and Ann have been accustomed to sole decision-making authority for many years, and will not be comfortable sharing this power. They will be tempted to second-guess every new decision that is different from what their own judgment might have been. The designated successor too will struggle with this dual decision-making arrangement. They will have a great deal of responsibility, but with limited authority to effectuate change. Further, the family office employees may have conflicts in loyalty, especially if they receive mixed messages from the two sets of leaders. I have witnessed several instances where valued long-time staff resigned in frustration during such a challenging transition.

As the new generation takes on more and more of a leadership role, Elizabeth will generally want to take steps towards professionalising the processes of the family office in order to broaden the services provided. As increased responsibility and authority is given to a widening team, and perhaps existing team members are being asked to leave, an important precaution is putting appropriate safeguards in place. The office should take this opportunity to undertake a review of its information security precautions, access to sensitive material, online access points, and the like. A review of cyber-security policies, procedures and precautions is never so important as when a leadership transition is underway.

Passwords should be changed periodically in any event, but after staff have been terminated it is especially critical. Office-owned equipment such as mobile phones, laptops or tablets, and physical keys, should be retrieved. Multi-party authorisation for expenditures over a nominal amount should be required. Access to sensitive information should be limited to a need-to-know basis, without inhibiting the ability of personnel to accomplish their responsibilities.

On a broader basis, the office might take the opportunity to consider implementing a policy around the use of social media. Seemingly innocuous posts about upcoming family holidays could lead to home break-ins as outsiders learn that the family home is unoccupied, or even kidnapping or other personal security risks depending on the holiday destination.

The final step in the transition is the ultimate transfer of sole decision-making authority. While, strictly speaking, this is a legal matter, John and Ann should not limit this final step to the simple act of signing some legal documents. As discussed more fully in the next section, the family office might plan a formal ceremony or other event to celebrate this culmination of all the planning, training and development.

Communicating the succession plan

Another reason that the transition process should be a gradual one is to allow for all stakeholders in the transition plan to acclimatise to the new leadership regime.

The non-management family members may have a more passive interest in the management of the family office, but will undoubtedly care very much about their continued financial interest in the ongoing family enterprise. They will need to be assured that there is a formal education programme in place to provide for an orderly transition of family office leadership.

Some may wish to opt-out of future participation in the shared family economic enterprise if they are not assured that the designated successor leader will continue the expected economic prosperity. As much as the family investment portfolio may be structured in such a way as to take advantage of a larger investment pool to participate in particular deal flows, it is wise to allow each member an individual exit option should they decide not to stay invested with the group. It can be limited in time, so as not to cause forced liquidation sales of investment positions that would disadvantage the rest of the family portfolio value.

In the Watts family with the nine grandchildren, we held a family meeting to formally announce the designated successor, explain why she was selected, and give everyone the opportunity to ask about what would change for them personally going forward. They were all provided with a three-month buy-out offer, should they decide to leave the collective family investment vehicle. In the end, everyone elected to stay invested in the collective family enterprise after hearing about the future plans and about Elizabeth's interest in a more inclusive approach going forward.

The organised and thoughtful communication to the family about the reasons behind the selection of Elizabeth and about the selection process itself defused any uncertainty and discomfort by addressing it head-on. Knowing that they had the right to leave gave them the freedom to decide to stay without feeling trapped. The family was assured that there had been a disciplined and considered review of eligible candidates rather than relying on favouritism or nepotism within family branches, and that there would be an extensive training process so that the new leader would be fully prepared to take over the reins.

In addition, there may be resentment about the choice of a successor, and family members not chosen, or members of their family branch, may seek to disrupt the planned orderly transition. Depending on how extended the family is, there may well be family members who thought they were qualified but were passed over for the top spot.

In order to overcome these and other objections of other family members, an ongoing programme of open communication should be established, providing the opportunity for questions and concerns to be voiced, and to allow for new ideas and ways of approaching the overall family office transparency.

Special roles might be created for these other family members to utilise their special talents on an ongoing basis. The Watts family created committees with many different purposes, and encouraged all the family members to join or head whichever committee interested them most. Some members volunteered to plan the annual family meeting soup to nuts, selecting the location, planning the social activities, even the meals. Another committee was formed to create a family newsletter. The family office took care of the administrative aspects of the newsletter, but the family committee members created original content and solicited newsy titbits year-round from the rest of the family. A third committee, comprised of members and spouses with investment expertise and interest, served as an advisory committee for the office's professional investment staff. And yet another committee was formed to advise the trustees of the family trusts – on a non-binding and non-fiduciary basis – with respect to various aspects of trust administration, including suggestions on the appropriateness, timing and amount of discretionary distributions for younger family members.

All these various committees were more than mere busy-work to appease family members passed over for the top spot. They each performed important functions for the family and strengthened the value that the family office provided to the family. Moreover, by working together on committees comprised of members across the lines of family branches, distant cousins came to know each other better and created bonds of trust that might not have been otherwise achieved.

Similarly, the family office employees will appreciate honest communication about the planned transition, and what is expected of them during and after the transition. They may have concerns about their continued future employment, and should be reassured to the extent appropriate. If staffing changes are expected, they should be communicated all at once, so that morale is not compromised by the uncertainty of ongoing terminations. Regardless of whether Charles the COO can be assured of his continuing employment, those staff who report to him need to know where they stand; if they are being kept on, then they should be assured, and if they are to be terminated, that too should be communicated with dignity, respect and professionalism.

Finally, John and Ann, as the retiring family heads, will often have complex and ambivalent feelings about their own impending loss of control. The power-sharing balance during the transition period may be especially difficult for the hard-charging entrepreneur who has traditionally had the final say. This may be part of the reason that the leader doubts that his or her children are 'ready' to take the reins.

John and Ann will have to come to accept, often over an extended period, that such a transition is not only inevitable but ultimately beneficial for the overall family enterprise. One technique that has proven effective here is to establish a new 'emeritus' role for the retiring leader, to smooth the personal emotional difficulties for the founder created by the transition. In this role, the retiring leader still retains a title, a continuing role with defined responsibilities, and some defined perks of his or her position as founder.

The family office should plan a big ceremony for the actual day that the new leader takes over.[3] This will accomplish three important purposes: to provide an opportunity to acknowledge and celebrate their leadership over the years; to welcome the new leader; and to serve as a clear demarcation of the date of the transfer in leadership.

The importance of this first purpose cannot be overstated. John and Ann are not only the founders of the family office, but they are the creators of the family's wealth. Their hard work over many years has assured the family of its comfort and privilege to make many choices in life. This should be celebrated in a meaningful way.

Secondly, the incoming successor should be encouraged in their new role and assured of the support and backing of all the family members as well as the professional staff. While the new position will undoubtedly have its perks and privileges, it will also carry with it much pressure and responsibility.

The third purpose will prove critical going forward, especially if John and Ann overstep their emeritus roles and attempt to veto decisions made by the new family office head. Having a certain date beyond which John and Ann no longer have final authority will provide the family office staff with a reliable yardstick going forward.

A carefully orchestrated transition planned well in advance may suffice to avoid many pitfalls of family office leadership succession. The existing leaders should select a successor well in advance, organise and plan for a detailed process to groom that successor, and be sure to communicate with all the stakeholders to ensure a smooth transition.

Susan R Schoenfeld, JD, LLM (Taxation), CPA, MBA, is CEO and founder of Wealth Legacy Advisors LLC based in New York City, USA, which serves as thought partner to families of wealth through personal attention and human spirit. She is an Attorney and CPA, with vast experience as an adviser to families and family offices on matters of generational wealth transfer, estate planning and education on the personal issues of wealth. A former Family Ambassador at a private Single Family Office, and Fiduciary Counsel at a prominent US trust company, Susan is a recognised speaker and author on family office and fiduciary matters.

1 Portions of the article appeared originally in *Trusts & Estates* magazine, August 2016, http://www.trustsandestates.com. The author thanks *Trusts & Estates* for permission.

2 All names in this article have been changed to protect client confidentiality.

3 The author thanks Barbara Hauser for reminding her of this effective technique to smooth ruffled feathers, as well as the emeritus role.

Having the humility to admit that, despite having our children's best interests at heart, we do not have a monopoly over knowing what is best for them, and investing the time to understand their wishes can similarly create impetus for next-generation engagement with the family's businesses and structures.

The right time to involve the next generation

Antoaneta Proctor

The apparent contradictions of human psychology never cease to amaze me. On the one hand, we identify deeply with our children and feel disappointed when their choices in life do not match those we would have made; on the other, we are painfully aware that our children are not us when it comes to involving them in, and passing on to them the baton of, business leadership, responsibility for investments and value creation choices, or the stewarding of family wealth. This is so even, or perhaps especially, in the absence of any realistic opportunity to test children's heir preparedness or leadership readiness. Yet we trust these same children to instantly develop the wisdom, sense of responsibility and financial sophistication to equal ours at the point of (forced) succession.

Likewise, wealth creators often feel compelled to put in place (what can be) elaborate succession planning: in terms of wills, trusts, private trust companies and detailed expressions of wishes. They do this for the protection of the family's assets for the benefit of children and future generations. Yet there is rarely any attempt at ascertaining, and thus testing assumptions about, what such children need, want or hope to achieve with their share of the family's wealth in direct discussions with them.

Putting assumptions to the test

One example which private wealth advisers are increasingly becoming familiar with involves next-generation family members whose understanding of social responsibility diverges sharply from that of senior generations. An assumption that such children would necessarily want their parents' wealth or can reconcile a values-driven business and investment approach with involvement in the family's traditional business(es) without seeking to redefine them, can create uncomfortable feelings of consternation and lack of appreciation.

> *The apparent contradictions of human psychology never cease to amaze me.*

Conversely, where the space exists for constructive and non-judgemental dialogue to take place within the family, parents may discover that allowing their wealth and children's creative energies to be channelled into new opportunities for investing with impact or philanthropic causes, can provide meaning which is larger than the family itself, and cohesion beyond what would have been possible had their original vision been pursued.

Another, somewhat surprising, real-life example is provided by the will planning of a patriarch who was convinced that fairness, rather than equality, would best meet the needs of his three adult daughters, two of which had married into families of very substantial wealth. The two sisters agreed. The third sister, however, vehemently objected: any departure from equality would have left her feeling like a second-rate citizen, deemed unable (along with her nuclear family) to forge her own way in life and be successful through her own independent efforts.

What is clear from these examples is that although estate planning and structuring options can provide a suitable framework for the orderly transfer of a family's wealth, on their own they provide at best an incomplete answer. This is especially so where such planning is designed to flex around the wishes and concerns of the incumbent generation, without much (if any) involvement from the next generation or sharing of the reasons and rationale for it with them.

Developing the self-awareness to bring to a conscious level the underlying assumptions which we invariably make – assumptions which reflect more who we are, than who our next generations may be or turn out to be – and the courage to ask meaningful questions of our children, which may return answers we did not expect or hoped never to hear, is directly relevant to whether and at what stage constructive family governance conversations can become a realistic possibility for the family.

Shaping needs and wants

Having the humility to admit that, despite having our children's best interests at heart, we do not have a monopoly over knowing what is best for them, and investing the time to understand their wishes can similarly create impetus for next-generation engagement with the family's businesses and structures. But this is not necessarily what we naturally do as parents.

Even rarer, in my experience, is any concerted effort, at least in first and second-generation wealth, at consciously shaping what next generations perceive to be their needs, wants and aspirations proactively: by holding focused family discussions and instilling in them a sense of responsibility and shared purpose, which is underpinned by the family's core values rather than the individual's lifestyle needs.

Timely and age-appropriate conversations are essential to: building a consensus as to the purpose of the family's wealth; healthy attitudes towards its enjoyment, investment and use for impact; and preserving the family's cohesion.

When to bring in the next generation

This is a question that many families struggle with. Start too soon, they say, and an entitled attitude creeps in where senior generations have been painstakingly guarding against it over the years by maintaining a lifestyle that is grounded in normality, responsible spending and sound work ethics. Likewise, you will likely have opened a Pandora's box of diverging attitudes toward how the family's wealth should be preserved, grown and used to benefit individual family members, family branches or generally, risking conflict and the erosion of familial trust. But if these are the underlying attitudes and dynamics within the family, would you not want to know that now, so that a realistic succession plan can be put in place?

Leave it too late, I say, and family members have drawn their own inferences about: the family's financial well-being, often inflated by their lack of involvement with the financial management of family assets or understanding of the maintenance costs involved; what they can expect by way of inheritance, with any gap between expectations and reality leading to disappointment; and their place within the family, family business and wealth-holding structures relative to siblings and as a matter of their parents' affections.

Why any time is a good time

Trying to pick a time that is just right is subject to at least six major caveats:

- worrying that the circle of trust is being expanded beyond the current generation of decision makers too soon, can mean that the family is too late to do it in a planned manner;
- in seeking to pinpoint the right time for engaging the next generation, most families focus on the disclosure of assets, values and structures. However, education must come before information. Family members must be trained to be responsible citizens, to appreciate the responsibility that comes with privilege and buy into the family's vision for the future before they can be trusted with shaping it;
- the right time for passing human and intellectual capital is appreciably earlier – it starts the moment a next generation family member is born. This is regardless of whether wealth creators are conscious of the messaging conveyed by their actions and attitudes: about the meaning of family, business ethics, success and wealth; or that this amounts to the passing of non-financial wealth (or occasionally the stunting of healthy attitudes developing, including towards wealth);
- it is premised on there being a right time. The reality is that different timings will be right when considering heir training, the sharing of information with next-generation family members, opportunities for participation in the family's decision making or the assumption of leadership for specific aspects of it. Even within the category of educating the next generation, a graduated approach will be appropriate, with the focus shifting from informing and observing initially, to learning by doing, and then involvement with stretch assignments of increasing complexity. What is right timing will also reflect the ebbs and flows of the family as a living organism, whose composition and functioning changes through death, incapacity, new in-laws, and exits on divorce or through personal choice;
- there is never a perfect time. Business families are typically engrossed in, if not the day-to-day, then certainly the strategic running of the business, in the context of which there is always

Timely and age-appropriate conversations are essential to: building a consensus as to the purpose of the family's wealth; healthy attitudes towards its enjoyment, investment and use for impact; and preserving the family's cohesion.

another urgent decision to be made. Creating the time and space for meaningful conversations with rising generations requires incumbents to keep in perspective what is important, albeit (to our current knowledge) not urgent;
- education, communication and next-generation participation are all processes, which need to be imbedded and occur regularly and consistently within the governance guardrails implemented by the family. Perfect timing is not always possible. But the longer a family has been practising, the more likely it is to successfully manage the inevitable consequences of being human in an uncertain world as they unfold.

Where does one start

By taking stock of where one is as a family.

Multi-generational families comprising numerous family members – including blended, culturally diverse and geographically dispersed family members – typically feel the need to put in place a formal family governance framework or rulebook for how the family wishes to manage itself, make decisions, communicate with each other and incorporate new family members.

Having a structured approach to training and the gradual inclusion of next-generation family members in the family's decision-making and governance structures; communicating it clearly, and applying it consistently ensures that expectations are managed in an objective and predictable way. Fairness of the process in turn contributes to outcomes being perceived as fair. This reduces the potential for grievances arising that are not addressed by the governance process and become full-blown family conflicts. It should also enable next-generation family members to feel part of a consensual vision for the family, which is not static but evolves as the family does.

How existing frameworks capture the next generation

If you are a family who already has a formal governance system in place, you may wish to consider the following questions in relation to it:

- Does it already include a programme for next-generation training?
- If so, what does it cover? Is it structured as purely an educational/workshop-style experience which covers the building blocks of financial basics (budgeting, earning an income, managing spending and savings), understanding investments and wealth transfers (in terms of understanding trusts and estate planning)? Or does it graduate into some form of experiential training, which provides hands-on involvement in actual (philanthropic) projects, opportunity to collaborate with others and contextual coaching?
- At what stage do young adults in your family have the opportunity to participate in and then lead on the selection of, pitching for finance for, monitoring of and reporting in relation to an investment or project? Who is available to support them with this and in what way? What accountability is there for coach and coachee?
- Is there a family bank or other mechanism for next-generation family members' ideas to be tested and, if successful, monetised with family support?
- What are the rules of engagement for family members to become involved in and progress within operating family business(es)?

Doing the governance process, rather than having it done to you

If your generation was involved in the creation of the family's rulebook, thought should be given to how next-generation family members are encouraged to own it also.

From the perspective of the next generation, being merely introduced to what senior generations have agreed to, before their time, can feel disempowering. This is unless rising generations also have the opportunity to debate certain of the family's governance provisions with their elders, gain an understanding of the rationale for the inclusion of those provisions and terms, suggest alternatives which the family can then debate and potentially agree to implement. This should keep the family's governance framework fresh and vibrant, with each successive generation having the ability to achieve participation and make its mark within the rules, rather than having to rebel against them.

When is the right time to invite such a dialogue would very much depend on the composition of the family. Ideally, a governance framework should not change too often in order to provide continuity and stability. A once-per-generation approach may work well where siblings are bunched up closely together, but would work less well where siblings are spaced out unevenly, there are significant age differences and complex blended family models.

Families with a seemingly blank canvas

Turning to families who do not have a formal or overarching governance matrix – as a deliberate choice (where, the feeling is, family circumstances do not currently justify this) or by default.

Just because there is no single document, such as a family constitution, which spells out the rules of engagement, it does not mean that there are not unwritten rules by which the family governs itself and

Where conversations with the next generation are currently being inhibited, it is important to distil the reasons for why this might be.

makes decisions. It also does exclude elements of written governance being present in a variety of contextual guises, such as shareholders' agreements, family office protocols or terms of reference for investment committees.

What it does mean, however, is that there may be less of a universally recognised path to incorporating the next generation into the family's governance framework. This in turn could open the door to inter-sibling rivalry, as well as perceptions (whether justified or not) of being treated unequally or others being preferred.

Depending on the personality and leadership style of senior family members, as well as the degree of trust that exists within the family, conversations around expectations of the next generation, how one becomes eligible to be considered for roles within the family business(es) and when might the rising generations qualify to be included in decisions that are being made for their benefit, may also be harder for rising generations to initiate, for fear of being perceived as power-hungry or money-grubbing.

Moving the dial

Where conversations with the next generation are currently being inhibited, it is important to distil the reasons for why this might be. If it is a fear by the current generation that rising generations are simply not ready, one needs to probe further and ask what will it take for parents to accept that their children are ready, willing and (often more than) sufficiently skilled. There is also the question of what is being done – by the current generation – to ensure that rising generations ready up, spurred on by the right combination of support and challenge.

Asking senior family members questions about how they might expect the family to fare in certain hypothetical scenarios and mapping their answers against stated objectives for the family and its wealth can be illuminating. This sort of comparison, if properly done, typically leads to two simple conclusions. First, that no matter how risky a governance conversation today might sound, postponing it only raises the stakes. This then leads to the second conclusion – that the best time to start is now.

The specifics of what this may involve will vary from family to family. Engaging an experienced facilitator with specialist governance skills will often be the most effective way of opening up discussions and setting the tone for the family to follow. Doing some investigative work first, in one-to-one conversations with the individual family members to gauge where they are each at, can be very revealing and will help identify immediate priorities for the family's governance efforts.

Flushing out concerns, identifying pain points and creating a safe space for possibilities to emerge is all part of the groundwork that needs to be done in order to start building effective, harmonious and rewarding next-generation engagement with the family, its wealth and its structures in due course.

Starting this work now can be invaluable. As Bil Keane, the American cartoonist, said: "Yesterday's the past, tomorrow's the future, but today is a gift. That's why it's called the present."

Extending the gift of the present to rising generations includes, above all, senior generations making themselves accessible: to guide, provide answers, listen, debate, mould and be moulded. They should be prepared to do this whenever they judge the next generation to be ready, whenever rising generations judge themselves to be ready and at any time in between. Doing something imperfectly now, is better than not doing it at all, not least because this gives families the chance of doing it again, but better.

Antoaneta Proctor is a private client partner at City law firm Wedlake Bell, focusing on international tax and trusts, family wealth structuring, cross-border succession and family governance. She is the author of the UK #1 best-selling book Generational Wealth: Why 99% of Families Fail to Establish a Lasting Legacy *(2022).*

In the context of bringing up children, parental expectations can be seen as a standard, ideas, a set of rules or even a framework if you like, that parents enforce upon a child, thinking it will lead to proper (successful) behaviour. From their perspective they believe that a certain way of life can lead to certain (excellent) achievements.

Parental expectations: effective guidelines or messy messages?

Raimund Kamp

Every parent wants their child to be happy, feel good about him or herself and lead a successful meaningful life. Parenting is a tough, challenging and sometimes overwhelming job. All mothers and fathers have expectations of their children, sometimes already pre-birth: what will our son or daughter look like and what will become of him or her? What is the purpose of expectations? Does it make a difference for children who grow up in an upwardly mobile, privileged, well-to-do environment? Families who have family offices are part of the wealthy environment, and it would help if their family offices have an understanding of these issues.

In this article, I will first explore what parental expectations are and how these intertwine with aspirations. The various types of expectations in wealthy families will be described in paragraph 2. What can parents do if setting high expectations does not guarantee excellence from children, to reach their full potential is the central question in paragraphs 3, 4 and 5. What can and may future heirs do with their inheritance will be answered in paragraph 6 and I finish this article with the ideal parental expectations of wealthy families.

1. Expectations and aspirations further examined

Let's first of all start with defining what expectations are and start with a look at the dictionary. The following definitions of expectations are given:

- a belief about (or mental picture of) the future;
- the feeling that something is about to happen;
- anticipation with confidence of fulfilment.

If you have great expectations, you think something good will come your way, but if you keep your expectations low you won't risk being disappointed. An expectation is a belief about what might happen in the future (eg, your expectation to be married with your partner your whole life). But it can also describe something that is supposed to happen, like a schoolteacher whose expectation is that everyone comes to class prepared.

In the context of bringing up children, parental expectations can be seen as a standard, ideas, a set of rules or even a framework if you like, that parents enforce upon a child, thinking it will lead to proper (successful) behaviour. From their perspective they believe that a certain way of life can lead to certain (excellent) achievements. Parental expectations can have a strong effect on a child's motivation and self-expectations. Healthy and realistic expectations can encourage a child's development and success. But there is a fine line. A tipping point when expectations become unrealistic. If this happens and a child can't live up to his or her parent's goals, this will lead to feelings of anxiety and discouragement. In an ideal world, parental rules and ideas about proper behaviour must be age appropriate and consider the child's maturity and skill level.

Besides paying attention to parental expectations, it is worthwhile to address aspirations to get the full picture of the parental challenge. According to the dictionary, 'aspirations' has the following meanings:

- a strong desire, longing, or aim; ambition (intellectual aspirations);
- a goal or objective that is strongly desired (the presidency has been his aspiration since boyhood).

2. Personal, social and professional expectations in wealthy families

What types of expectations are there in wealthy families? In this paragraph I present insights into a qualitative research Wealth Transfer in the Netherlands. Together with Marijke Kuijpers MSc and in cooperation with professor Ad Kil of Nyenrode Business University, I have researched the upbringing of 18 heirs in wealthy families, how they are prepared for the inheritance of family capital and their experiences with inherited wealth. In our research the following five expectations were dominant:

- tapping into talents;
- etiquette;
- future partner;
- studies and academic performance; and
- career and work.

We categorised these in three distinct areas of expectations: personal, social and professional.

Personal	Social	Professional
• Tapping into talents	• Etiquette • Future (marriage) partner	• Studies and academic performance • Career and work

Personal expectations: tapping into talents

The parents of a number of heirs want them to harness their talents. They expect the child to do his best to get the most out of his own capabilities. These capabilities are intelligence, talents and skills. One of the greatest fears of wealthy parents is for their children to use the wealth of the family as a safety net, no longer putting any effort into doing things for themselves. Parents believe that harnessing their children's talents would contribute to their high self-esteem and a happy life. One heiress worded her wishes for her son in a way we often encountered during the course of this study:

> *What we really want is for our son to use his talents, so that he becomes proud of who he is and goes on to do whatever makes him feel good for himself. I would really like that. For him to believe in himself, I find that to be the basis of everything.*

Social expectations: etiquette

Expectations about etiquette have to do with the behaviour expected of wealthy people, and in particular how they spend their free time and how discrete they are with their money. In new-money families, there tends to be more expectations about leisure activities. Parents make sure their children do certain sports like horseback riding, tennis and hockey, or that they receive music lessons.

The goal of the etiquette expectations of new-money families is to find a connection to the higher social classes. The set of norms and standards of the higher classes is passed on by newly rich parents to their children. These will enable the children to find a connection to the higher social classes more easily when they are adults.

In old-money families, it is important to teach each generation anew the standards that will make them be considered 'good people'. Etiquette expectations in these families tend to deal with discretion, in particular not speaking about money and wealth. An heiress from an old-money family mentioned that to her family etiquette meant dressing neatly, having good table manners and writing thank you notes, among other things.

Social expectations: the future (marriage) partner

Not a single male heir indicated there was any kind of expectation regarding his marriage partner. In our study, the most commonly cited expectation regarding daughters' spouses is that they needed to be brainy and well educated. These very features were behind the decision of some daughters to pursue further studies, as it was an excellent chance to meet a fitting partner, as one of the heiresses said:

> *We didn't have to get PhDs per se, but it was better to do so because that put us in a whole different category in what came to life partners. If at least the husband was it, you wouldn't see that the partner wasn't it.*

The intention of the parents, and especially of the fathers, is for a daughter to find a good candidate. To these parents, good often means with as high a level of education as possible. The higher the level of education of the partner, the higher his potential to be financially successful. If a man makes good money himself, there is less risk of an unequal relationship between the wealthy heiress and her husband. Another definition of a good candidate seemed to be that of a man who comes from an old-money family. When a wealthy heiress marries into such a family, her social status rises.

Professional expectations: studies and academic performance

The differences in expectations regarding studies and academic performance were staggering among the families in our research. Some parents had planned well-defined schooling or study trajectories for their children, going far beyond school performance alone. This was the reason some girls were made to follow a particular programme, or sent to boarding school, so they could later get the right life partner to bite the hook, so to speak. In some of the families the standard was to reach a university level of education, even if the child struggled to achieve that level. Representatively put: "It was a given that I would study. My brother and I both did. I think that if you assume that your children will go to university, you are setting the bar rather high."

A small number of heirs found their parents' academic expectations to be too low. If the child struggled with certain subjects, he would immediately get private tutoring or perhaps be transferred to private school. In retrospect, these heirs believe their parents could have put more pressure on them to do better instead of simply arranging for private lessons or private schooling. Low academic expectations motivated some heirs to go the extra mile to prove they could achieve more than was believed of them.

Recent psychological research[1] on study and academic performances found that high parental aspirations led to increased academic achievement, but only when it did not exceed realistic expectations.

The drawback to parental expectations of entrepreneurship is that not everyone has the talent to become an entrepreneur. For heirs that lack this talent, or who have it in lesser measure, it becomes difficult to accomplish what is expected of them.

When aspirations exceeded expectations, the children's achievement decreased proportionately.[2] Establishing healthy academic expectations plus communicating these can be an important key to fostering success in school. When parents have high hopes for their children's academic achievements, they tend to do better in school, unless those hopes are unrealistic, in which case the children may not perform well in school.

Professional expectations: career and work

The parents of our interviewees had remarkably few specific expectations regarding the careers and work of their children. Children can follow their own passion. When there are certain expectations about career and work, they mostly tend to be related to the family business and entrepreneurship. If the family owns a company, there is a big chance that it will affect the child's career choices to a certain degree. Our interviews indicate that expectations for an heir to go into the family business tend to grow gradually. Both the parents and the child grow into the idea.

There were also families with family businesses which didn't expect their children to take on the weight of the company. These parents encourage their children to choose their own path when it comes to work outside the company. An interviewee said:

It was my father's business and not a family business. He also never brought it up at the time: if you drop out of school you'll have to come and work with me... On the contrary, I was to go and find my own path.

In addition to expectations regarding the family business, expectations of entrepreneurship were also mentioned during the course of this study. In certain families of successful entrepreneurs the younger generations were bottle-fed entrepreneurship since birth. Some (grand) parents would go as far as to tell their children that any career path other than entrepreneurship fell nothing short of a disqualification. One heir was strongly influenced by his grandfather's ideas:

On my father's side we come from a lineage of entrepreneurs and on my mother's side from an intellectual family. The atmosphere, especially around my grandfather, was that only independent people are successful, and the rest are just those who work for others. That was more or less the norm. My father and his generation really took to it as they grew up and they also passed it on to us. So that set the tone and determined to a large extent the choices that we made.

The drawback to parental expectations of entrepreneurship is that not everyone has the talent to become an entrepreneur. For heirs who lack this talent, or who have it in lesser measure, it becomes difficult to accomplish what is expected of them. Career choices are not determined by considerations of what family members may be good at or what their real passions are. As one of the heirs aptly remarked:

In such an environment, you are driven to make certain choices that aren't always the choices you would have made from the standpoint of who you are, what you know and what you are good at.

Our conclusion is that most parents want their children to focus on making their own life and career choices, without letting these be determined by the wealth of the family. When there are family businesses, the family's wealth plays a less obtrusive role in the choices of work and career. Expectations regarding entrepreneurship are much more difficult for heirs to fulfil because talent and passion determine the outcome to a much greater extent.

3. Degrees of expectations

Our research shows that the group of interviewees' parents had high, low or unclear expectations of their children. Naturally, this had a varied effect on the children which might even impact them in their adult lives. Parents with high expectations nullified their children's initiative. Fear of failure prevented the heirs from taking on certain tasks to avoid disappointing the parents. One heiress described how her sister dealt with her parents' high expectations: "My sister thought: I won't start this. I won't even try it once in case I make a mistake. We used to call our sister Switzerland: always neutral. A bit of this, a bit of that".

These high expectations could of course also function as source of motivation to perform better in some cases, even to this day. The personality of each individual heir plays a crucial role here. One heiress is very demanding with herself because her father emphasised that nobody should ever choose the path of least resistance: "If I don't immediately get how to do it, I hate myself".

We noticed that a number of heirs' parents had remarkably low expectations. Our interviews showed that the intention behind these low expectations was to protect the children from disappointment.

Besides high and low expectations, we talked to heirs who had parents with unclear expectations. When children have no idea what their parents expect but feel they are not meeting these expectations, they carry a mental burden. One heiress:

> *I have a very strong feeling that I have to accomplish something, but I cannot describe what it is. But I am not accomplishing it, and my sister feels it even more strongly. And she carries the mental burden that she is not quite meeting the standards.*

4. Unrealistic expectations of wealthy parents

A frequent complaint of children who grow up in a wealthy environment or successful business family is the pressure to achieve. American psychologist and heir John Levy paints a picture that growing up and being a part of a wealthy family often comes with high expectations. He categorises the individual expectations to perform excellently in three areas: personal, social and professional. According to Levy there is an additional, more generic, expectation for future heirs to sustain and grow the family capital.

High parental expectations can work out well for children who can cope, but are a disaster when the expectations are unrealistic. According to Levy, quite a few parents do not look at the diversity and the capabilities of their children and use the same standards for all their children.[3]

Lee Hauser, an American psychologist and expert, distinguishes three different categories of unrealistic expectations: expectations of excellence, of maturity, and of communality. Expectations of excellence means that parents think: why should we not have the best child? Because they own the best companies or have the best careers and live in the most beautiful houses, why should they not expect that their child is superior? Hausner points out that the goals are not based on the interests and abilities of the child, but on what they subjectively believe represents success. The consequence is that they create unbearable pressure on the child, as his achievements must be outstanding (eg, at school or sports) in order to please the parents.[4]

The expectations of maturity, the second category, involves a preconceived notion that their children develop quicker than their chronological age, because of the upward mobility. Their sophisticated lifestyle exposes their children to other travel, cultural, social functions and therefore they acquire different knowledge and experiences. Parents have the tendency to put their children in situations that require them to behave or think beyond their chronological age.

The third type of expectations – commonality – are those that demand the children to grow up exactly as their parents, a family member or a friend's child. This expectation to be like someone else presumes that their interests are the only valid ones and denies the child's unique individuality. When imposed rigidly the child may be afraid to express his own feelings and desires and very often leads to intense frustration, anger and resentment.

What they will expect from their children will be based primarily on what they fantasise of what they will become and not necessarily on what their children are capable of or interested in becoming. Affluent parents frequently want nothing short of the best for and from their children. Their unrealistic expectations can become a burden when a child is put in a position of having to please the parents first and himself second. According to Hausner, the lifelong pain children experience as the result of unrealistic parental expectations is usually far greater than the pain from which the parents are trying to protect the child.

What can parents do if setting high expectations does not guarantee excellence from children, to reach their full potential? People, whether children or adults, are most successful in activities in which they are internally motivated; that is in which they personally choose to be involved and enjoy. According to Hausner, parents can encourage an innate drive for excellence only if they respect the unique interests and passions of a child and allow him to be involved in setting his own goals. Parents can foster a healthy climate supporting their child's goals by their emphasis on process and not on product. This encompasses a shift in priorities from parents from results (product thinking) of a child to the effort itself (process thinking). Although these two concepts are

High parental expectations can work out well for children who can cope, but are a disaster when the expectations are unrealistic.

very much intertwined, it is important for parents to recognise the difference in focus. Children are always involved in some type of process; however not every child will always be able to obtain the sought-after final goal, the ultimate product.

5. Ego involvement

In the context of wealthy families, children will perform tasks that are (extremely) easy; who can't drive in a sports car, attend fancy cocktail parties or travel across the world, all financially sponsored activities by mum and dad. This can lead to a low self-esteem of an individual and even a feeling of being locked up in a system. This is an emotional consequence of luxury that is not earned by the child.

Research about aspirations provides interesting insights into internal motivation to reach goals and the psychological impact on self-worth. How does this work out? When you are personally involved in an activity or task we can say that your ego is involved or at stake. It has an impact on your feeling of self-worth, because it does not feel good if you fail the activity or task. The feeling of success or failure is related to carry out a task within a realistic goal. When a task is extremely easy (shopping with a credit card of your parents) or extremely hard (learning to write in Dutch in a week if you are not a native) you (and your ego) will not be personally involved. Carrying out a very easy task will not increase your self-worth, neither does failing an extremely difficult task decrease your self-worth. In short, when there is a realistic degree of complexity, perceived by the individual who carries out the task, there will be ego involvement. This has a positive impact on the motivation and the feeling of self-worth when the tasks are completed successfully.[5]

6. Expectations of family wealth

What can and are you allowed to do with your inheritance? The interviewees' parents had all kinds of expectations (see above). I have not yet described their expectations regarding the family wealth and how the heirs have dealt with this. The big question is which role the family fortune may play in the lives of the next generation? The respondents cited three objectives of the capital:

- preservation;
- facilitate your own life;
- sharing and giving it back (philanthropy).

Objective 1: Preservation

Almost all parents find it important that their children preserve the built-up family wealth. The question is how they communicate this message. Our research shows that there are large differences between families. In the majority of cases, parents tell their children almost nothing, and the desire to preserve the capital is only given implicitly during the upbringing. The message that children especially remember is to not use the wealth for consumptive reasons. Perfectly illustrated by the following quote: "I've always felt that we were not allowed to 'consume' the wealth".

During the upbringing, some parents explicitly explain to their children about the meaning and goals of the wealth. An heir said about the objective of wealth:

> *It's a challenge if you get an inheritance. The purpose is to preserve this and pass it on. This is closely related to the way one has been brought up. I also inherited the wealth and try to pass it on in a responsible manner to the next generation. When they use their inheritance for an education, illness, care and better living, then it is not an issue, if done in a responsible manner. Like a good steward. Ensure that the wealth is managed in a good way.*

Preservation and the famous stewardship clearly resound in his quote.

When a family business is involved, the message of preservation is a top priority and always communicated explicitly. In a family business, it is not so much about the value of the company but rather its history and the aspirations for the future. Because of the employees attached to the company, it is a logical idea to pursue preservation. In short, the continuity of the business is paramount and the individual wishes of the heir are of secondary importance. Summarised in the following quote: "I am damn sure that this business is something that should continue in the family, that I am just an administrator for a certain period, yes, I'm a steward of the heritage".

The wish to preserve wealth for future generations is an almost crippling goal for heirs with limited financial knowledge and experience. As they have absolutely no idea how to achieve this important family goal, some of them just ignore their financial matters and hope for the better. During and after the financial crisis of 2008 a few of them became suddenly aware that their lax attitude needed to change. An heiress said: "It always went well so I thought it will be good forever. Only in the last few years with the crisis I have a little more contact with the bank. Everyone does".

We have seen in some families that the financially talented family member picks up the ball and looks after the affairs of the untalented relatives. In some cases, these financial high fliers were not only able to maintain the inherited family wealth, but they also increased it substantially. This sounds like a perfect model to sustain wealth but the drawback is the huge responsibility these financially savvy heirs feel for their untalented relatives. At the same time, some untalented heirs were unhappy with the overdependence on their sibling.

Objective 2: Facilitating your own life

Heirs of old-money families are often used to a certain lifestyle. Parents strive to ensure that the next generation can maintain this level. The inherited assets may support their children's goal. It is implicitly or explicitly made clear that there is a difference between expenses associated with 'sustainable expenditures' such as houses, and consumptive expenditure. For the purchase of a house the family fortune should support the next generation (unconditionally). With respect to consumer spending there are limits determined by family rules: there are expectations that a family member lives within their means and the expenditure must be really necessary.

In addition to purchasing a house, parents facilitate special life events that have a large impact, such as an education and starting a business. Children regularly get the opportunity to purchase an enterprise through a friendly loan from their parents. The wealth may also be used to change jobs or to work less.

It takes many heirs a lot of effort to spend (a part of) their inheritance because emotionally they feel the wealth is not theirs yet, even when it's in their own name. One heiress had to get used to the idea too: "It took a while before I could enjoy it. I had a wish list and I could have done things earlier, but one way or another I did not."

Objective 3: Giving back and sharing

The third and final objective of the family wealth is about sharing it with other people and/or feeling the responsibility to contribute towards society. Some families have been active with charities for decades, often through their own family foundations. The next generation is familiar with this and aware that this is one of the objectives of the family fortune. If parents are not role models in giving back and sharing, it is (more) difficult for heirs to pursue this objective at a later stage.

To summarise the conclusion: parents communicate the three objectives of the family capital often too implicitly to their children, which leads to confusion and ambiguity in the next generation.

7. The ideal parental expectations and aspirations

In an ideal family situation, wealthy parents who bring their children up and want the best for their children and not from their children, should consider the following:

- Many affluent children fail to live up their potential because they were pushed. Most of them do not suffer from a lack of motivation, only from the wrong kind of motivation: external motivation, rather than internal drive.
- Parents can foster a healthy climate supporting their child's goals by their emphasis on process and not on result.
- A child will be motivated when he successfully completes challenging tasks with realistic goals where his ego is 'at stake'.

It is my experience that families find it difficult to establish a family culture with balanced expectations, to have a dialogue (not a discussion) about the meaning of wealth and to develop a plan to involve the children in a role they really want based on intrinsic motivation. An adviser can play an important role and assist the family with the challenging task to raise children in a well-to-do environment. A good start is to give feedback on the parental expectations and aspirations. Being able to look beyond the regular scope of traditional financial, tax or investment services, an adviser can help wealthy parents to have clear parental expectations that are effective guidelines instead of messy messages.

Raimund Kamp is an entrepreneur, researcher, author and speaker in the international field of family offices and business families. His special expertise relates to families who are in transition and the transfer of the wealth/family business to the upcoming generation.

1 K Murayama, M Suzuki, R Pekrun, S Lichtenfeld and H Marsh, "Don't Aim Too High for Your Kids: Parental Overaspirations Undermines Students' Learning in Mathematics", *Journal of Personality and Social Psychology*, 16 November 2015.

2 The study of 3,530 secondary students and their parents assessed math achievements and parental aspirations and also measured parental expectations. The aspirations of the parents were defined as how much parents wanted their children to earn a particular grade. Expectations were measured by how likely parents thought their kids could actually achieve those marks.

3 JL Levy, *Inherited Wealth. Opportunites and Dilemmas*, North Charleston: BookSurge Publishing, 2008.

4 L Hausner, *Children of Paradise: Succesful Parenting for Prosperous Families*, Los Angeles: Jeremy P Tarcher Inc, 1990.

5 Hilgard, 1971, adjusted by professor AJ Kil, *The Golden Rucksack – Handbook for Wealthy Families*, Boom Publishers, 2013.

To be successful over generations, the family office must be viewed as effective, trustworthy and relevant to each generation it serves.

Not the founder's family office: evolving to meet the needs of rising generations

Amelia Renkert-Thomas

A 23-year-old woman, granddaughter of a highly-successful wealth creator, has a question about a recent decision made by the family office's investment committee. At her mother's suggestion, she calls the CEO of the family office. What happens next?

- She leaves a message for the CEO, who responds by email, suggesting that she review the minutes of the investment committee.
- Her call is answered the CEO, who is frazzled. He pulls the Investment Policy Statement up on his computer, but is interrupted by a call from the CIO, who has been ordered by another G3 family member to vet a deal pitched by his buddy, today.
- Her call is answered by the CEO's assistant, who promises a response. Nothing happens. When the granddaughter follows up, she's told that she should send her question to the CIO.

Over generations, single-family offices play a role in the lives of family members. But what kind of role? How will the relationship between the clients and the office change as the family's composition and needs evolve? Seemingly simple decisions made by founders and their advisory teams concerning staffing, structure, governance and family involvement will shape family office governance and the attitudes and behaviours of the office's clients, decades later. Interactions between the office and next-generation family members can enhance or exacerbate the relationship.

To be successful over generations, the family office must be viewed as effective, trustworthy and relevant to each generation it serves. How can a family office recognise challenges that were planted at the time of its creation and make adjustments to become the family office that rising generations need?

Three family offices – The Vault, the Concierge and On the Fly

Imagine, if you will, three different family offices.[1] In each case, the founder (G1) is no longer living and the office serves G2, G3 and, in some cases, G4. All three family offices have substantial assets under management, deeply experienced and capable staff and structures comprised of various trusts and entities that promote tax-efficiency, protect assets and spell out governance. The founders intended to create wealth management vehicles that would generate attractive returns, preserve and grow assets, and weather difficult financial times, including family conflict. The founders worked with knowledgeable and experienced advisers to structure the office. But, as you will see, the three family offices are quite different in their attitudes and perspectives toward governance and family involvement. These attitudes and perspectives – the consequence of decisions made decades ago – now determine the involvement, relevance and relationship of the office to G2, G3 and beyond.

The Vault

The family office we'll call 'the Vault' was created by the founder when the family business was taken public following a bitter disagreement between the founder's son, who was in line to run the business, and the founder's daughter, whose husband ran the largest and most profitable division. Relationships between the son's and daughter's branches remain strained. The family office investment team has systematically sold the company stock and diversified the portfolio, following an endowment model. The office operates with 100% non-family staff. The family office staff and a board made up of independent directors and trustees manage and govern the office, respectively. The governance of the office focuses on transparency – family members have full access to performance information and copies of foundational documents such as trust agreements, and receive monthly distributions based on generation and age according to a schedule published annually.

The Vault was structured as an institution, intended to protect family wealth from family disputes. Its policies of prohibiting family involvement in operations and governance while ensuring equality of distributions, and providing full transparency with respect to information, highlight the founder's fear of family conflict and priority of risk avoidance. The trusts that hold assets managed by the office provide for distributions of income for G2 and G3 but do not permit distributions of principle except in the event of an extraordinary emergency, to prevent disparate requests and any grounds for accusations of unfairness. Requests for additional funds or services are politely but firmly denied. The office is extremely formal and precise in its dealings with family members. Scrupulous transparency coupled with equal distributions suggests to family members, "You can look but don't even try to touch". The Vault is effective within its narrow scope, but does not leave room for next-gen engagement. How will it meet the needs of a changing family?

The Concierge

The family office we'll call 'the Concierge' was created by the founder to invest distributions from the family's operating business. The business is run by one G2 family member hand-picked by the founder before his death, and continues to expand into new markets. The rest of the family is not involved in the business. The office provides various services to the business and also manages a portfolio of publicly-traded securities and alternatives. Family members play limited roles on committees that advise the trustees of family trusts, but otherwise the entire wealth-holding structure is operated by staff and governed by independent directors and trustees. Following the practice of the founder, who rarely shared information about the businesses with his children, there is little transparency or communication with the family regarding the business, investment performance or family office operations. The family office staff provides services for family members, upon request, as they did for the founder. These include getting theatre tickets, paying bills, arranging for home repairs, planning travel, and vetting one-off investments.

The Concierge, whether intentionally or not, has come to replicate the role of the founding parent, who focused on the business and tended to deal with family members reactively, rather than proactively. The office provides many of the same investment management services provided by the Vault, and with an equally competent investment staff, but it operates as a black box, with little or no transparency – an echo of the business culture created by the founder. Furthermore, the office is viewed by the G2 CEO as just one more issue to be dealt with. The office lacks a strategic focus, and operations can be chaotic and misaligned. The Concierge does cater to the family's concierge requests for services, but on a selective basis – there are no established boundaries, so the office chooses on a case-by-case basis which requests it will respond to and which it will not. Often, the requests delivered at highest volume or with greatest emotion are dealt with first, so the office seems to cycle through states of emergency. The lack of transparency, coupled with an erratic attitude towards concierge services, suggests to family members, "You'll get what we think you should get, unless you scream loudly enough, in which case you may get more". The Concierge was organically formed but never clearly defined. It is helpful to the family in some ways, but how can it improve effectiveness and fairness for the coming generations?

On the Fly

The family office we'll call 'On the Fly' was created 50 years ago by an executor, following the wealth creator's accidental death, to manage a complex portfolio of multi-national business and investment assets. The deceased, Will, a successful entrepreneur, was survived by a young wife and two daughters under the age of 10. Because Will had not done much estate planning, his executor (his brother, John) found himself creating an office overnight. Since Will's death, the businesses have been sold and the proceeds invested in well-designed portfolios. The office was run by John for 30 years with substantial help from Will's CFO and right-hand man, and is now run by Alice, who served as Controller under the CFO. Services have focused on the needs and interests of the founder's surviving spouse, who is now in her 80s and battling cancer. The founder's daughters, who had no involvement with the office while growing up, now have young adult children of their own.

On the Fly was structured not by Will, the wealth creator, but by his brother/executor, John, and so choices regarding structure and practice are based less on Will's express wishes, and more on John's interpretation of them. John has an indelible memory of a conversation that occurred just after Will's wedding, "I've signed an estate plan and made you executor – if anything ever happens to me, just make sure my wife has everything she needs". John followed Will's instructions – perhaps to a fault. Because the estate was substantial and the office's team made smart investment decisions, the portfolio has performed well. But the distribution rate has been increasing, and slowly eating into principal, particularly as the wife's collection of residences has

Family members play limited roles on committees that advise the trustees of family trusts, but otherwise the entire wealth-holding structure is operated by staff and governed by independent directors and trustees.

Wealth creators, who often have strong personalities, forge the family office environment and culture and shape the career paths and decision-making habits of those who will operate the office after their exit.

grown. The office was created in a time of crisis, based on very narrow wishes. It has never taken the time to consider its governance, presently or for the future. On the Fly remains rear-facing and extremely narrowly focused because of the calamitous circumstances of its formation. How can it look to the future while honouring its purpose?

The decision-making practices of the Vault, the Concierge, and On the Fly offices, and their styles of involvement with next-gen family members, come from many sources. Three of the critical elements that shape the relationship of the family office with family members are:

- the attitude of the founder towards use of – and decision-making around – family wealth, as set forth in writings or as remembered by family, advisers or staff;
- the office's leadership and management practices; and
- the legal structure of the office and the vehicles that hold the wealth it manages or oversees.

The impact of these factors tends to grow over time, often creating issues that have an outsized effect on rising generations of family clients, and yet they are rarely explicated and evaluated for their effects on the family office system.

Attitudes of the founder

A family office founded by a wealth creator typically bears the founder's unmistakable stamp. Wealth creators, who often have strong personalities, forge the family office environment and culture and shape the career paths and decision-making habits of those who will operate the office after their exit. Consciously or not, these opinions, habits and attitudes are adopted by staff and advisers as a set of shadow rules or guidelines for family office decision-making, often perpetuated by default, and they can condition the rising generation's involvement with the office.

We can see this force at work in all three of our fictitious offices, where the decisions of the office – particularly around governance, office services and distributions – are guided by the founder's words or choices made decades previously. The Vault's unilateral decision-making and transparency reflect the founder's concern that differential treatment and secrecy create conflict. The Concierge's black box, business-first style mimics the culture the founder imprinted on his enterprise. On the Fly is organised around an emotion-laden comment made by the wealth creator, along with the brother's memories and best intentions. The challenge is that no founder, however successful, mindful, longsighted and well-intentioned, can predict the entire future for his or her family and family office. The staff of the family office must take what direction they can deduce from the founder's comments, writings and choices, and use those to make decisions regarding administration and investment of complex assets for the benefit of a growing group of people with increasingly heterogeneous interests.

This highlights the importance of having detailed conversations with the founder about challenges that might arise if his or her preferences are codified and enforced over a long term, particularly if the composition of the family turns out to be different from his or her expectations in terms of number, ages, abilities, interests, experience or readiness. At least some founders will be interested in debating the trade-offs, and ultimately might come to advocate for flexibility over time, if they are asked. But when the topic is not addressed, and the founder doesn't fully consider long-term implications, the staff are left with the uncomfortable task of weighing the founder's expressed thoughts, the opinions and needs of the founder's children, and their own best professional judgment, to set a course. Helping the founder think through future governance when the office is being founded might lead to more useful precedent and governance that can be adjusted as the business and the family change.

The office's culture and management practices

A second input that shapes the relationship between the rising generation and the family office is the culture and management of the family office itself.

Some family offices are planned from the ground up – the founding family recognises that their collective capital would benefit from centralised management and administration and develops a plan.

The founder specifies which assets the family office will manage, and, working with a development team, sets forth a clear purpose, mission and vision for the office. The development team, which includes experienced legal, investment and fiduciary advisers, lays out an organisation chart illustrating critical roles and reporting lines, develops position descriptions with appropriate compensation and hires capable staff. They engage counsel, investment consultants, custodians and other critical advisers and service providers. They spell out accountability throughout the structure and identify and prepare trustees, family leaders and other trusted individuals to participate on boards, committees and other forums throughout the structure to ensure proper oversight.

However, most offices come into being in a far more organic fashion. The Concierge is a good example. The founder had created a substantial and geographically far-flung operating business, and as the ownership of the business became more complex and distributions were funnelled into new investments, the founder asked the CFO to handle ownership-level administration. For years, the CFO and the founder's administrative assistant worked valiantly to maintain files of the most critical documents, keep track of investments, send out Crummey letters for the insurance trusts and prepare tax filings. Much of the time, business issues took priority and the investment and trust decision-making was done hurriedly, if at all. After the founder's death, the eldest son and hand-picked successor hired a full-time family office CEO. The family office CEO, who had previously been a senior partner at a highly-regarded firm, pushed to add some formality to the structure. He advocated for bringing in an in-house CIO and appointing an investment committee, developing investment policy statements and individual asset allocations, replacing spreadsheets with a feature-rich reporting package, and implementing more sophisticated strategies to minimise income and gift/estate taxes.

Interestingly, while the family office CEO was successful in getting approval to add more sophisticated features and systems, he has been largely unsuccessful in changing the overall culture and management of the office and in expanding its role in supporting the wider family. The office was low on the founder's priority list, and that assessment has seeped into the culture of the office and the entire family enterprise. Family office accounting staff are not assertive, and they find themselves unable to get important information from the business staff on a timely basis. Committee heads (who often have other roles in the enterprise) prioritise other projects. The only work that is reliably considered short-fuse is concierge services for the G2 CEO, who, as an integral part of the operating business, gets preferential treatment from the family office. Because of this, the wider family has adopted the tactic of communicating a heightened urgency for their requests in order to receive services. This further exacerbates the divide of priority between the operating business and family office, and the G2 head and his siblings' families.

G3 family members have found the Concierge frustrating to deal with. The CEO is the face of the family office operation, but in a family culture where power is the most valuable currency, he commands very little. He has little decision-making authority, can't answer important questions, and lacks clout compared with others in the family's orbit. Furthermore, it is clear to all that, while talented and knowledgeable, his management skills are less impressive. Beneficiaries sense the disorganisation of the office, and that sense is compounded when they get incomplete or mixed messages from the office about the business. (The family CEO finds it useful to direct all family inquiries about the business through the family office.) While the office has a fairly impressive track record when it comes to investment performance, its ineffective and unfocused management system means it has little else to offer.

Legal structures and hybrid governance

Family offices typically play a leading role in carrying out the governance of the wealth-holding structure. Once a wealth-holding structure has operated for multiple generations, the family office (and the family) may find that governance of the entities and the interplay of decision-making roles of family

---

A family office is typically structured as a legal entity that does not itself hold wealth, but rather provides services to individual family members, family trusts, operating businesses, real estate and other investments, themselves held in legal structures.

Depending on the mindset and interests of the founder, the governance provisions may have been highly customised to his wishes or may simply reflect the default terms of the law firm's model documents.

members and staff has become complicated, confusing and misaligned.

A family office is typically structured as a legal entity that does not itself hold wealth, but rather provides services to individual family members, family trusts, operating businesses, real estate and other investments, themselves held in legal structures. All of these may be subject to various agreements (such as buy-sell agreements, shareholder agreements, voting trusts, etc).

Legal structures, entities and agreements are intended to facilitate the effective operation and governance of the overall family enterprise, but they bring with them additional layers of complexity. Sometimes, the same legal team will have created the family office and most of the entities (and corresponding agreements) that the family office serves, with the goal of developing an organised structure with unified governance. Other times, the entities and agreements will have been developed independently, over time, sometimes by different firms, as the wealth was created. Depending on the mindset and interests of the founder, the governance provisions may have been highly customised to his wishes or may simply reflect the default terms of the law firm's model documents. Regardless of the provenance of their creation, these structures specify which individuals or groups control the entity, and how those controls will be exercised. Particularly when the entities don't have a common vocabulary and an organised, overarching governance system, the result can be a structure that is internally conflicted and increasingly difficult to govern and administer over time.

'Hybrid governance' results when formal governance – the terms of governance set forth in the entity's documents and related agreements – is ignored or modified in practice. Hybrid governance can become common practice when the specified governance terms and processes are silent as to a given situation, or too complex or clumsy to follow in the face of the exigencies of day-to-day operations. In complex systems such as family wealth-holding structures, hybrid governance can become the norm, especially when the governance provisions of the various entities set forth a hodge-podge of unrelated and misaligned rules, processes and procedures. It can be difficult or impossible to convene different boards or management committees with different nominating and governing systems, and possibly with named members who are at best ineffective and at worst incompetent or no longer living. Hybrid governance is risky – even dangerous – because it can lead to decision-making that is inconsistent, possibly unenforceable, and potentially actionable.

Consider that a next generation family member who asks a simple question may find herself in the midst of an unanticipated and uncomfortable situation, if that question happens to surface an instance of hybrid governance. Perhaps she is being treated as a member of one generation for the purpose of distributions by virtue of her age, when she is in fact a member of a different generation, with the result that the distributions she receives are larger (or smaller) than they should be according to the document. Perhaps a trust for her benefit is being invested outside the risk parameters originally agreed upon due to liquidity issues elsewhere in the structure. Perhaps cash is being funnelled from trusts to prop up a failing business, without proper fiduciary oversight. So revealed instances of hybrid governance cast the family office and the overall structure in a negative light at best, and put it at risk of litigation, at worst. Even if the outcomes of the hybrid governance decision-making do not rise to the level of malfeasance, they can shake the next generation's trust in the family office and create a message that the office serves some at the expense of others.

This is the situation that next generation clients of On the Fly find when they deal with the office. The brother/executor marshalled all of Will's assets – two businesses, 24 real estate entities holding properties used by the businesses (seven of them outside the United States), vacation homes in Taos and Cabo san Lucas, and investment portfolios with four different advisers (Will was reluctant to trust anyone and was 'trying them out'). Will's personal and business legal work was done by different firms (and Will had often put off talking with his lawyers). With all efforts focused on supporting Will's widow, stabilising the businesses and other assets, and completing estate tax reporting obligations, alignment of the governance provisions of the various legal entities and development of an overarching governance structure was simply not John's priority. While he longed for the experience and perspective an independent board could bring to the family office, other events such as the sale of the businesses demanded his attention. Counsel has proposed a to-do list that includes creating an investment-holding vehicle to be overseen by a properly-constituted investment committee, and decanting trusts to clarify fiduciary responsibilities, but as yet the work has not been undertaken. And so, On the Fly continues to lurch its way from issue to issue.

Looking to the future: becoming relevant to the rising generation

As we have seen, family offices are shaped – and can become constrained – by attitudes, decisions and actions long since passed. Producing strong investment performance and keeping track of family and trust assets aren't enough to maintain a positive relationship with family clients. Will the family office be seen by the rising generation as a relevant and proactive force for growth of all the family's forms of capital? Or will it be deemed irrelevant or, worse, an impediment to the family's purpose, leading rising generation family members to seek an exit?

What is it that rising generation family members need from the family office?

Fundamentally, a family office must be viewed as effective, trustworthy and relevant by each generation it serves. Recognising outdated attitudes, strengthening management and weeding out hybrid governance can all help. Three additional initiatives – helping young people learn to manage wealth, helping them develop productive awareness of what it means to have access to wealth, and developing the rising generation's engagement and oversight capacity – can increase the value of the family office in the lives of the rising generation family members it serves.

The basics

At a basic level, a young person needs help navigating wealth – dealing with distributions and taxes as well as managing money, dealing with financial institutions, understanding investments, handling credit, buying real estate, maintaining privacy and security. The family office can be a useful resource to a young person, particularly if their parents aren't knowledgeable or aren't comfortable talking about money. The family office can be particularly valuable if it is proactive and offers help early, through simple transactions (opening a bank account, choosing and then managing a credit card) that lay a foundation for more complex interactions, such as developing a financial plan or dealing with substantial trust distributions or terminations. These kinds of interactions can become commonplace in an effective family office, and staff members can work to foster relationships with family members, anticipate their needs, and offer their services through calls, emails, newsletters, lunches or even events. Beginning early helps – staff members who are familiar and friendly faces to young family members more easily become trusted resources as those family members move into adulthood.

The three fictitious family offices presented in this article – the Vault, the Concierge, and On the Fly – likely would all face challenges providing this basic level of assistance to rising generation family members. While the staff at the Vault is well-positioned to provide the basics, the office is constrained in what services it can provide by its culture of risk aversion and its foundational premise of maintaining equal access to a fully-defined and highly-limited range of services. The staff at the Concierge is used to providing services, but lacks a coherent vision of their work and a mandate from family leaders. The staff of On the Fly has been so focused on Will's spouse's needs and the sale of the businesses that they have shortchanged their relationship with G2 and, especially, G3. All three would benefit from beginning an open dialogue with G3 (and their parents) about how the office can help them.

Developing productive awareness

At a higher level, a young person will need help understanding what wealth means, how their wealth may affect the ways they navigate the world, and how others will respond to them. Growing up with wealth does not necessarily lead to understanding and making thoughtful choices about wealth. In fact, it can hinder that awareness by virtue of the safety net that substantial wealth can offer. The goal for a family

Producing strong investment performance and keeping track of family and trust assets aren't enough to maintain a positive relationship with family clients.

> *Without informed input and choice-making from the family, and without the family coming to a consensus about its vision for the future, the family office will find it very difficult to sustain its work over the long term.*

office with respect to its young adult clients is fostering what might be called *productive awareness* – an understanding of the opportunities wealth opens and the possible consequences of their wealth, positive and negative, over their lifetime. Some parents are good at this task, but many are not, and the family office staff can bring real value to young adult clients struggling to come to grips with their personal circumstances. The family office staff can also help rising-generation clients see how their financial capital enables them to build their individual human capital – to see wealth as a tool for harnessing their passions to add value in the world, rather than as an end in itself.

This role is necessarily more subtle and delicate than providing education about financial matters. It requires that the family office leadership understand the family's values and its collective attitudes and unspoken rules about access to and uses of wealth. Is every family member expected to have a pre-nup before they marry? Is it expected that family members will have completed a degree or have a job as a precondition to receiving distributions, or distributions above a certain level? Is entrepreneurialism encouraged (and funded) or is preservation of principal a higher priority? The family office staff may find that, as the family grows, different branches may come to have different values or priorities, and that some of those may be internally inconsistent or in direct conflict (hybrid governance certainly exists in families as well as operating entities!). In such situations, the family office staff can bring a broader perspective or identify and engage useful resources such as seminars or consultants to help the family clarify expectations and help the rising generation expand their productive awareness of their wealth in all its forms.

None of the three fictitious offices have invested in creating the capacity for helping young adult clients with these questions, whether through education programmes or bringing in outside resources. As a result, there is heightened risk that the family's views on the role of wealth in family life will splinter. Such a splintering increases the risk of polarising views and increased conflict both within the family and between the family and the family office.

Building engagement

Ultimately, for the office to become a valued and useful part of the lives of each successive rising generation – beyond being a source of funds, investment advice and tax preparation assistance – it will need to engage rising generations in the process of making critical decisions about the future of the family office and the investment and administration of the family's wealth. The point is not that family should manage the office, but rather that they should play a role in governing and overseeing it. Without informed input and choice-making from the family, and without the family coming to a consensus about its vision for the future, the family office will find it very difficult to sustain its work over the long term.

Engagement is not a single conversation or an occasional meeting. Engagement requires that adult family member clients be part of an ongoing discussion with the office about collective vision and how it will be achieved. In such an exercise, the clients come together to articulate the shared purpose for investing their wealth together through the office, rather than individually, and to spell out a vision for the role of wealth in the family's future. Is it a continuation of a legacy? A steady and predictable source of income? Seed money for new entrepreneurial efforts? A safety net for family members? Once the family clients have reached consensus on the shared purpose and vision for the family office and the family's wealth, forums such as a family office board of directors, client council, or investment committee can be instituted to serve as oversight bodies through which capable and interested family members deploy their human capital in service of the family and the assets. The shared purpose and vision then become the foundation for strategic planning by the office team, focusing the family office and the oversight work of the forums. Young clients seek meaning and purpose in their lives, and making them part of the governance and oversight of the family office can enable them to be valuable contributors to its future.

Developing engagement can seem like an impossible task to a family office that lacks status in the family enterprise system, like the Concierge. Who would want to do the work? On the Fly would also find it daunting, because its focus on the needs of Will's widow and the demands of major liquidity events have led it to shortchange its relationships with G2 and, particularly, G3. The founder of the Vault sought to avoid engagement completely, fearing that it would increase conflict. Yet, how those offices cultivate relationships and build engagement with their rising generation family members today will determine whether they can inspire trust and provide services that are relevant to and valued by their family clients going forward.

To achieve the goal of being seen as effective, trustworthy and relevant to every generation it serves, a family office must develop awareness of how its culture and operations are viewed by its clients, and how it promotes or impedes productive client relationships. The founder's attitudes, the office's culture and operations, and the legal structures and agreements that govern the family office and the entities it oversees all shape the way the office views rising generation clients. Building successful relationships for the future requires that the office recognise and deal with the potential issues that its legacy might create, while also recognising the distinct needs of rising generation clients for assistance, information, education and engagement.

Amelia Renkert-Thomas is the founder of Renkert Thomas Consulting LLC, the author of Engaged Ownership: A Guide for Owners of Family Businesses *(Wiley, 2015) and Professor of the Practice of Family Business at the University of North Carolina Kenan-Flagler Business School. Renkert Thomas Consulting LLC works with family enterprise owners on issues related to strategy, ownership and governance.*

1 The three examples set forth in this article are fictitious composites of family offices I've worked with during my career as a family enterprise governance consultant.

Children of affluent homes are considered to be among the happiest group of people in the world, but in fact as teenagers they are more at risk of depression, anxiety, suicide and substance abuse than their middle-class counterparts.

Let's do it the SMART way: a practical guide for the raising of affluent children

Philippe J Weil

Introduction

One might think that children of wealthy families have everything going for them; they get the coolest toys, nicest clothes, are educated in the best schools, have private tutors, grow up with nannies, have the best doctors care for them and seem to lack nothing, but the truth is it is not easy to grow up with all these 'things' with the stigma of a 'rich child' or a 'trust fund baby'.

When you read about 'at-risk' children, you envision children from underprivileged neighbourhoods, from broken homes, street kids, etc and can hardly envision the kids of the top wealth percentile to be children 'at-risk'. What a surprise that a recent research body has added a new 'at-risk' group of adolescent youth – children of affluent homes. A study of public school students, conducted by Suniya S Luthar shows: "that as many as 22 percent of adolescent girls from financially comfortable families suffer from clinical depression. This is three times the national rate of depression for adolescent girls" [1].

The documentary film *Born Rich* [2], a controversial and much discussed work by Jamie Johnson, a member of the Johnson & Johnson family, shows interviews with 11 children of the super-rich and their struggle to find their own place in life. The film portraits a young man struggling with depression, and another one telling about the common use of LSD in one of the leading and most prestigious boarding schools at the young age of 12. Another highlight in the film is Ivanka Trump telling how she discovered that her parents were filing for divorce by the headline in the newspaper and was surprised by a big crowd of journalists following her to school on that day.

In my practice as multi-family office executive I have seen more than once that families have 'that one problem child' who has not completed school, has used drugs, is struggling and wants nothing to do with the family. These kids show up at the family meetings, but make sure to be drunk or high and to embarrass their parents and siblings.

I am helping a family in which one sibling has fallen into drugs and alcohol 35 years ago and has pulled down the entire family into disputes, financial terror and mistrust. The trustees are now working with us to repair the family and not to repeat the same mistake done by previous generations again in the next generation.

Children of affluent homes are considered to be among the happiest group of people in the world, but in fact as teenagers they are more at risk of depression, anxiety, suicide and substance abuse than their middle-class counterparts.

This phenomenon should be worrisome and alarming for affluent parents and for the educators of their kids. Barbara Blouin, in her book *Inheritors & Work* calls it very poignantly: "the disadvantage of having all the advantages" [3].

Eileen Gallo, PhD and Jon Gallo, JD, in their book *Silver Spoon Kids* have a very good listing of the 'double-edged sword' of the Effect of Affluence [4], as shown below.

What are the reasons that so many of the next generation in affluent families struggle and are 'at-risk'; why do the negative effects so often dominate the positive ones?

- There is the prevailing assumption that rich

Effect of affluence

Positive	**Negative**
Financial security	Lack of motivation to work/achieve
Freedom to learn/explore	Laziness
More interesting things to do	Activity overload
Exposure to the finer things in life	Overindulgence
Philanthropic opportunities	Sense of entitlement
Friendship with other bright, affluent kids	Insularity and snobbery
Appreciation for the rewards of hard work and ambition	Extreme materialism

people have no problems: Here a quote from Ivanka Trump [2]: in answer to someone asking her how it feels to be wealthy and to never have felt any pain she is upset and concludes "... to think that with money comes happiness!"

- Parental isolation: "It's so odd that I feel my mom is everywhere and nowhere at the same time." Being "everywhere" is about intrusion, being "nowhere" is about lack of connection" [1]. Many parents are so busy with their own schedules and priorities that they forget to be with their children.
- High parental expectations and big doubts: "When parents place too much pressure on a child to achieve at unrealistically high levels, they may give that child feelings of hopelessness and anxiety ... The end result may be that [the child] does not try at all" [5]. A good article on this topic was published in the December 2016 edition of this journal ("Parental expectations: effective guidelines or messy messages?" by Raimund Kamp).
- Walking in the founder's shadow: John Seabrook is quoted "When you inherit something, you always have that doubt: Could I have done it on my own?" [3]. The overpowering image of the all-successful founder is that the parent is in the eyes of the others very difficult to measure up to by the next generation.
- Feeling of entitlement: "... the kids have come to expect privilege as their due, not something they have to re-earn, sustain or nurture" [6] having the power of money and status causes the next generation to have a distorted value system. See also *Born Rich* [2] and the excellent TED talk by Paul Piff: "Does money make you mean?" [17].
- Lack of meaning, challenges and little motivation: "... There is a kind of boredom and despair I often see in these people: they can't figure out how to actually be of use ..." [3]. The previous generations have already done everything and achieved so much, what is there left to do for the next generation?

"Seek first to understand, then to be understood"

Stephen R Covey. [16]

Not many families see that their kids are actually crying out for help and that it's not the monetary help the kids need.

In my work with families I focus on five areas of importance as a guideline to prevent families from experiencing the above described phenomena. For this article I have arranged them in a SMART way:

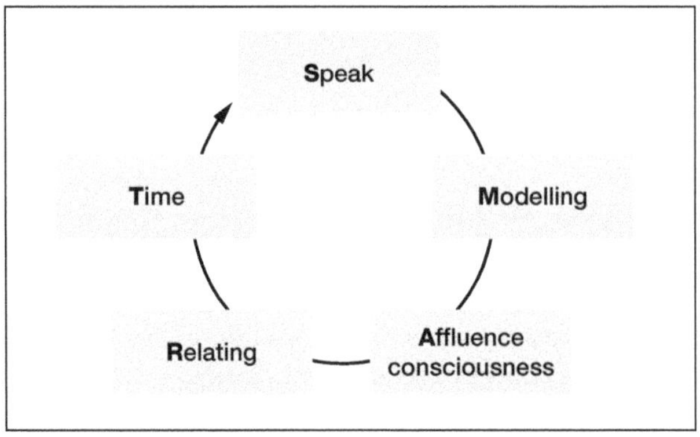

Speak

It might sound trivial to emphasise speaking as the first step to prevent the problems of the affluent children. Speaking is not difficult – or is it? In today's world of WhatsApp, texting and instant communication it seems we have lost the natural capability to 'just' talk, tell stories, communicate opinions and feelings, have a civilised discussion (even if we do not agree) and to listen to others.

Do we still have the skills needed for a real conversation with our parents, partners and children? We have them instinctively, we have just forgotten how to use them.

What was common in the past, to sit around the fireplace or the dining table and have a conversation, today requires an effort from all the participants. You have to take a break to invest in mutual communication. Families need to be aware of the importance of talking to each other, of having valued time together. You cannot express all feelings and emotions in an instant conversation.

In meetings with families my team and I find ourselves guiding families on basic communication skills such as listening, listening effectively, articulating and conveying feelings. We speak with them about effective conflict resolutions and the rules of a respectful conversation.

What you should do in a conversation

- Listen until the end
- Clarify and find out more details
- Check understanding
- Pay attention to body language

The 'do not's' in a conversation

- Pretend you are listening
- Hear only what you want to hear

- Interrupt the other
- Prepare your 'defence' while the other talks

We remind parents that the more they share their experiences with their children, the more the children will share theirs with them. It is not enough to preach to the next generation; it has to be a genuine conversation where both participants listen and understand.

Many destructions of families could be avoided if the conflicts are addressed, talked about and resolved early instead of avoided. "Since conflict often involves misunderstandings and misinterpretations, the perceived disagreement may become considerably exaggerated, be it in the heat of the moment or simmering over time" [7]. Conflict resolution instead of conflict avoidance; it might be a very difficult undertaking, but considering the alternative – a worthwhile investment.

Modelling

Some of us have difficulties with speaking, never find the right moment and are afraid of the confrontation. So, besides speaking, how else can we communicate our values and legacy? How do you communicate with a next generation member who does not listen? "The deeds you do may be the only sermon some persons will hear today" (Francis of Assisi); yes, by doing, by being an example, a role model, you can also send a very clear message.

I once witnessed how one of my clients got angry at his adolescent daughter during dinner at the hotel for using her smart phone in a foreign country (and creating a few euros of roaming costs) and at the same meal instructing me in front of his daughter to cancel the chartered yacht for the vacation starting next week causing a loss of the very expensive down-payment (thousands of euros). What does the child learn from the father's behaviour? Which set of values does this event convey?

As we all know, humans instinctively absorb and imitate their parents' (or caretaker's) behaviour from a very early age. So often we see our children's play behaviours, quotes, words and gestures clearly reenacting our own.

What we outlined above with the speaking is obviously also true with modelling; don't think your kid is 'just a child' and does not understand. We often hear parents saying: 'not in front of the children', but already by this statement you have modelled a message that has its implications to the understanding and behaviour of your children.

If words can be hidden from children, actions cannot. The way you treat the nanny, the way you talk to (and about) people working in your household has an effect on your children. 'Leading by example' is actively – not just verbally – communicating values [8].

Practising what you preach: "... by passing on well-thought-out values to our children, we help them achieve value-based happiness and give them a moral compass with which to navigate their way for years to come" [4]. Last, when your children are born you need to sit down with your spouse and discuss the values you want to instil and teach them – and then also apply those values to yourselves. Our way of living and our behaviour must reflect those values and beliefs, otherwise it is a confusing message.

The Money, Meaning & Choices Institute published a booklet called *Children and Money, The Impact of Wealth on Raising Children of All Ages*. In there you can find the following list of best practices of *Financial Parenting*:

- Communicate and reach consensus of your core money values.
- Reach an agreement with your partner on how you will live your money values.
- Practise effective money communication.
- Know your child's developmental readiness to learn about and responsibly handle money.
- Model and teach money management skills and work ethic.
- Model and teach philanthropy.
- Communicate your intentions and conditions about distributions and estate plans [9].

As Jay Hughes points out, there is not only the Financial Capital to look after [10]. Only once the Intellectual, Human, Social and Spiritual Capital are well looked after, is the Financial Capital in good hands.

But it is not only your behaviour in front of your children that counts, it's also how you value other people's contribution that teaches your kids about values and beliefs. Your children are exposed to all sorts of role models. It is you who have to point them in the right direction and help them understand the various messages received.

Affluence consciousness

This is the capability of an affluent family to cope with their wealth, position in society and have a

---

"I know what I have given you...
I do not know what you have received."

Antonio Porchia

---

healthy relationship to money. In their book *Facilitating Financial Health* Brad Klontz, PsyD, Rick Kahler, CFP and Ted Klontz, PhD describe Financial Health as having a balanced, comfortable relationship with money [11].

Money is something we do not like to talk about. But making it taboo is not helpful for an adolescent growing up in an affluent household. I am not saying that one has to discuss the tax declaration with a 13-year-old child, but the elephant in the room has to be addressed; the fact that the family has wealth, that they are in a privileged situation compared with their peers is something that creates difficulties and questions for everyone and especially for the rising generation. Barbara Hauser and Suzan Peterfriend have written a very helpful book *Mommy, Are We Rich?* with a lot of helpful answers to these questions from a small child, a teenager and a young adult [12].

"Of course your kids know how much money you have", said Lee Miller, regional director of the New York Office for Glenmede Trust, which caters to the wealthy. "Parents are wilfully disbelieving that their children are not connecting the dots" [13].

But how do you convey the message? Speaking and Modelling is not enough; you also have to teach your children to have a healthy relationship with money.

In legacy families[1] very often addressing the issues will make the children discover that their parents went through the same struggles in their adolescence and that the children are not alone with their feelings.

The conversation is about learning together how to live a financially healthy life with affluence and not falling into the many pitfalls I listed earlier.

Such a healthy relationship includes the following:

- Understanding the unconscious beliefs, or 'money scripts' one has learned about money, and being able to change those that are detrimental to one's financial health.
- Knowing enough about money mechanics to be able to invest and manage funds appropriately.
- Communicating openly and honestly within the family around financial issues.
- Having clear financial goals and plans for meeting those goals.
- Making financial choices and taking financial actions that are consistent with one's values and purpose.
- Experiencing low levels of financial stress.
- Experiencing high levels of financial satisfaction.
- Using money, not as an end in itself, but as a tool to help achieve what is most important in life [11].

(This is not the complete list from the book, but the ones relevant for our purpose.)

As I always say: "our generation has already learned to talk about sex ... we are proud of our liberal approach to parenting ... but when did you last speak to your partner or children about money and the effect it has on you/them?"

Emily Post, the author of *Etiquette* [14] writes: "Only a vulgarian talks ceaselessly about how much this or that cost him. A very well-bred man intensely dislikes the mention of money, and never speaks of it (out of business hours) if he can avoid it."

JP Morgan is famous for having said: "I'll go to jail rather than discuss my personal affairs."

So no wonder it is difficult to speak about money:

- It is considered a private matter;
- Money seen as taboo;
- Connotation of dirt ('filthy' rich);
- Talking about money might bring up conflicts and disagreement;

Table 1

Stages[2]	Responsibilities	Actions
Apprenticeship (5–18)	Develop financial vocabulary; establish early financial habits and values; practice saving, spending, earning, and philanthropy	Manage allowance; hold first job; begin community involvement
Starting out (19–30)	Establish identity and independent lifestyle; experiment	Acquire education and/or life/career experiences; establish savings and a good credit record
Taking charge (31–50)	Build assets; establish a foundation for self and/or family	Acquire assets; build career and family; explore life interests
Looking ahead (51–65)	Take stock; mentor; contribute to next-generation needs	Reassess life choices/goals, and re-energise plans
Third wave (66+)	Relinquish some responsibilities; plan for the next generation	Live and give creatively

Table 2

Age/stage	Social/emotional development	Appropriate money skills to master
Stage one: 5–8	Is curious Has short attention span May have very high energy Begins to view fairness as important	Counts coins and bills Understands the value and purpose of money Learns to differentiate between wants and needs
Stage two: 9–12	Growing fast, body is changing Feels self-conscious Begins self-expression and independence Developing social conscience Becoming aware of hobbies and careers Strongly identifies with peer groups	Can make change Shows initiating behaviour and entrepreneurial spirit Shows awareness of cost of things Shows awareness of earned money Can balance cheque book and keep up with savings account
Stage three: 13–15	Focuses primarily on the present; has only a vague sense of the future Egocentric, self-conscious and anxious about personal behaviour Begins to think independently Conforms to peer group norms and behaviours Highly experimental phase; tries different roles	Can shop comparatively Understands time-money relationship Begins to earn money; initiates small ventures Commits to saving goals Has basic understanding of investment Connects money and future Understands philanthropy Can read bank statement Understands interest and dividends
Stage four: 16–18	Has increased capacity for logical thought and planning Preoccupied with acceptance by peer group Experimenting with independence Confronts serious decisions about life	Actively saves, spends, invests Connects goals and saving Experiences responsibility for others and self Able to talk about money and plan future Understands money as power Can read a pay cheque, do simple tax forms Shows developing capacity for economic self-sufficiency

- High emotional significance of money (positive/negative);
- Avoiding difficult issues related to money.

When educating children we all know that setting boundaries, discipline and limits is key. It gives the children a framework and strengthens their feeling of responsibility. It also teaches them that not everything is allowed. So the same is true with money. If your child thinks because he/she has money she/he is entitled to a special treatment, then all the alarms have to go off! Entitlement is in my eyes the biggest enemy of affluent families. There is an excellent TED Talk by the social psychologist Paul Piff: "Does Money make you mean?" [17]; where he shows that once wealth increases, companionship and empathy decreases and deservingness and ideology of self-interest rise.

A survey of US TRUST in 2007 shows that 95% of parents surveyed recognise the importance of their children receiving a solid financial education but only 24% feel that their children are adequately prepared for wealth. The survey further showed that 53% of the parents were concerned that children will be adversely affected by wealth. So it actually means that even though everyone sees the importance of financial literacy, when it comes to the personal money and wealth of the family, we prefer to keep our children in the dark.

Just last week I met a woman of 70+ years, a member of a prominent industrial family, who told me that the first time she was invited to the meeting of the family trust was at the age of 58! Why didn't her trustees involve her at an earlier age?

In the 21st century, where reaching 100 years will

not be an exception and 'children' inherit when they arrive at retirement age, it's about time to rethink the way families handle wealth. It is essential that one educates the next generation to deal with the family wealth and to include all the living generations of the family in the financial planning.

Financial literacy is economic self-defense. And our collective responsibility as caring adults is to arm the next generation with the skills and knowledge they need to handle themselves in a world in which financial safety nets are being replaced by the imperative of financial self-sufficiency [15].

Financial education, to be effective, must be a continuous process, not an annual event. Joline Godfrey calls it "The Drip, Drip, Drip Method" of consistent, repetitive experiences that accumulate as financial fluency over time. She further enforces her argument by referring to mastering a sport, learning a language or playing a musical instrument – all skills that develop in a process.

Joline Godfrey's Key Stages of Financial Development (see table 1) call the childhood years the 'Apprenticeship'. She divides the Apprenticeship into four stages (see table 2). [15]

It takes structure, practice, drill commitment and resources to prepare your children to be affluent conscious. It is fruitless to expect family members to function as responsible owners without having basic financial fluency.

Relating

Relating to the other and society. Once your children are affluent conscious it will help them with coping with the fear of being used, exploited and measured only by their wealth. We have to help our children relate to the environment. The longer we keep them separate from the 'outside' world and disconnected from the reality of life, the more they become detached and have it hard finding themselves, be a productive member of society and be affluent conscious.

"I want to leave my kids enough money so that they can do anything, but not so much that they can do nothing."

Warren Buffett

It is a very slippery road to become a spoiled 'trust fund baby' whose values are completely detached from reality. To find the balance in life you need to relate to your inner self, to your surroundings and to society at large.

Children from affluent homes are very often popular with their peers because of the wrong things; the nice swimming pool, the cool games, the freezer full of good ice-cream, the fancy cars, the tickets to concerts, etc.

Peter Buffett (Warren Buffett's son) is quoted to answer to the question of how he reacted when his father first appeared on the Forbes list of richest Americans: "Well, that would be about the time that we found out how much money we had as a family. I'm not kidding, it was when I was in my 20s that my mom and I talked at some point, because there he was, on this list. And we laughed about it, because we said, "Well, isn't it funny? You know, we know who we are, but everybody's treating us differently now."

Warren added: "and they [the kids] knew who their friends were, and their friends were their friends because they liked 'em, and not because they were the rich kid on the block or anything of the sort".

Many children of first generation wealth creators remember their hard education around money. The constant reminder that their parents started at zero, that only through hard work do you achieve the riches, etc.

But if the wealth is inherited? In *Born Rich*, the documentary by Jamie Johnson, you will see how isolated these children are and how they are afraid of being exploited. Ivanka Trump points out that she is looking for sincerity in friends, as she was afraid that people get close to her because of her parents' wealth [2].

What can we do to strengthen the self-esteem of these young people? What will occupy them and instil passion in them? What will balance their relationship to money?

In my practice I have discovered that philanthropy is a wonderful and non-threatening tool to bring young adults closer to the issue of money. We empower the next generation with establishing the charitable foundation, discussing the mission and value system of the foundation, work closely at building philanthropic governance of the family. This activity – by itself satisfactory – has the wonderful side-effect of connecting the various generations of the family and involves all the members of the family, the ones in leading positions as well as the ones on the sidelines. It is the foundation for a lasting legacy.

Sometimes the activity on the charitable side of the family enables estranged members of a family to get to know each other again and to break prejudicial opinions about the next generation. This then opens the door to having serious discussions about the core wealth of the family and helps shape the family of wealth in all domains.

> *"It's good to have money and the things money can buy, but it's good, too, to make sure you haven't lost the things that money can't buy."*
>
> George Lorimer

Family members learn that all this wealth is not only a burden but an opportunity to do 'good' and to become a leader in their community.

This way the next generation can relate to the family history, be part of the shapers of the family legacy and history and also find their right place in society.

Time

Time is always of the essence! We all know that 'time is money' – but in the case of education of affluent children it is exactly the opposite. *Not investing time* will cost money;[3] investing time with the family is like planting seeds, the fruits will come with the growth of the next generation.

Time flies, and the formative childhood years of the children are a unique window of opportunity to give them the tools to become responsible, productive, positive and happy members of the family and society at large. You have to invest in the family, in the children; only this way will you be able to guarantee a continuation of the special legacy that only your family has.

To build a legacy a family needs much more than just a family business or family wealth. The vast majority of families fall apart after the third generation; investing in your family the SMART way, increases the chances that the family becomes a legacy family. SPEAK, be a role MODEL, giving the family members tools to cope with affluence, invest in their financial health and become AFFLUENT CONSCIOUS, helping them to find their own path and RELATE to their environment and, last but not least, spend TIME with your family!

Bibliography

[1] Madeline Levine, PhD, *The Price of Privilege*, New York: HarperCollins, 2006.
[2] Jamie Johnson, *Born Rich*, 2003.
[3] Barbara Blouin, *Inheritors & Work: The search for Purpose*, Halifax: The Inheritance Project/Trio Press, 1996.
[4] Eileen Gallo, PhD and Jon Gallo, JD, *Silver Spoon Kids*, s.l, Contemporary Books, 2001.
[5] Lee Hausner, *Children of Paradise*, Los Angeles: Tarcher, 1990.
[6] Family Office Exchange, *Preparing the Next Generation for the Responsibilties of Ownership*, 2007.
[7] Hausner and Freeman, *The Legacy Family*, New York, Palgrave Macmillan, 2009.
[8] Michael Schrage, "Like it or not, you are always leading by example", *Harvard Business Review*, 2016.
[9] Goldbart, DiFuria and Jaffe, *Children and Money*, San Francisco Money, Meaning & Choices Institute, 2004.
[10] James E Hughes Jr, *Family Wealth*, New York: Bloomberg, 2004.
[11] Klontz, Kahler and Klontz, *Facilitating Financial Health*, Cincinnati: The National Underwriter Company, 2008.
[12] Hauser and Peterfriend, *Mommy, Are We Rich? Talking to Children about Family Money*, Minneapolis: s.n., 2001 and 2014.
[13] Paul Sullivan, "How the Wealthy Talk to Their Children About Money", *New York Times*, 2017.
[14] Emily Post, *Etiquette in Society, in Business, in Politics and at Home*, New York: s.n., 1922.
[15] Joline Godfrey, *Raising Financially Fit Kids*, Berkeley: Ten Speed Press, 2003.
[16] Stephen R Covey, *The 7 habits of Highly Effective People*, New York: Fireside, 1990.
[17] TED, *Does Money make you Mean?* [perf] Paul Piff, 2013.

Philippe J Weil TEP, an established Swiss banker, is the founder and managing director of PJ Weil Ltd, a multi-family office boutique with offices in Tel Aviv and Zurich. He is personne de Confiance for a few selected Global Families of Wealth.

1 Families where the wealth has been created in earlier generations.
2 I think since 2003, when this table was composed, the age groups have widened and each phase from 'Taking charge' to 'Third wave' should widen by 10 years to 'Taking charge' (31–60), 'Looking ahead' (61–75) and Third wave to (76+).
3 Estate lawyers, trustees, psychologists, rehab clinics, etc.

The importance of financial education for securing wealth transfer across generations

Peter Brock

Unless you are a banker or a financial planner/adviser, you will not normally have been taught techniques for structuring your own wealth. This is never part of the curriculum at any school or university – only few mainly post-graduate or executive education courses exist in this area of expertise. If you are due to inherit a significant amount of wealth or call it your own already, many advisers, banks and wealth managers will be wooing or even chasing you with investment products and services. But how do you ensure you make the right choices and be in the driving seat when optimising your individual wealth structuring?

In this article, it is intended to raise your awareness that every individual in the context of families of wealth needs some financial education and how the different aspects of wealth structuring as well as family organisational aspects come together in sustainably transferring wealth across generations with success.

Wealth structuring aspects

Some principles are important for you to consider when interacting with the wealth management industry:

- External advisers of all kinds are great and will be able to assist you a lot, but only if they are truly independent and if you are able to instruct them according to your individual requirements. Without some basic understanding about financial planning, it will be almost impossible to pick the good ones.
- You can delegate most of the financial work, but only if you can fully rely on and trust your service providers or your own team. But ultimately, wealth will always remain your responsibility and final decisions cannot be delegated away – so you cannot escape from dealing with your wealth anyway!
- Always consider your wealth on a holistic basis, taking into account all the different asset classes you own – from entrepreneurial activities, possibly your family business, your more liquid private wealth, but also your human and social capital, as well as your family value. Only by taking everything into consideration can you make wise decisions at top level about your strategic asset allocation. Too often advisers only know part of the story or deal with part of your wealth – in that case it is up to you to bring it all together.

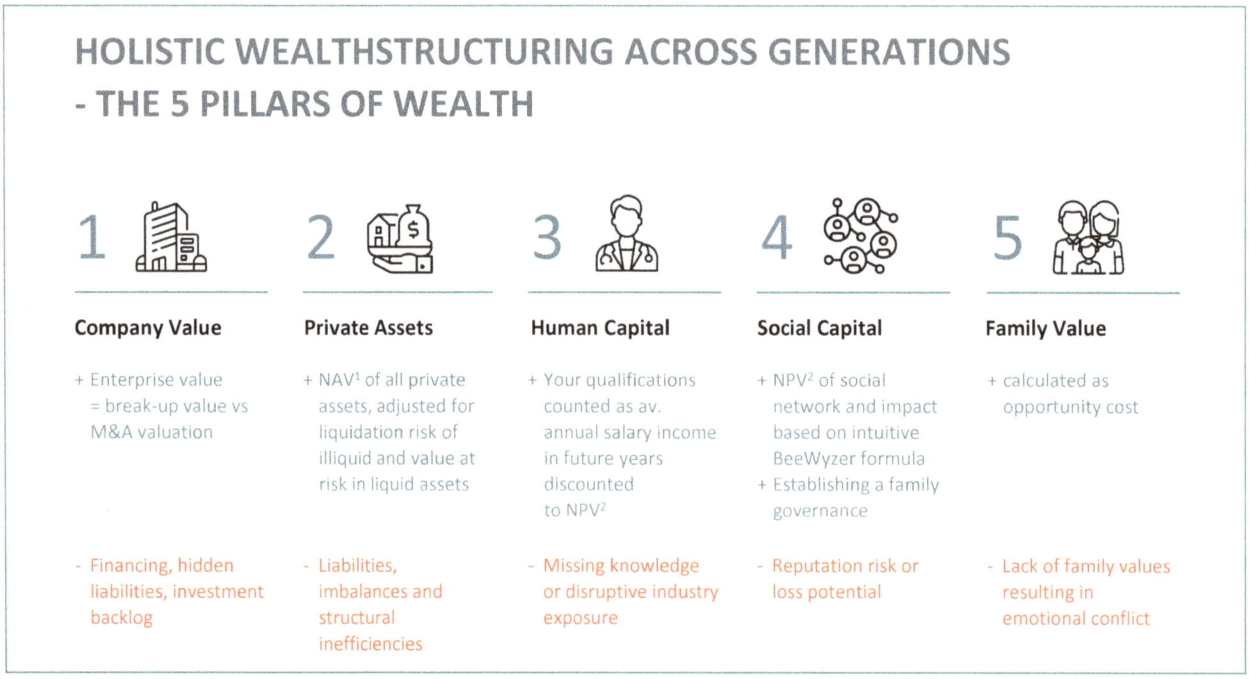

Copyright: www.BeeWyzer.com

Once you, the wealth owner, have obtained a solid understanding of both the liquid and illiquid asset classes – the status quo – of your portfolio, and a good overview of your potential future income from your human and social capital, as well as your future cash flow requirements, you can start planning your strategic asset allocation. Either you do the principles yourself or you do the exercise together with an experienced and truly independent adviser. But it remains your responsibility to set the scene.

The Strategic Asset Allocation (SAA) divides total assets into asset classes or categories. It factors in your risk appetite, your return expectation and your own personal liquidity needs. This strategic financial planning is done with a time horizon of five to 10 years with annual revisions. Broadly, it picks the asset classes to invest in and defines ranges for each of them. It covers fixed assets such as your business, private equity or venture capital or real estate you hold permanently as well as your private, more liquid assets like cash, equities and bonds. Liquidity or income needs, tax restrictions, sustainability targets and other long-term investment objectives are also factored in. Personal affinity or aversion to specific asset classes may be covered by completely excluding an asset class or by giving it a bigger share than the numbers would otherwise suggest – a sort of 'human overrule'.

The SAA divides your total assets across the asset classes you have chosen to invest in. You either aim at the highest possible return for a given risk budget or at a target return for the lowest possible risk. And – possibly most importantly today – you would also factor-in sustainability aspects to ensure that your capital is invested mostly to contribute to make the world a better place. Future risk and return are figures based upon market expectation as seen in futures contracts and other instruments. Or you make an economic forecast, starting with present values, factoring in historical developments in similar circumstances and extrapolating it into the future. In this sample (see chart on left below: example portfolios for different risk profiles) you see the neutral value for each asset class in a given risk profile. The neutral value is in between the upper and the lower limit of the range for each asset class. Within this range, tactical asset allocation (TAA) and eventually the selection of managers or individual investment vehicles (see pyramid chart on the right below) do their job during the year by changing the exposure to that asset class.

The old school of portfolio theory and research attributed a performance contribution of 90% to the SAA. More recent research for specific markets has also shown lower levels, but never below 60%. So the SAA remains the most important base of your performance pyramid. This confirms that it is of utmost importance to get the general allocation of asset classes right in order to optimise your results. A bad selection to start with cannot be corrected by a good manager selection process or the tactical asset allocation.

Financial planning for private wealth has been around for some decades now and has certainly done a lot of good – people started to treat their personal finances with more care, applying a systematic approach and the concentrated knowledge of trained advisers.

It always starts with the individual wealth balance sheet – a good financial hygiene for everybody as it

STRATEGIC ASSET ALLOCATION - SAA

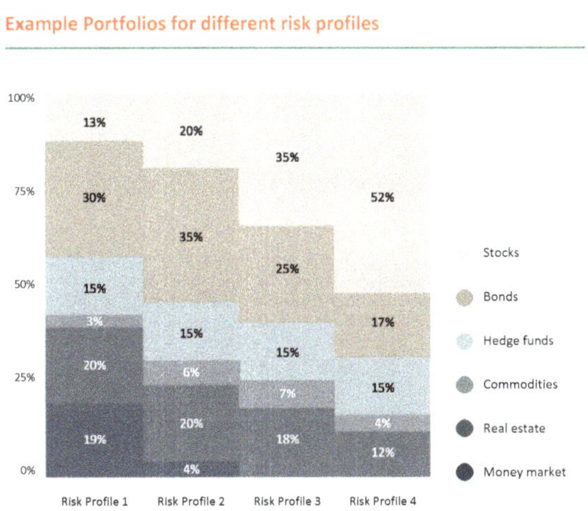

THE IMPORTANCE OF PERFORMANCE CONTRIBUTION

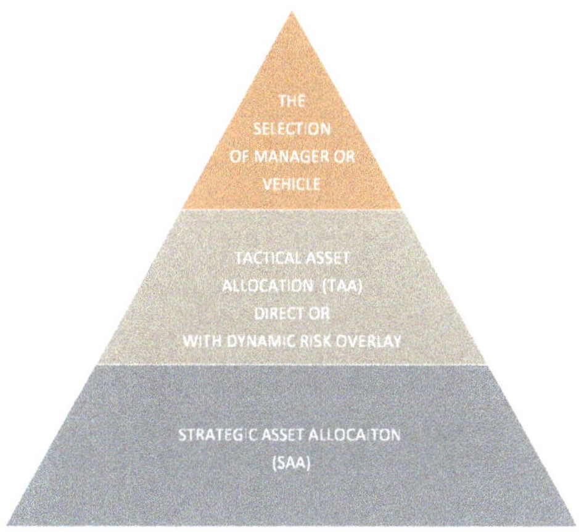

Copyright: www.BeeWyzer.com

> *Everyone wants their wealth to be organised in a sustainable way and it should be robust against the current insecure investment climate.*

forces you to look at your status quo once a year. Shortcomings in that balance sheet as well as personal aims and needs help to define a goal for the size and structure your wealth should have in the future. And the journey from status quo to that goal allows you to identify a strategy for your investment approach.

Adding solid cash flow planning, including your life expenses and income flows from investments or salary-kind of income, complements the balance sheet to an integrated financial plan – as it is done in corporations. Why shouldn't you plan your private wealth just as professionally as your entrepreneurial activities?

Unfortunately, financial planning often became a standardised practice, doing the whole exercise even for smaller or less complex wealth, thus overdoing it at times. And for substantial wealth it often showed irrelevant dimensions, eg pension planning or insurance issues that may be irrelevant or immaterial.

The balance sheet approach should ideally take this issue to the next level, focusing not only on corporate and private wealth, but on human capital, social capital and family values also. Generally, it should take all assets into account in a holistic way. It just makes sense in a complex family wealth setting. Combined with this solid financial education the basic SAA becomes a simple process where no complex maths is needed – after all this is not too difficult, if you are at least aware of the basic principles. In our experience, this gives a helpful orientation for wealth structuring – sufficient in most situations. But if the complexity is higher – you can and should bring in a financial planner for the fine-tuning. Such advisers could also work for or alongside you on questions that may come up along the way. For example, on cost controlling or risk management, when you are not sure and need a second check. This may be money well spent, when your own knowledge and insights are insufficient.

The robustness of your wealth

Everyone wants their wealth to be organised in a sustainable way and it should be robust against the current insecure investment climate. When I use the term 'sustainable', I mean two things: investments should contribute to making this world a better place; and investments should be structured to withstand external shocks.

Diversification is usually the name of the game here and it is no bad thing to diversify and thus de-risk your wealth. But it does not in itself get you to the robustness you aim at – here are the reasons:

- As we learned during the financial crisis, in a general market shock even historically negative correlations tend to regress to positive mean or average out – driven by liquidity shortages. The most diversified portfolio of wealth might turn out to be undiversified with all asset classes behaving almost the same way, ie downwards.

  So a diversification that works even in times of difficult market conditions has to go far beyond traditional asset classes and tap assets which investors seldom think about, such as farming, gold, diamonds or food and drugs, things that people will always need or want to buy. On top of that a higher quota of liquidity is needed than investment professionals usually see as efficient. Because you will not be able to create it when you need it.
- External shocks are often 'black swan' events. You do not know what is coming and you do not know when it is coming. And nobody can run a diversified investment mix based on researching historic financial data that tackles an external shock not known at all. A diversification that possibly works here has to cover the recommendations from the first point and add the topic of resources – besides your financial resources, the liquidity and the broader diversification, you have to make sure to have access to all physical and intellectual resources needed in times of external shocks. This way you will be able to move your assets, to unwind old inadequate structures or businesses and start new ones, to win suitable staff for it, to secure material and physical resources or the like.
- Most people think only about their business assets and their private assets, in effect limiting their diversification potential in the sense of everything described above.

  But as personal financial planning is about your life, it should go further than that. We think that your individual holistic wealth balance sheet should consider the following five dimensions of wealth: the company value and private wealth, but also human capital, social capital and family value, in order to make your wealth more robust.

That is why financial awareness and education are crucially important to deal with a broader holistic balance sheet approach. Based on this knowledge, you are enabled to deal with an easy-to-understand robustness tool for your wealth.

So, in a nutshell, unless you want to rely completely on others, you need to have at least a basic understanding of the different asset classes from listed equity and debt to real estate or private equity/venture capital investments or simple derivatives. Some basic understanding of the economy and relevant markets as well as the business models in the financial services industry will help you to avoid being misled and also help you to navigate the complexities in today's difficult market situation with increasing inflation and interest rates, the Covid-19 pandemic, the war in Ukraine and the over-indebtedness of most countries.

Furthermore, the trend towards an ever-increasing number of family offices being set up also highlights the need for more financial know-how of the wealth owner. While a great family officer that you may or may not have can take the heaviest burdens off you, global regulation and common sense requires that any wealth owner should have at least a basic understanding of his or her overall wealth situation. This is supported by the trend of using more and more robo-advisers in managing wealth. Clearly, any family office team as well as any robo-adviser needs some input from the wealth owner as to the overall willingness or need to invest in certain asset classes, the required returns and the risk propensity. These key criteria are individual to any wealth owner and will form the basis of any asset allocation and wealth structuring exercise.

Family organisational aspects

The same is true for the family aspects in dealing with your wealth. Many things are very different in various cultures, but the main lessons on how best to transfer wealth to the next generation and how to organise your family structure are the same in every country, culture or region. And some tools or references are true globally:

- For example (at least) larger families (either regarding the size of the wealth or the size of the family) should ideally have a family governance in place in order to have an orderly framework for dealing with wealth, succession and the education of the next generation.
- As part of the governance framework, it definitely makes sense to establish a family or individual investment policy (or investment policy statement) in order to avoid discussing the same questions over and over again. The family values will be the basis for any investment policy and will guide you on how serious you take sustainable investment approaches or if you might want to go deeper, for example into impact investing.
- Setting up regular family gatherings and a representative family council to simplify the decision-making process within the family are also typically very helpful measures. The family council should then be enabled to overlook or even manage the family wealth structure.
- Regarding the wealth management aspects within the family network, it remains an individual decision to set up your own family office or work with an external multi-family office. The differences are manifold and it is important you are aware of them and what they mean for you individually.

No matter from what angle you look at wealth, financial education is the basis for everything, whether you have your own single-family office or you are using a multi-family office for external services. The relevant know-how and competencies allow you to base trust on understanding, replace chaos with processes and combine financial return for your capital with sustainable impact. For example, it is just too easy at the moment to get fooled by lots of ESG products, unless you understand what the differences to honest impact investing are and how to avoid greenwashing.

In a recent article on wealth protection, the German *Manager Magazin* (February 2022 issue) reported on large entrepreneurial families like the Metzlers, Mercks or Freudenbergs and how they have secured their wealth over many generations. The most encouraging insight was that many pieces of advice do not require a degree in economics or finance, but a willingness to understand some practical lessons. The article mentions:

- Invest in stocks/equities as a core of your wealth strategy;
- Invest strategically considering your holistic wealth;
- Practice beats theory in these difficult times;
- Reduce fees/commissions charged by your bankers and advisers; and
- Acquire basic knowledge, so that you stay in the driving seat!

Setting up your own asset manager or single-family office is what families of wealth increasingly do, like nextgen Jonathan Steinhardt, a Berlin-based film producer. He comes from a German Mittelstand family enterprise. Jonathan studied economics, but he was still certain that he needed tutoring on wealth issues. And as a newcomer to Berlin, he turned to BeeWyzer, a start-up that specialises in financial education for entrepreneurial families. The founders Christian Stadermann (56), formerly managing director of the Quandt sisters' multi-family office, and ex-investment banker Peter Brock (55) have produced more than five hours of video material with basic knowledge about company succession, governance in entrepreneurial families and asset organisation. The video learning comes with worksheets and tools to apply the knowledge to the individual's own situation. Most clients do not aim to become investment experts themselves, says Stadermann, "It's about creating a balance sheet with our tools to develop an investment concept and to be able to select and evaluate service providers. Nevertheless, we show instruments for investment strategy, risk management and in-depth controlling – a good starter kit for those who want to do something themselves."

A fully fledged financial education course for wealth management should typically include both the family structuring subjects as well as the more technical finance literature. This includes defining the family values based on the existing family legacy, defining and dealing with family and generational conflicts, as well as subsequently setting up your own family charter or governance. A nextgen client put it very clearly: "Any family governance needs revision every few years to adapt it to the current circumstances and to the currently most active generations. It needs to be relevant for the current generations and they need to buy-in! ... otherwise, the charter just collects dust on grandpa's cupboard." To make the discussion about family values more relevant, this can be linked directly to the family's investment policy by discussing, for example, "What does the family think about sustainability? And how do we want to invest in order to make the capital work to save the planet with strategies like sustainable, ESG or impact investing?"

Sustainable investing today is a mega subject – not only for nextgens – and directly links to the family and any individual's own set of mind and values. So the combination of the soft and the hard skills is increasingly important to create a coordinated action and set of rules for the whole family in transferring wealth across generations. This includes a modern approach to philanthropic activities. While in the past the entrepreneur wanted to return something to society towards the end of his or her career, today a modern philanthropic strategy is becoming more common – this entails clear aspects of CSR (corporate social responsibility) throughout the whole entrepreneurial career in the family business, possibly investing in social entrepreneurship or venture capital. Often not just ESG-integration in the liquid portfolio, but also a move towards the application of more stringent impact investing strategies across the wealth portfolio. Any wealth owner should be clear about his or her competencies and should design their level of involvement in structuring the wealth as a learning journey.

The famous Three-Circle Model (see below, developed by Renato Tagiuri and John Davis at Harvard Business School, starting in 1978) typically depicts three different positions you can be in – the owner of the business or the wealth, a manager in the business or simply a family member. Within such family systems, every participant should carefully reflect on his or her own position, should review his or her respective skill set and also the desires and

The Three Circle Model as adapted by BeeWyzer

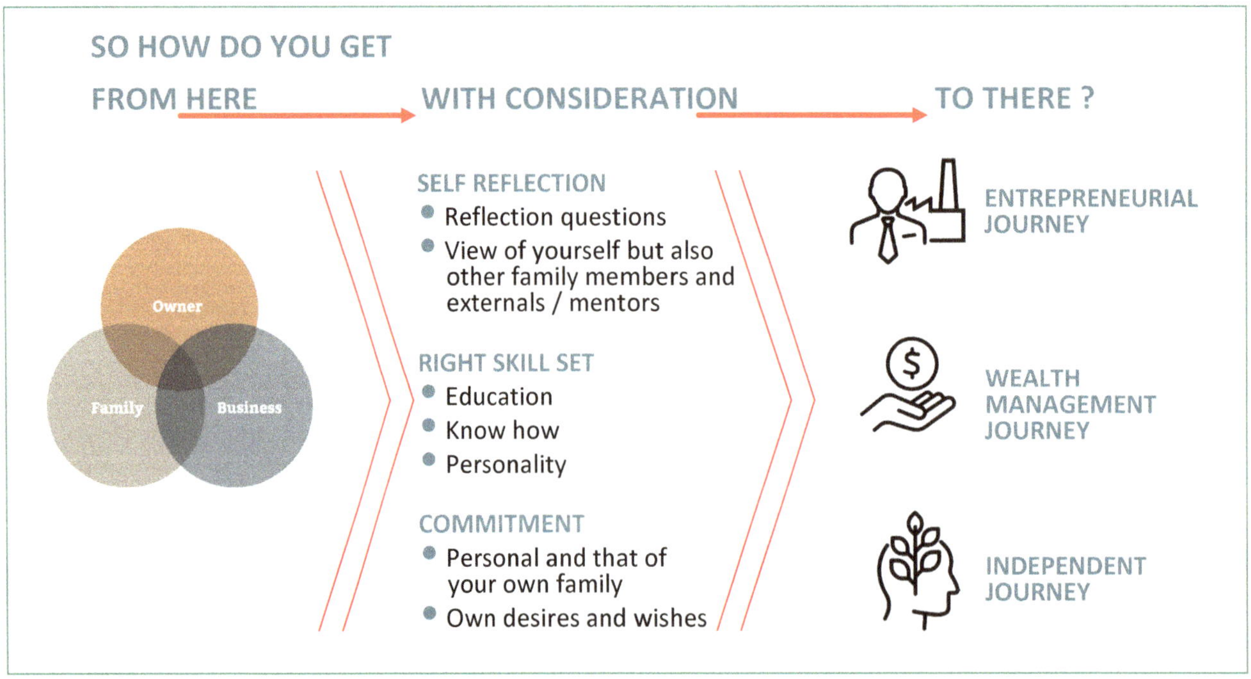

Copyright: www.BeeWyzer.com

wishes that he or she may be working towards. An optimal concept of financial (and family) education enables the individual to define the role positioning: is it more an entrepreneurial focus with operational responsibility in the family business (entrepreneurial journey), or is it a deeper involvement in the wealth management activities of the family (wealth management journey) or – alternatively – is the individual going on a more independent journey in life outside the entrepreneurial or wealth responsibilities. But even if it is the latter, some basic and relevant financial education is necessary for this person to understand the basics and decide on the optimal wealth structure and reporting mechanisms in order to stay on top of the matters. Either way, financial-know how provides the basis for all and enables the individual to tackle both soft and hard wealth issues by themselves.

For film producer and nextgen Steinhardt, the financial education programme has fulfilled its purpose: "After that, I knew what questions I could ask when I spoke to the investment manager." For any nextgen like Jonathan Steinhardt, it is crucial to be aware of their own skills and competencies in order to evaluate how best to interact with the family, the family business and also the family wealth.

Whatever your personal journey, you will need some training in relevant know-how to deal with your wealth. It comes with duty and, in many cases, a family legacy. Your responsibility for dealing with that cannot be delegated away completely – so live up to it, equip yourself and enjoy your own individual journey while educating yourself for managing the wealth transfer process better and sustainably across generations!

Peter Brock is the co-founder and managing partner at BeeWyzer GmbH (www.beewyzer.com), an independent, holistic and enabling step-by-step online video training programme for better wealth organisation. It enables wealth owners to develop strategies to grow, secure and transfer wealth successfully to the next generation.

I'm successful, but can't talk to my children about money! Help!

Maya Prabhu

Conversations about money are often difficult, especially when clients are concerned about how their children will adapt to a sudden increase in family wealth.

"Are we rich?" Lina was shocked when she arrived home from work to be faced with this question from her nine-year-old daughter Natalie. She had tried so hard to ensure her children led normal lives in spite of the success of her business. Yes, they went on some exciting holidays and lived in a comfortable house, but nothing extravagant. What would happen when the press announced her share of the proceeds from the sale of her company in a few weeks? Would it completely distort the sense of purpose and values for Natalie and her two older brothers? Would their friends treat them differently?

Families of significant wealth have always faced special challenges: How do we raise children without sapping their ambition to work? What is the best time to reveal the magnitude of the family's assets? When should children take a seat at the family governance table? How do we teach them about philanthropy? Young people who may eventually manage substantial assets also need to be particularly financially literate. Academic literature and the experiences of our advisers make it clear: great advantages go to children whose parents, grandparents or other family members consciously and consistently teach them about the mechanics and implications of wealth. So how are you supposed to accomplish this lofty goal in the middle of a busy life? The answer is simple: Teach them, one activity at a time, starting early and continuing as they grow. Each engaging activity can be tailored to a child's developmental stage and is designed to teach key lessons. Our experience of working with wealthy families has taught us that it is never too early to learn, and never too late to teach.

All children need to develop a basic understanding of financial matters. They are tasked with navigating an ever-proliferating array of financial choices and tasks, and this responsibility starts earlier than you might think. As a parent, grandparent or guardian, the most effective way you can empower your children in money matters is by focusing on the right lessons for the right ages. Children also make tempting targets for cyber criminals, and this can threaten the entire family. It has never been more important to teach children about wealth.

It has never been more important to teach children about wealth.

How do I talk about money with my children?

When families consider what they want their offspring to know, there are universal goals common to raising children to be responsible adults. However, many families express their concerns around discussing wealth, and the hardest part comes when they have to initiate the conversation: *"How do I talk with my children about money?"*

It is true that talking to children about money can be problematic for many reasons. In some cases, it comes from cultural beliefs, where it is taboo to talk about money. In others, people are concerned about taking away their children's sense of motivation and purpose in life, or are worried that they may see wealth as a burden, rather than an opportunity. However, avoiding talking about money altogether can have unintended consequences, such as children feeling untrusted, dismissed or unprepared. Lack of communication about money and its purpose, and not having a clear process for decision-making on financial matters, can negatively affect family harmony. A study conducted in 2003 showed that 70% of families failed to successfully transfer their wealth beyond the third generation, and the main reason for this was the breakdown of communication and trust in 60% of cases.

How do I teach my children about money?

Even if we do not realise it, we are constantly teaching. Children closely observe our attitudes and behaviours; how we handle money is no exception. Wealth can create opportunities and challenges for the younger generation that can have positive and negative outcomes. We have worked closely with a leading educationist, Susan Doty, to develop a practical guide for parents and grandparents on how to prepare children for wealth: financially, socially and emotionally. There is no magic formula, but what children need to learn about money can be introduced in a phased and age-appropriate way.

The aim of such activities is to help them master key concepts and habits over the years. Children's understanding of money is created cumulatively over time by verbal and non-verbal cues.

Within the process of empowering your children in money matters, the first step is to understand what they need to learn. Our experts have identified seven skills that can help them handle wealth effectively, supporting the decision-making process in line with family values (see figure 1).

Figure 1: Understand what your children need to learn

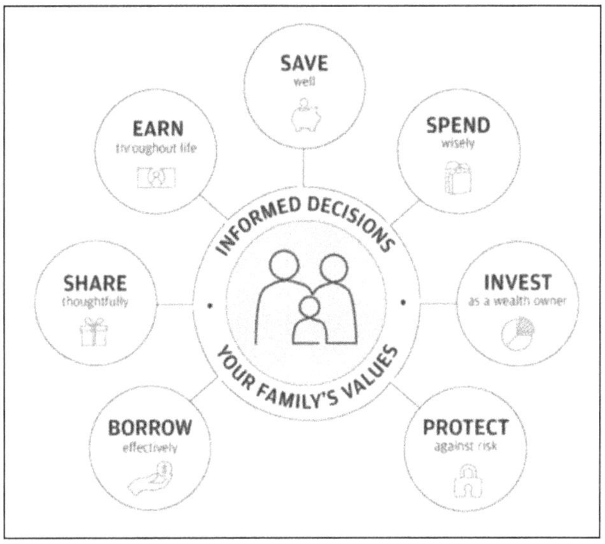

Source: JP Morgan, Teaching Your Children About Wealth – A Guide for Parents and Grandparents, 2018

The seven skills above are admirable, surely – but how are parents and grandparents supposed to help children acquire them? Timing is everything. A child might ask a significant question in a moment of serious reflection or simply on an absolute whim: "If we are rich, can I give money to my friends?" As any teacher knows, the ideal response matches the cognitive ability of the learner.

For preschoolers, for example, keeping a piggy bank might help reinforce the idea of delayed gratification. Early childhood age is an appropriate time to introduce an initial allowance, with the simple piggy bank. When the child desires a certain special toy or activity, encourage them to save for it in the piggy bank and help them to track progress towards the savings goal. Learning and understanding the benefits of this behaviour at a young age will provide an important foundation for the future. As time goes on, this can evolve into three clear jars with 'spending', 'saving' and 'sharing' labels. Allowing the child to make a choice as to the allocation of their personal money, and encouraging them to articulate the reason for this, will begin to shape the way they think. The journey develops into further expense planning and stock market games in the teenage years, culminating in a life plan and potential future expenses when they are young adults.

The best thing about using activities like this is that there are no formal rules or limits as to the context in which they can play out. Indeed, it was at the grocery store when one of our clients learnt the significance of using a fun activity to educate his 10-year-old daughter as to the importance and value of money. Every time they went shopping, his daughter would relentlessly ask him to buy a certain cereal that came in a box plastered with cartoons. Of course, he had seen it advertised on morning TV – a situation that all parents will be familiar with! The same type of thing would happen when they passed a toy store. The daughter would beg for 'Transformer Legos' or cheap action figures from Star Wars. Her father soon realised that it was time to teach her something about companies and their clever marketing techniques. As it happened, they often watched business news together at breakfast time. His daughter loved it when the anchor would announce news related to the company where her father worked; she was especially pleased when the stock went up! It was at this point that the father realised that investing in the stock market might be a fun way to teach his daughter about companies.

They started out small – he allowed his daughter to buy any stock she wanted, as long as she paid with her allowance or money that had been received as gifts – and he would then match his daughter's contribution. She was immediately drawn to companies that she could relate to, be that computer stock or shares in Manchester United. She was so enthralled by the idea that she soon started asking how she could invest

Her father soon realised that it was time to teach her something about companies and their clever marketing techniques. As it happened, they often watched business news together at breakfast time.

Figure 2: Use activities to help turn goals into realities

Preschool 3-5 years old	Early childhood 6-8 years old	Middle childhood 9-11 years old	Young teens 12-14 years old	Teenage 15-18 years old	Young adulthood 19-22 years old
				Part-time job or startup	
			The monthly allowance	Mini portfolio	
Piggy Bank savings		Allowance contract	Future expenses	Credit sccore	Independent budgeting
Coin sets and songs	First allowance	First budget	Family borrowing	Intro to (auto) insurance	Define life goals
Shopping trips	Three jars	Entrepreneur interviews	Stock Market games	Intro to good causes	Philanthropic engagement
First chores	Lemonade stand	Bank account	Volunteer and fundraise	College fund	Family governance
Identity protection	Online safety	Cyberself	Cyber limits	Cyberfamily	Cybersecurity awareness

Source: JP Morgan, Teaching Your Children About Wealth – A Guide for Parents and Grandparents, 2018

in her favourite restaurants; if they too had stocks. When they travelled together on an airline with TVs, his daughter promptly decided that this would be a great buy because other airlines didn't have them. Not only did this game teach the young girl a bit about companies and their motivation, but it also taught her that money can be invested, not just spent or saved. And, of course, not every stock went up and that was a lesson in itself. Father and daughter also got to spend some really enjoyable times together.

A year on, the now 11-year-old daughter spent the recent holiday period lecturing her older cousin on how to use his holiday money. "Don't buy toys", she informed the very surprised older boy, "You want to invest for the future". She has performed a similar role for her younger brother, aged eight, who is keen to understand when he too can buy stocks. The relationships between father, daughter, cousin and brother in this example illustrate some classic family dynamics: children astutely observe both parents and each other's actions. Moreover, older children love to actively teach and serve as a role model for younger siblings. However, one of the most powerful aspects of the approach highlighted in this story is that, instead

As your children grow comfortable with stocks, you might consider allowing them to branch out to other types of investments: similarly small amounts of simple equity, fixed income, REIT and gold index funds.

As children reach the teenage years, it is fundamental that they gain an understanding of how 'oversharing' online can be detrimental to them, the family and the family network.

of simply paying for the daughter's stocks, the parents insisted she use some of her own money to purchase the stocks that interested her. Taking this approach can empower and encourage your children to be mindful about researching their stock choices, and how they spend their money. Using your money to match your children's investments will then boost their enthusiasm further.

As your children grow comfortable with stocks, you might consider allowing them to branch out to other types of investments: similarly small amounts of simple equity, fixed income, REIT and gold index funds. You'd be introducing the concept of diversification and, over time, be able to show how different assets behave under different market conditions.

This example also illustrates how important it is to be a good role model for your children by articulating and demonstrating your family's values. Shared values can bring your family together, help define your attitude to the purpose of wealth and guide decision-making on financial matters. As the old adage goes, "actions speak louder than words", and how you and your family live by your values is critical. To that effect, if parents are keen to reinforce frugal spending as one of their values, then they might want to be more thoughtful about, for example, taking multiple luxury holidays and how these are positioned to their children.

How can I ensure my children are safe online?

As technology fast pervades all areas of our lives, a focus on, and an understanding of, cybersecurity is becoming more important than ever. Whether or not your children have an online presence, their personal information may still be exposed; a compromise can go undetected for years and can put the whole family at risk. Once your child reaches age six, it would be an appropriate time to start teaching them the core skills of cybersecurity and online safety. There are a number of steps that can be taken to ensure children of all ages are both safe and aware online, and it is never too early to start. The most important action you can take is to establish an open and ongoing dialogue with your children about cybersecurity, discussing the positives and negatives of being online, stressing the fact that 'online is forever' and offering some cautions about strangers. It can be helpful to establish some basic family rules from the outset. Children are often more likely to abide by rules to which the whole family is subjected.

Even before your children have started school, there are steps you can take to lay the foundations of a safe, sensible and secure online presence. Examples include establishing and freezing your child's credit rating by contacting each of the three major credit bureaus. A credit freeze will prevent a person, merchant or institution from making an inquiry on your child's credit report unless you temporarily lift or remove the freeze. It would also be prudent to secure all paper and electronic documents that contain your child's personal or other sensitive information, such as birth certificates, and to shred documents you no longer need.

As children get older, online safety becomes a crucial lesson. You can consider connecting the ideas of online protection or 'hygiene' to the more common health and safety protections that children are also learning at these ages. Just as the use of bicycle helmets and seat belts become second nature to your child, so should the rules of online safety. You can help them by setting time and content limits for digital media and devices, and explaining 'why' so that children can comprehend the concerns and the underlying risks.

Perhaps most concerning to parents these days is the realm of smartphones and devices. One way you can have some control over your child's exposure and engagement with this world is by applying the strictest (age-appropriate) content-filtering on each phone, tablet or computer and explaining why. Children are inherently friendly and curious. While you do not want to quash these impulses, you should explain that being online requires an extra layer of vigilance; they must not communicate with strangers. To that effect, teaching your children to report a text, call or email from someone they are not familiar with, and not responding, is just as important. Again, personal example is key. If children observe their parents spending a lot of time – for example at family mealtimes on their phone – they would likely think that this is desirable and will then resist their parents setting time limits on their own internet use!

As children reach the teenage years, it is fundamental that they gain an understanding of how 'oversharing' online can be detrimental to them, the family and the family network. It is during these 'tween' years that children are going through rapid changes and are often obsessed with discovering their identities, especially with their own peers. However, it is important to remind children that photos, emails, texts and social media posts leave permanent records that might come back to haunt them. Moreover, putting personal information in an email or text message can make it easier for hackers to take advantage of it.

Approaching adult age, cybersecurity begins to take on a whole new meaning. Children start to take more responsibility for their own personal finances both off and online. It is imperative that online financial accounts are set up safely and securely, for example without personal information in usernames, with strong passwords, online activity alerts and the ability to identify fraudulent activity.

How can I involve my children in money matters?

A key question that clients ask us is whether they need to reveal their balance sheet to their children in order to enter into these conversations about wealth. The answer is no. As illustrated by the father-daughter investment activity above, there are many ways in which discussions around principles, purpose and values can take place without mentioning numbers, which can then be shared when everyone is more comfortable talking about money. Despite this, it goes without saying that parents must be mindful of the power of the internet and that, in today's world where a lot of information is readily available online, children (or their friends) may know or guess the family's financial status anyway. In our experience, these discussions are always best led by, and deliberated as, a family.

So, how did Lina respond to her daughter Natalie's question? She explained that they were financially comfortable and would have more than they needed after the sale of her business in a few weeks' time. Lina then asked her daughter what had prompted her question. Natalie responded that her best friend told her that she had heard her family is very rich.

Lina arranged a meeting during family time on a Sunday evening as she had a project she wanted to discuss. With the sale of her business soon completing, she said she would like to set up a charitable foundation to share some of the proceeds. This reflected the core family value of 'sharing' – a word very familiar to Natalie and her brothers as they heard it constantly, especially when they argued over toys. The family project involved choosing a name for their charitable foundation. Lina invited Natalie and her brothers to discuss it themselves and propose a name at their next family meeting in two weeks' time. The children did their homework and after much debate proposed the name 'The Happy Foundation', as they wanted to make other children happy through their charitable work.

Natalie is now 28 years old and, along with her older brothers and parents, is a steward of the family wealth and a trustee of The Happy Foundation. She describes the foundation as the golden thread running through their identity and purpose as a family. It is the crucible to discuss the meaning and purpose of their wealth; to set the foundations of their family's communication and decision-making on money; and learn crucial financial lessons by examining charity balance sheets and investing the foundation's endowment.

Natalie also says the foundation has given her and her brothers a sense of fulfilment by making the world around them a better place. Each of the siblings also had the opportunity to contribute first a part of their pocket money and now their salaries to The Happy Foundation, providing them with a strong sense of ownership over the family's philanthropy. Aside from philanthropy, family projects on planning a holiday can also be an enjoyable way to learn about prices and financial choices.

Preparing the next generation for wealth can be a rewarding journey that brings the family even closer together. There are many ways to approach this process that fit with your family's values and preferences.

Maya Prabhu is managing director and head of wealth advisory for Europe and the Middle East, JP Morgan Private Bank. Maya is passionate about helping families talk and plan for the future on a range of topics including the meaning and purpose of their wealth, how they stay close as a family, how they wish to manage and make decisions about their money and their family business and how they prepare their children and grandchildren for the opportunities and challenges that wealth brings.

The hows and whys of enterprising families reinterpreting timeless tales for their NextGen

Asher Noor

Overview

You are the bows from which your children
as living arrows are sent forth
Gibran Khalil Gibran

Those born with a silver spoon may not necessarily understand the tenacity it took the previous generation to get to the top of the ladder and the discipline it takes to ensure an enduring stay there.

It is hard work to get the privileged next generation (NextGen) to comprehend not just the real merits and virtue of wealth, but also its trappings and fleeting nature. It certainly is a tough assignment to bequeath the same values and grit.

No amount of executive education, family retreats or off-sites, mentoring sessions, gap years and charitable stints in third-world countries, outside work experience or threats of cutting off the trust fund handouts have been surefire recipes to make every privileged NextGen understand their burden of merely being custodians of wealth.

In today's world, where people stumble across wealth created out of thin air, it is a herculean task to drive home the message that there is another way to attaining and retaining the wealth status. The dull way, ie through focus, planning, hard work, determination and perseverance.

Enterprising families are known to have tried mixtures of coaching or cursing, brainwashing or beseeching, instructing or indoctrinating with the NextGen, but it has not always yielded the desired results.

Realising that no amount of normal manoeuvring will ordinarily shape the mindset of those born in privilege, that wealth is more of a burden than a bonanza, some enterprising families have resorted to a different playbook.

The aim of this article is to try lifting the lid on a recipe that has made some of them raise a mature brood who are receptive to the duty entrusted to them. They have been able to inculcate in their NextGen the instinctive understanding that their mandate is to continue the legacy and manage wealth instead of misusing it.

In order to give their NextGen a leg up, what such enterprising families have been able to do is to rewire their brains from an incredibly young age by providing an alternative commentary and outside perspective to the obvious and the ordinary. One such vessel they use are the timeless tales, fables and stories which are universal, warm and fuzzy but with a bit of overanalysing can yield invaluable business lessons.

They discuss with them these bedtime stories but do not stop at the end when it says, "they lived happily ever after". That is where the conversation actually starts. Those conversations then lay the groundwork and provide the toolkit of street smartness that allows the NextGens to develop a keen business acumen and a respect for wealth creation and preservation.

The brain rewiring of course does not happen under the scalpel. This surgical strike is by tapping into the super power that such enterprising families have of being shrewd psychologists. They woo their children's subconscious. They subtly sermon, speak and sing to their children's subconscious. It might sound shady but in reality that is what clever parenting is getting to be all about.

It starts when the child is born and the wealthy parents, who are striving to evade the 'shirt sleeves to shirt sleeves' curse, are at the top of the game on this.

Make no mistake that it is both exhilarating and necessary to be obsessed with documenting the nutritional and developmental milestone of one's progeny, as is the case with ordinary parents. However, enterprising families are in a different league for a reason. They are laying the foundations of a head start, because they have an eye on the future! From the get go, they are speaking to their children's subconscious with a clear underlying goal of securing the path of extraordinary for them.

So what exactly is the subconscious?

The reason man may become the master of his own destiny is because he has the power to influence his own subconscious mind.
Napoleon Hill

In functional terms, the mind is what the brain does. This is until the identity theorists have us believe that the mind is the brain. The consensus that is gaining traction though, is that the mind is more than a brain. From being described as an infant's blank slate to

Freud defining it as a hydraulic and electromagnetic system, in today's tech world the relatable way would be to call it a super computer.

Our mind is meant to absorb all sorts of information which comes its way, repurpose it into knowledge and then utilise that knowledge for necessary action.

The mind has been dissected into various components, categories or parts. In simple terms, there are two basic areas. The conscious mind and the subconscious mind. The conscious mind is the familiar part that we are aware of. The subconscious mind is the data bank with an unlimited storage and retrieval option that stores beliefs, values and past experiences. If the conscious mind is the gardener planting seeds, the subconscious mind is the fertile soil where those seeds germinate.

It is not only the genetic similarities with parents that make their children relatable. The children are sponges when it comes to imitation. They soak up the behaviours and habits and will follow parental examples more often than they follow their advice.

Ordinary parents do significant damage to their children's subconscious with careless choice of words or actions. That radically influences the young mind, which could either fail to understand the right from the wrong and could also lead to lack of confidence or trust issues etc.

As they say, ordinary parents worry that their children are not listening to them. What they should actually be worried about is that the children are always observing them and are keen to mimic – consciously and subconsciously. It is the early formative years that demand the most from parents.

Enterprising families have thus realised that it is easier to create than restore. It is in the formative years that most subconscious beliefs and habits are hard coded in the minds. There is no filter to judge right from wrong, there is no critical editing and judgement and all gets a place in the infinite repository.

Parents might practise what they preach to satisfy the imitation aspect of raising children who like to copy more than they care to listen. However, the enterprising families who are keen on giving a head start to their NextGen, take the pain early on, to rewire the subconscious. Their thesis is that in later life their children can then act and react in the blink of an eye in ways productive to their well-being by tapping into what they have helped store in their subconscious.

Timeless tales – subconsciously guiding NextGens

A timeless tale, or for that matter any tale, will have components of a protagonist, a villain, a plot, a twist and then a solution that makes one feel good. With timeless tales there is always a bit of improbability interspersed with ingenuity and incredulity to deliver an interesting closure.

Timeless tales might be a good method to put the kids to sleep, but as we know in later life what really fires up our imagination and success are the dreams that stop us from sleeping.

Enterprising families do not just read these timeless tales to their children to end with a "they lived happily ever after" solution as an antidote for all the complexities in life. These parents are able to provide a different perspective and they keep talking about it in such a way that it really does seep into the NextGen's subconscious. For that, they need to repeat these timeless tales, with their interpretation often and convincingly enough until for their NextGen that becomes the real aftermath and is parked in their subconscious as the undeniable truth.

Given how useful these timeless tales can be in later life for the big decision-making, the NextGens revert to let the subconscious decide based on the way these timeless tales were interpreted and explained to them.

In this article, we will see how morals, conclusions, interpretation and context in some of these timeless tales are distilled by the enterprising families. This alone is worth its weight in gold compared to the learnings from any case study at an Ivy League school. The learnings from the case studies may not be around forever. The lessons gleaned and hammered into the subconscious from these timeless tales are lifelong.

Timeless tales will come back to the NextGen repeatedly all during their lifetime from myriad sources. Enterprising families preempt those repetitions where it reduces it to the lowest common denominator of good versus evil. They are helping to immunise their NextGen from mediocrity. While even the lowest common denominator moral offerings are useful, worthwhile and relevant, the obsession with enterprising families is to secure a head start for their NextGen.

Our mind is meant to absorb all sorts of information which comes its way, repurpose it into knowledge and then utilise that knowledge for necessary action.

Telling tales is a powerful communication. Warren Buffet believes communication is key otherwise it's as pointless as winking in the dark to attract attention.

The sceptic will always say Bah Humbug!

Detractors will always lean on Ebenezer Scrooge to blast a Bah Humbug. Their main argument is that the timeless tales have a notion of magic and a knight in shining armour coming to the rescue while the real world is devoid of it. They believe that tales of yesteryear may turn the NextGen into softies. Their gripe is that rags to riches does not happen, simply because they have yet to be the beneficiaries of that. However, the reality is rags to riches happens daily. Most likely, vice versa too.

Fairy tales can trigger innovation because you can create something out of nothing where there are no barriers to imagination and that brings magic into our daily lives. It reinforces courage. Data cannot rally the troops. Stories can.

Telling tales is a powerful communication. Warren Buffet believes communication is key otherwise it's as pointless as winking in the dark to attract attention.

Timeless tales – wrapped in new layers of exploration

Below is a sample of some of the stories I have heard enterprising families narrate to their NextGen with their own vested wrapper of reasoning and analysis. It is with this new lens that apparently the NextGen find a different perspective and a head start in life, especially in terms of leadership, entrepreneurship and wealth custodianship. I am just the storyteller here.

Emperor's new clothes

The emperor is conned into donning a non-existent suit that is invisible to the 'hopelessly stupid'. Fearing to come across as stupid, neither the emperor nor his courtiers question the obvious, until a child cries out, "But he isn't wearing anything at all!"

The emperor parading about in a suit that is not just invisible but also non-existent, has a lot more to offer than embarrassment, for the emperor and his sycophants. There is certainly more to it than what meets the eye.

It can be hypothesised from the tale that one should tell the truth as one sees it, without being fearful of the backlash. A similar real-world example would probably be Jack Welch calling shareholder value "the dumbest idea in the world". Not sure if anyone else was as blunt and forthcoming about a mantra everyone else swears by. Honest communication and feedback is key to the success of an enterprise. If something is wrong or does not add up, one should still speak up if no one else does. Age does not matter. A young person might know better than an adult might. Speak up if one believes they have something important to say. Vanity can lead to spectacularly poor decision-making.

Enterprising families, however, have more varied and worldly interpretations to offer their NextGen. Oft repeated, these then morph from conjecture to certainties, ensconced in their subconscious. In later life, the NextGen do not then fall into the trap of the herd mindset. Some of those varied and worldly interpretations include:

- Governments lie through their teeth with promises that they know they can never keep. Corporations speak of serving all stakeholders while singularly focused on their selfish agendas. People live fake lives on borrowed money that they cannot afford to repay, to impress neighbours, friends and strangers. They are all wearing the invisible clothes, but collectively applaud, encourage and support the vicious circle of make-believe that is self-serving. Those who can see through the charade are still the ones that end up being criticised.
- Do you have someone in your circle who will whisper in your ear that, "Emperor, you are not wearing anything". That kind of advice is something that usually money cannot buy. We are all emperors of our lives and, in that, we need to beware of obsequious yes-men, as they do more harm than good.
- Grown-ups routinely do a group lie by turning a blind eye to the obvious truth. They usually do so by ignoring bad news and posturing with the status quo. Raise issues of seeing things as they are and not necessarily as they are presented (even if vouched for by everyone).
- The procession does not have to go on. Good leaders stay the course but great leaders are not shy in making U-turns. It is better to admit a mistake and reverse the course than continue parading about one's folly.

The ugly duckling

Child of a swan whose egg is rolled into a duck nest leads to a life of misery. Cast out of the pond for looking different and hence deemed ugly and a misfit by ducks, hens, geese, old woman and her cat, he yearns to be like the beautiful swans that he considers out of his league. Only upon seeing his reflection in the pond does he realise that he too is a royal bird – a beautiful swan!

Those in the know are acutely aware that this is probably the shortest autobiography of all times. The author of the fairy tale was merely sharing his own life's worth of anguish and misery in a parable fashion. They are also aware of the backstory of how the author of this tale had his rags to riches story happen when he was bribed with jewels by the monarch of his time, so that he desist from writing political satire. Thus, they are not going to let a loaded story such as this be parked in the deepest recesses of their NextGen's subconscious, without putting in enough markers to help them navigate during their darkest times.

It can be hypothesised from the tale that don't try too hard to fit in for if it's proving hard, maybe one doesn't necessarily fit in in any case. Beauty is relative. Peers considering one an outcast based on appearance are the ones at fault.

Enterprising families, however, have more varied and worldly interpretations to offer their NextGen. Oft repeated, these then morph from conjecture to certainties, ensconced in their subconscious. In later life, the NextGen do not then fall into the trap of the herd mindset. Some of those varied and worldly interpretations include:

- The transition from ugly duckling to a swan is not overnight. It is a personal journey. If ugly is where one is right now and swan is the phase one wants to get to, it is a journey of self-reflection, courage, resilience and having the right role models and aspirations.
- Your *raison d'être* is to find your tribe and stick to it.
- You are a different breed regardless of the ecosystem you find yourself in.
- Fulfil your desire or potential as a swan by imitating and aspiring to be a swan and not a duck.
- Ugly duckling could be a benchmark or reference necessary as a contrast to outshine.

Rumpelstiltskin

A miller boasts to the king that his daughter can turn straw into gold. The daughter is put to the impossible task but saved by a goblin who bargains the girl's gold chain, to weave the straw into gold. The greedy king wants more straw turned to gold and when there is nothing left to barter, the girl offers the goblin her future first-born in exchange. The king marries her, they have a baby and the goblin reappears to remind the now queen of her promise. Horrified, she begs to be let off her promise and the goblin puts the condition that she needs to guess his name. She by a stroke of luck is able to guess it – Rumpelstiltskin – and saves herself and her family, destroying him in the process.

It is indeed an improbable tale that has its stressful signposts all throughout the story. The macho tendencies of the three males in the story – the boastful miller, the greedy king and the overconfident goblin are on full display.

It can be hypothesised from the tale that is crucial to do due diligence and be wary of doing business with strangers on an impulse. Background checks with those one wants to engage with contractually will be ever useful. Verbal contracts are weak and difficult to enforce unless parties consider their word their bond. Even with all the money or magical powers in the world, our dependency on others remains. Nothing in life is free.

Enterprising families, however, have more varied and worldly interpretations to offer their NextGen. Oft repeated, these then morph from conjecture to certainties, ensconced in their subconscious. In later life, the NextGen do not then fall into the trap of the herd mindset. Some of those varied and worldly interpretations include:

- The king is the decaying mindset that believes old ways of doing business can still turn straw into gold. Innovation at the hands of rank outsiders like Rumpelstiltskin can still produce gold/profit but once their name/knowledge is stolen from them, they are disposable. The likes of Rumpelstiltskin can transform organisations and processes but similar to consultants might wish to jealously guard their knowledge or charge exorbitantly for it.
- Do not fall for the asset liability mismatch of making long-term decisions and commitments for needs that are short term in duration.
- Bartering baby for gold is an unfairly priced

The transition from ugly duckling to a swan is not overnight. It is a personal journey.

Sibling rivalry destroys any collective good that could have come about from harmony and a united front, while wicked or demanding bosses can scare away good talent.

trade but if one can pin down the desperation of the counterparty, any tradeoff is possible.
- Close to closing one's best deal, it pays to keep one's mouth shut and the glee bottled up instead of singing or gloating about it, incorrectly assuming no one is listening or watching.
- For all his efforts, including spinning gold and waiting for the delivery on his contract, ie the child, isn't Rumpelstiltskin defrauded in the end? If one is perceived as the outsider, there may not be a forum where one could petition for justice. Fairness is not how most business transactions are structured to conclude.

Cinderella

Held hostage by her wicked step-mother and jealous step-sisters, Cinderella is only able to attend the royal ball thanks to the fairy godmother. However, in her rush to get back before the magical transformation wears off, she leaves her magical shoe behind at the ball. The prince searches high and low until he finds the foot that fits the shoe and is thus reunited with her, marries her and they live happily ever after.

Marilyn Monroe once said, "With the right shoes, a woman can conquer the world". Surely, those shoes could be their education, their experience, their personality or a mixture of all these and more. With a bit of a nudge, Cinderella could actually be fathomed as an ambitious woman determined to change her fate.

It can be hypothesised from the tale that showing up at the ball is half the journey accomplished and, despite being nervous, it is all about seizing the initiative and when an opportunity such as a glass slipper fits, to wear it.

Enterprising families, however, have more varied and worldly interpretations to offer their NextGen. Oft repeated, these then morph from conjecture to certainties, ensconced in their subconscious. In later life, the NextGen do not then fall into the trap of the herd mindset. Some of those varied and worldly interpretations include:

- Sibling rivalry destroys any collective good that could have come about from harmony and a united front, while wicked or demanding bosses can scare away good talent.
- Having contacts in high places like the fairy godmother do come in handy. In addition, the fairy godmother could be a mentor, a business degree or even a book.
- A clock striking midnight is like the perfect storm of a pandemic, lower oil prices, tanking economy, cratering real estate and stock markets, disrupted supply chains and waning demand for one's business offering – all happening at the same time. The threat of 'midnight' bankrupting one in the blink of an eye is real, even if statistically improbable without the passage of a standard interval.
- The prince is after a very niche clientele and can only get through after protracted market research. Your business can and will eventually find the customer for whom the shoe fits perfectly but they will not come to you. You will have to go to them, even if you are the prince.
- Clients do get impressed with first looks. When given the chance do not be shy in making a grand impression.

Little Red Riding Hood

In the forest, on the way to delivering food supplies to grandma, the young girl meets a wolf and speaks of where she is heading. The wolf rushes ahead to grandma's house, eats her up and awaits the young girl's arrival. When the girl arrives, the wolf pretending to be grandma in her clothing entices her into the house and eats her too.

It is a graphic story with the bad wolf winning the day. Variations to the story have a huntsman arriving later, cutting open the sleeping wolf and rescuing the two. In any case, it is difficult to find any overarching moral in a story where the innocent girl is the victim.

It can be hypothesised from the tale that people are usually not what they pretend to be and blindly trusting them inevitably leads to increasing one's susceptibility. Being innocent is no shield from the evil that lurks around us. It is a big bad world out there. Volunteering too much information is unnecessary and making one's whereabouts known is almost certainly putting one into a vulnerable position. If one does not focus on the task, is easily distracted and is not alert to the oddity of extra care and attention from strangers, one is going to learn it the hard way.

Enterprising families, however, have more varied and worldly interpretations to offer their NextGen. Oft repeated, these then morph from conjecture to certainties, ensconced in their subconscious. In later life, the NextGen do not then fall into the trap of the herd mindset. Some of those varied and worldly interpretations include:

- Packaging could transform a wolf into a grandma. If you are the customer, do not fall for a product based on its packaging. If you are the business, do not forget to pay extra attention to detail when it comes to packaging. Until the consumer wises up, it might actually help rack up sales on a mediocre product.
- Away from the security of the watchful eyes of one's parents and sanctity of one's own home turf, the world out there has no sympathy for the naïve.

Three little pigs

Three little pigs go out into the world to make a fortune. The first little pig uses straw to build a house. The wolf finds him, blows the house down with a puff and eats the pig. The second little pig uses sticks to build a house. The wolf finds him, blows the house down with a puff and eats him too. The third little pig uses bricks to build a house. The wolf tries to huff and puff his way in but failing that and a few other tricks, climbs down the chimney. He lands in boiling water and the pig eats him instead.

It can be hypothesised from the tale that there could be fatal consequences of surrendering on quality.

A very enterprising reinterpretation to come about is by flipping the narrative and perspective and reimagining the story from the wolf's perspective! In this scenario, the wolf is merely calling in on his pig neighbours in the quest for sugar and destroying the pigs and their houses accidentally by sneezing and ends up being vilified. This vilification stems from historical precedents of those of his ilk never being known to be on the right side of the law.

Enterprising families, however, have more varied and worldly interpretations to offer their NextGen. Oft repeated, these then morph from conjecture to certainties, ensconced in their subconscious. In later life, the NextGen do not then fall into the trap of the herd mindset. Some of those varied and worldly interpretations include:

- Complacency can undo anything that has been built and assumed to last. Attackers are always on the prowl. Active monitoring is essential and it would be wise to always be prepared for the unexpected.
- Think of the story in the context of the importance of cyber security. The brick design provides the impenetrable structure that straw and sticks cannot provide.
- In addition, what if we are the hardworking entrepreneurial pigs building our empires or nest eggs and the wolf is but the myriad of economic variables that we can fear but cannot ordinarily control.

Conclusion

Some day you will be old enough to start reading fairy tales again.
CS Lewis

Enterprising families use timeless tales to show the NextGen the reality that lies beyond the obvious. This is like a super power if one can embrace it fully of being able to connect the dots and look beyond the apparent. In today's world, seeing is most certainly not believing. This is where the subconscious and subliminal play a crucial role.

Enterprising families subconsciously influence and park ideas, thoughts, vision, mission and values that end up being the North Star for the NextGen. The lessons of timeless tales, oft narrated from a varied lens, turbo charges the NextGen's senses and puts them on autopilot on decision-making for life.

Enterprising families know that they have to initially do the heavy lifting and once it's done successfully, it is pretty hard to undo the subconscious. Want to test this? The Humpty Dumpty rhyme does not at any point explicitly state that it was an egg. Yet, how else have we ever imagined Humpty Dumpty?

Asher Noor is the Chief Investment Officer for AlTouq Group, a sophisticated Saudi Arabian single-family office.*

* Editor's note: Asher Noor is now the founder and CEO of Odyssey SFO, based in Melbourne, Australia. He can be reached at ashernoor@gmail.com.

Large global family enterprises and the professionals who oversee them are well-advised to employ creative planning and management tools to create and maximise the characteristics of nimble decision-making and flexibility – and ultimately resilience – which provide the best chance of success during tumultuous times.

Generational resilience through the integration of governance into structure

Carly E Doshi, William J Kambas and Michael S Schwartz

Architects of large family enterprises may be tempted by the simplicity and clarity of focusing exclusively on tax efficiency, but at what cost?

Recognised areas of global uncertainty, such as political and social unrest, stock market volatility, global pandemics, and an ageing population erode stability and create challenging environments for the general public, but large enterprises may be particularly susceptible. It is frequently suggested that a family's resilience in the face of adversity is one of the key predictors for their long-term enterprise success.[1] Large global family enterprises and the professionals who oversee them are well-advised to employ creative planning and management tools to create and maximise the characteristics of nimble decision-making and flexibility – and ultimately resilience – which provide the best chance of success during tumultuous times.

In this article, we advocate for the incorporation of resiliency planning into family systems, concurring with other recent scholarship on resiliency as a goal of family governance work. We will expand this further, by mapping family resiliency to a technical application, including components of a legal advisory framework and against recent cases where this has proved relevant.

Today's challenges and the importance of proper structuring

One of the central roles of family planning is risk management. At no time has this been more apparent, and more critical, than in 2020, given the litany of global challenges which have arisen during a short period. A steady hand in the face of such challenges is one of the hallmarks of effective risk management. Ultimately, resilience is the way that families will be best equipped to weather the current storm.

Scholars have long observed that many wealthy families establish and then lose their wealth within three generations, absent well thought-out planning. While typically losses of wealth are thought of as negative, if wealth decline is planned then it doesn't have to be. For some families of significant wealth, the ultimate legacy is a large charitable endeavour, not wealthy generations of heirs. Such a view has, in recent years, been made more public via Bill Gates and Warren Buffet's "The Giving Pledge".[2] Still, the classic example of a family losing wealth remains – a family growing in members but stagnant or depleting in its resources, combined with a prevailing sense of entitlement among the future generations.[3] As subsequent generations continue to hold onto the lavish lifestyle of their ancestors, the pot must get further divided, until it dwindles. The problem is compounded when future generations do not have the same enthusiasm or interest in taking an active role in the family wealth, through participation in operating businesses, board membership or roles within the family structure. In the classic example, by the end of the third generation, the wealth is gone.

Among scholars and advisers who focus on this dynamic, the agreed-upon 'insurance' for high-net-worth families seeking to preserve their wealth and achieve their goals across generations is by demonstrating urgency to address this paradigm, and a commitment to developing a well thought-out family governance structure and system.[4] Just as important as the structures themselves are the actors and family members who play a critical role in preserving wealth and managing risk. They steer the ship and are integral in perpetuating the values and vision of the family and making sure that the stated objectives are maintained (or adjusted as needed). And at the heart of the capability of these actors is resilience. Resilience trumps the fear of uncertainty and can lead to protection from an unstable framework and economic loss in turbulent times.[5]

However, the broad ideas of resilience and family governance are not in themselves enough for families to protect their wealth and achieve their goals. Families need to actively cultivate resilience by folding it into the fabric of the family system, including their legal structures. Within these structures, tax efficiency and investment returns are very important, but the success of a family will depend on its ability to cohesively govern itself within the structure. Below are our suggestions for integration of family governance into legal structures.

Recognising the triggers: instability and unpredictability

Although it is impossible to predict what challenges a family may face over time, certain events test a family's bonds. These triggers are moments that shock the system, are often emotional, and take family members' focus away from the continuity of the system and their individual, day-to-day roles. It is crucial to identify these potential inflection points, and build in mechanisms to help deal with them when or if they arise.

Some triggers may be easily identifiable by technical family advisers, as a result of their training in tax planning or investment management. However, many triggers involve interpersonal relationships and family dynamics and require an understanding of the various actors and larger social landscape in which they operate. Triggers may be internal to the family members or might be external, coming from the surrounding environment. Internal triggers include births, deaths, illness, incapacity, divorce and retirement. These triggers impact the family system itself – the size and members of participants and/or their ability to fulfil a given role. Whether through the addition of new family members (marriage, births) or subtraction of others (death, divorce), the definition of 'family' itself is changed in some way. External triggers include geopolitical events, market volatility resulting in dramatic declines in capital, political or social unrest, and natural disasters. Both types of triggers put strains on the structure and are key drivers in why families need a solid governance with resilient people at the helm. Leaders of family enterprises are wise to be aware of triggers and to have a risk management plan for addressing them in advance.

Changes in global tax compliance and reporting obligations for families is another potential trigger. For example, in June 2020, the US Internal Revenue Service (the IRS) announced the re-formation of the Global High-Net-Worth squad, formed to take a holistic approach in addressing high-net-worth taxpayers and to look at the complete financial picture of high-net-worth individuals and the enterprises they control.[6] IRS Commissioner Chuck Rettig once referred to audits by the Global High-Net-Worth squad as being "audits from hell", and the reviews will include interests in US and foreign partnerships, trusts, subchapter S corporations, C corporations, private foundations, and gifts between family members.[7] Increased regulatory scrutiny demands cohesive and well-functioning governance, where the participants are adhering strictly to the purposes, structure and formalities of the system. As any practitioner who has navigated an IRS audit can attest, the process can be trying for even the most organised of taxpayers. A solid and organised governance structure with intelligent and capable people can help mitigate this risk.

When dealing with triggers, it is often the perception of a risk that increases the stress response.[8] Humans, whether individually or as groups, are not typically at our best when faced with a decision to fight or flight.[9] Without proper training and structure, family members may push for quick and simple solutions, or may act reflexively and impulsively. Decisions made in a moment of stress frequently fail to account for the long-term problems or risks that erode economic fortunes.

A better plan is to prepare when times are not urgent, and equip family members and other relevant actors with the tools and skills to handle triggers effectively. Under calm circumstances and with level heads, a family is best-positioned to build a system for decision making which can be practised over time, and then utilised when triggers appear.

The solution: family governance integration

Family advisers have a variety of tools at their disposal to maximise wealth and provide for efficient transfer across generations. But while traditional advice may prevent some triggering events from taking root or delay the impact of others, it may not adequately prepare a family and its members for dealing with unexpected or inevitable triggers. This is when resilience is required.

Fortunately, the process for developing effective governance can be easily mapped against resilience by applying the three component parts of resilience: shared beliefs, organisation and communication. Professionals can assist in this by counselling families through these decisions based on professional experience, and drawing on known family fortunes that have been squandered. In quick summary:

Beliefs

The first step to forming an effective governance structure is for a family to turn inward and consider its mostly closely held beliefs and values. Helping family members to articulate family values is critical, as it binds individuals together and is the test against which future actions are considered. It is also the bedrock upon which a family will rely when a crisis hits, giving it the resilience it needs.

Leaders of family enterprises are wise to be aware of triggers and to have a risk management plan for addressing them in advance.

Organisation

While unpredictable triggers lead to uncertainty, proactive organisation enables efficient and effective decision making. For family enterprises, this involves developing systems for clear management. Which individuals should be involved in key decisions? Do the relevant persons include those with both formal and informal roles within an operating business? How does a group convene, vote and effectuate its decisions? Who receives material benefits, and what benefits should they reasonably expect? A tax-efficient structure that does not contemplate these issues will inevitably lead to problems, and a family mired in bureaucracy will succumb to inaction during a crisis.

Communication

Finally, family resilience demands clear communication with a spirit of collaboration. Family member roles may differ, and indeed in a complex enterprise the level of participation is likely to be varied.[10] But the importance of feeling included and informed cannot be overstated. Failing to communicate with key parties – even those who lack current authority, but whose future interests are nonetheless at stake – is the surest path to family discord, and ultimately to potential litigation. Communication should not wait until a structure is in crisis mode. If possible, it should occur all throughout the planning and operation phases of the structure.

Importantly, the goals, process and organisation are the prelude to the structure. These three elements, and their codification through a family governance deliverable such as a family constitution, may be viewed as sitting 'above' trust structures in the organisational chart of a family system. Taken together, they transcend all individuals, operating businesses or other holdings, even tax and legal planning, and provide both stability as well as flexibility.

Design and implementation

Once the family have established their goals, and have a clear articulation of their desired organisation and communication channels, they can then move on to designing and developing the structure. During this phase the estate plan is formulated, including more precise details of the overall structure, its benefits and implications, and the documents to memorialise it. While legal and tax advisers are frequently in the driver's seat, this should remain a collaborative process between counsel and the family.

Before drafting, advisers charged with setting up or managing a system should:

- take the time to understand the symmetry between the family's personal goals and business goals;
- explain various governance structure options to the family (family entities, trust companies, family offices, etc);
- consider the family's own closely held beliefs and long-term goals;
- include various roles in the structure, in keeping with the family's own identified way of organising themselves;
- build in opportunities and channels for family communication; and
- help the family identify any service providers that will be needed to implement and maintain the structure.

Finally, jurisdiction can be a very important question at this stage with wide-ranging considerations and implications for resiliency. At the highest level, determining foreign or domestic status is critical, but from there the options quickly multiply. Both US states and many countries globally offer compelling and persuasive tax regimes, governance flexibility, privacy and protection of property rights. But others, particularly the older, larger and more structured jurisdictions, are more restrictive. While considering the most important factors to a particular family, convenience should also not be overlooked. Many a family office has struggled to recruit top talent due to their physical location; virtual offices in major hubs may be a sufficient work-around, but add additional complexity and overheads.

Once these considerations have been navigated with care, and appropriate jurisdictions identified, only then does one turn to the legal documents. The legal implementation should be reserved to the end of the process. In other words – measure twice, cut once.

Once the family have established their goals, and have a clear articulation of their desired organisation and communication channels, they can then move on to designing and developing the structure.

> *Many families consolidate wealth in a family holding vehicle; in many cases, this is in the form of a limited partnership.*

Looking closely at the legal documents

For a resilient system able to withstand a crisis, legal documents are as important as the codification of the family governance plan. Extending the family governance work into the legal documents takes some effort and creativity, but the resulting system is most likely to address a family's own values, organisation and communication – and therefore provide the greatest chance of resilience.

While a traditional estate planner may focus primarily on a client's last will and testament, there are other crucial documents that should and often do form part of the plan.

Trusts

In many US family governance structures rooted in estate planning, trust agreements are often the central documents. This is true for many other common law jurisdictions across the globe. A trust, in essence, is an agreement whereby a settlor (the person currently holding wealth) makes an arrangement with a trustee (a competent, experienced, party suitable to oversee wealth) to manage wealth (whether assets or property) for a set group of beneficiaries (often, but not always, descendants of the settlor and charities).

Trusts are ideal documents for family governance. At a high level, the trust instrument clearly defines roles and provides clarity around expectations. This includes setting forth the fiduciaries and beneficiaries. Trusts also clearly define the terms by which future power holders or beneficiaries step into their roles – potentially mentioning specifically the triggering events about which a family is likely to be concerned, such as the death or incapacity of an older generation. While the trust does not prevent the trigger from happening, it does provide clarity and structure so that the individual actors can proceed in an orderly and organised way.

Other estate planning documents

For individuals, basic estate plans include financial powers of attorney and healthcare directives setting forth wishes in the event of incapacity. Both documents have significant implications for family dynamics, and care should be taken when counselling a client about who to name in such roles. This is particularly the case for a financial power of attorney – unless restrained by the power of attorney instrument, the attorney-in-fact can typically freely make decisions that the individual himself can make, including wiring money into or out of bank accounts, and selling or acquiring property. While tradition might prescribe that an oldest child or male heir be given authority, this may not always be the best choice for a family with multiple children, particularly where distrust is an issue. Even worse is when the person to be named suffers from addiction or other issues. Therefore, there is value in considering these decisions carefully, appointing individuals who are well-equipped to be good stewards, and ideally build flexibility to make adjustments as needed.

Partnerships

Many families consolidate wealth in a family holding vehicle; in many cases, this is in the form of a limited partnership. The governing document of a partnership agreement establishes general partner and limited partner roles; each of these roles include specific responsibilities and benefits which should be considered (in addition to the traditional tax reasons for doing so). For example, in the case of a cohort of siblings, are each equally well-suited to participate in such an arrangement? Will one or more not honour the formalities? This can lead to undesirable results in the future. The partnership agreement may also contain various withdrawal and transferability restrictions, as well as guidelines and procedures for managing the partnership, which can be helpful in providing flexibility in the future as circumstances surrounding the assets held in the partnership or the participants change. But careful attention should be paid to who holds a particular power, and how the legal drafting may actually create unintended imbalances of power among related people.

Family limited partnerships offer opportunities for integrating management collaboration and family values. Determining who will participate in a partnership should not be a foregone conclusion. It is an opportunity to make important decisions fostering family involvement. While some families do not require structured engagement, such as when a family is merely pooling portfolio investments managed by an external adviser, this is not the case when a family limited partnership is concerned; engagement here is highly valuable.

For example, consider a hypothetical family limited

While traditionally families make decisions around the dining room table (or a family meeting that occurs over a holiday), roles, responsibilities and decision-making authority in those situations are subjected to the natural governance of the loudest family members.

partnership which has six limited partners and one general partner who has sufficient income generated from outside the family. The general partner may not be focused on managing the assets within the partnership, and instead may retain an investment adviser with limited vetting, and may charge that adviser with managing the assets with limited oversight. These situations occur, and the results can be significant, particularly where the chosen delegate lacks appropriate experience and skill.

Alternatively, if this same family established a family office, and undertake to hire employees, vetting of skills and experience become folded into the process. A chief executive officer can be hired and compensated accordingly, and such families are often able to retain top talent from hedge funds and investment banking. This formality and infrastructure can be helpful to a family to maintain its wealth.

Holding companies and limited liability companies (LLCs)

In the United States, the LLC is used almost interchangeably with the limited partnership. But they are not identical. An LLC operating agreement functions similarly to a partnership agreement, establishing whether the entity is managed by managers or members, and it will dictate roles and responsibilities. In the United States, a default classification LLC will be taxed identically to a partnership, unless it has only a single member. The LLC operating agreement can be drafted to graft in the committees and positions that mirror either a partnership or a corporation. Again, as above, consideration should be paid to who is appointed to these roles and the family dynamics which exist today and are anticipated in the future.

Especially outside of the United States, families often find value in using holding companies, however, there are compelling reasons to incorporate a family holding company (of sorts) in certain US situations as well. A holding company is typically established as a corporation (or an LLC that elects to be characterised as a corporation), or in the European tradition, a *société anonyme*, but could be a private limited company as well. Shareholders of these types of holding companies will memorialise their governance with a corporation's bylaws, which function similar to the LLC agreement but may include additional roles such as boards and officers, and may include various restrictions on transferability of shares, among other parameters of operations not otherwise dictated by state statute. While some families may benefit from these additional roles, which can bolster organisation, facilitate communication and enhance feelings of fairness, not every family needs this level of detail, and for some the additional complexity may be undesirable.

Other operating business documents

While traditionally families make decisions around the dining room table (or a family meeting that occurs over a holiday), roles, responsibilities and decision-making authority in those situations are subjected to the natural governance of the loudest family members. For entities with employees, such as private trust companies and family offices, the ongoing demands of running a complex network requires clarity of organisation and communication. For these entities, the list of important and relevant legal documents can be quite long: employment agreements, training manuals, employment road maps, internship programmes, independent contractor agreements, commercial lease agreements, and contracts for dealing with third-party vendors.[11] The nature and character of these documents evolves as the structure continues, and often the library grows over time. Resiliency here may hinge more on organisation than the other two factors, due to the sheer volume of the information and documents involved, but these documents can also be tools for communication and articulation of values.

Legal documents related to the structure of such entities are ideal for incorporation of family governance. In the corporate and business context, these documents offer an opportunity to define various positions and explain the entity's approach to these positions. For example, the purpose clause of key documents can be a cornerstone provision. In developing a purpose clause, a family essentially reiterates the products of their family governance work: the goals and objectives, values, desire for communication, and family organisation. Functionally, the question may be, "why is a legal entity being established, and what objectives should future decision makers keep in mind?" but underscoring the response is the work done by a family to articulate its own purpose. Ideally a purpose clause strikes a balance between allowing for flexibility, while also providing meaningful guidance to future participants. Depending on the context, it may make sense to have broader statements in certain documents which govern investments or other holdings which will change over time, with more refined objectives outlined in testamentary letters of wishes, which are nonbinding.

Where employees are concerned, key legal documents often serve to bring employees into the system in a clear and organised fashion, and provide new employees with an understanding of the expectations of their role. A thoughtful employee handbook may include the family's values, so they are known to all who work there. These statements of values are often a point of pride for a family, and employees may also feel an affinity for the mission of the family. The employee handbook can also offer guidance to those active in the operation on how they should act and react in different situations. In particular, the employee handbook should include directions for how to resolve conflicts within the appropriate hierarchy, thereby potentially eliminating threats to the system before they arise.

Training and educational programmes may sound rudimentary, but offer valuable benefits for employees and family members alike, in terms of fostering communication and bolstering the resilience of the system. Family training programmes might incorporate how to be good stewards of the family wealth, communications over succession, management training, and oversight over operating businesses and investments, and the family philanthropy. Who participates in such a meeting, how it is run, and the frequency with which it occurs are all variables to be determined by the family, but including key employees in some sessions is not unusual. Ultimately, active engagement will allow family members and their advisers to anticipate actions, expectations and the realities of operating a family enterprise.[12] Inviting rising generations into the enterprise creates opportunities for them and for the best and brightest within the family to feel they are an integral part of the family ecosystem. This can, in turn, have both educational and practical benefits in terms of building resilience.

The importance of following the formalities

One of the principal tenets of any family governance structure is that the key actors must follow the rules that are established. If a system is to be resilient, risk must be managed, and orderly operation is a must. Not only is this essential for operational reasons, but also for tax reasons, depending on the applicable jurisdiction. Failure to follow the rules as established can lead to disaster.

In *Lender Management, LLC v Commissioner*,[13] a court analysed a family's centralised control and management structure. The question at hand was whether a tax deduction was permissible under the US Internal Revenue Code (the US Code). Under the US Code, a deduction is allowed for all expenses paid or incurred in carrying on a trade or business,[14] but sporadic activities such as a hobby do not qualify.[15] The rule requires that "the taxpayer must be involved in the activity with continuity and regularity and the taxpayer's primary purpose for engaging in the activity must be for income or profit".

For the Lender family, oversight and management of the family's investment strategy had been executed through Lender Management LLC (Lender Management), an LLC formed under the laws of the state of Connecticut. It operated as a fund manager and had been in continuous operation for 25 years. Lender Management elected to be treated as a partnership for US income tax purposes and it provided direct management services to three LLCs (each family investment consolidation vehicles). The overall structure was created as part of a reorganisation, the goal of which was to accommodate greater diversification of the managed investments and more flexible asset allocation at the individual investor level.

Training and educational programmes may sound rudimentary, but offer valuable benefits for employees and family members alike, in terms of fostering communication and bolstering the resilience of the system.

Lender Management's managers ran the operation in an extremely professional fashion, and they spent significant time exploring hedge fund and private equity opportunities, closely monitoring the holdings, and meeting with family members to discuss their financial needs and investment risk tolerances.

Lender Management offers a good illustration of the professional attributes reflected in a carefully constructed structure that serves the family's robust investment strategy. In this case, we see that clearly defined roles and responsibilities including meetings, reporting and a formalised professional approach solidifies family member positions on both the management side of a family enterprise as well as those benefiting from being purely passive investors. In Lender Management, the professional arrangement mirrored, to a large degree, that which is used in a private equity or venture capital context, where a general partner promises to manage assets according to a strict investment strategy and attracts limited partners with a similar objective to the investment programme. Investors, including family members who may be passive investors, are attracted to a strategy that is operated consistently and predictably to meet their cash-flow needs. Without clearly identifying the cash-flow needs and memorialising it in a binding legal arrangement, limited partners would not have confidence in such an investment. Such predictability and stability fosters resilience, and these formalities were noted by the tax court's analysis.

Another example of high-quality management and structuring, when presented with a legal challenge, is the case *Estate of Barbara M Purdue v Commissioner*.[16] In *Purdue*, the court held in favour of a viable family partnership, and the corresponding tax planning that had been achieved in its formation, when both family engagement and a significant non-tax purpose were evidenced. As part of an intentional and well-planned consolidation, an older generation member before her death contributed assets including marketable securities and a building within a single-family partnership that was managed by a single adviser. The older generation member received interest in an LLC that was proportional to the property. Additionally, the decedent had retained sufficient assets outside the LLC that could pay for her living expenses, and she did not commingle her funds with the funds of the LLC. While the IRS had argued that the entity was formed and funded primarily for transfer tax savings, the court found that the consolidation of assets for management and control purposes was a significant non-tax reason to form and fund the LLC. This was true even though partnership assets were ultimately needed for estate expenses.

The court opinion in *Purdue* also provides a reference for similarly situated families. The court described at length the professional management of the family partnership including the maintenance of its own accounts in the use of its own funds for partnership business. Meetings were held which had written agendas, minutes and summaries. The family members knew their role and responsibilities and respected them in a professional and diligent manner. All of these facts were important factors in the court's opinion, and adherence to the structure led directly to the taxpayer's success. Additionally, *Purdue* is an important lesson on how honouring the legal structure actually served to provide stability in the face of a legal challenge, and therefore rendered the family structure and its members more resilient.

However, not every example of family entity planning has been positive. In *Estate of Howard V Moore v Commissioner*,[17] a taxpayer transferred his farm shortly before death to a family limited partnership. The stated rationale for forming the entity was that the family could hold and maintain productive use of the actively managed farm and real estate. Five days after the transfer, the family limited partnership sold the farm. Throughout the process, the decedent maintained a high level of control over the entity, and no members of the taxpayer's family expressed interest in managing the taxpayer's assets. Unsurprisingly, the tax court found against the taxpayer. The court noted that the sale of the farm had been contemplated before the family partnership had been formed, and then proceeded immediately after the partnership was in place. While the maintenance of the farm and its operational activities could be a good and supportable reason for a family to consolidate family assets into a family partnership, the subsequent sale and continuing control by the decedent shattered the business purpose to a point it could not be reconstructed. Without any other non-tax reason for the transfer, the transfer was invalidated and the court brought the value of the farm back into the taxpayer's estate for the purpose of taxing it.

Investors, including family members who may be passive investors, are attracted to a strategy that is operated consistently and predictably to meet their cash-flow needs.

Conclusion

While the considerations and factors facing individual families vary widely, long-term resiliency is a goal for most. Crises are unpredictable, but families will be best positioned to weather the storm through proactive thoughtful incorporation of resiliency factors via family governance. A good model for achieving governance is applying the three components of resilience – shared beliefs, organisation and communication – to a given situation and then formalising the system via an appropriate structure. This should, in turn, be incorporated into legal documents and legal frameworks.

By integrating family governance into structures and including resiliency factors into legal documents, the entire system becomes more resilient – able to withstand changes to internal family dynamics, endure external pressures such as pandemics and recessions, and even overcome legal challenges. This work requires time and effort, but the risks involved with not doing so are grave. Particularly in today's environment, family resiliency is needed more than ever.

Carly E Doshi is the Head of Philanthropy, Family Governance, and Family Office Advisory for HSBC Private Banking, Americas.
William J Kambas is a Partner and the Regional Division Leader of the US Private Client and Tax Team at Withers Bergman LLP.
Michael S Schwartz is a Partner in the Private Client Group and Co-Chair of the Trusts and Estates Practice at Curtis, Mallet-Prevost, Colt & Mosle LLP.*

1 See, eg, James Grubman, *Strangers in Paradise: How Families Adapt to Wealth Across Generations*, Family Wealth Consulting, 2013.
2 The Giving Pledge, "A commitment to philanthropy", givingpledge.org/.
3 Roy O Williams, and Vic Preisser, *Preparing Heirs: Five Steps to a Successful Transition of Family Wealth and Values*, Robert D Reed Publishers, 2015.
4 HSBC Private Banking's annual Essence of Enterprise Report, 2017.
5 For more on the topic of family resilience and its role in a crisis, see "Family resilience: strengths forged through adversity" in F Walsh, *Normal Family Processes: Growing Diversity and Complexity*, Guilford Press, 2012, pp329–427.
6 www.irs.gov/businesses/large-business-and-international-lbi-division; https://www.irs.gov/irm/part4/irm_04-052-001.
7 www.forbes.com/sites/jasonbfreeman/2020/06/21/the-irs-intends-to-audit-more-high-wealth-taxpayers/#291e010c596e.
8 See, eg, Tagiuri and Davis, "Three Circle Model", Harvard Business School, 1978.
9 F Walsh, *Normal Family Processes: Growing Diversity and Complexity*, Guilford Press, 2012, pp399–412.
10 Tagiuri and Davis, Harvard Business School, 1978.
11 See, eg, "Structure and Integration: The Architecture of Succession", by N Todd Angkatavanich and William J Kambas, FFI Practitioner, 27 August 2013, https://ffipractitioner.org/structure-and-integration-the-architecture-of-succession/.
12 See "Engaged Ownership: A Guide for Owners of Family Businesses" by Amelia Renkert-Thomas, https://www.engagedownership.com/engaged-ownership-book.
13 *Lender Management, LLC, et al v Commissioner*, TC Memo 2017-246.
14 IRC Section 162(a).
15 *Commissioner v Groetzinger*, 480 US 23, 35 (1987).
16 *Estate of Barbara M Purdue v Commissioner*, TC Memo 2015-249.
17 *Estate of Howard V Moore v Commissioner*, TC Memo 2020-40.

* Editor's note: Michael Schwartz is now at Day Pitney. He can be reached at mschwartz@daypitney.com

Reframing succession in a disruptive era – a business family perspective

Roger King and Jeremy Cheng

Succession has long been a key concern for many families in business. When it comes to the point of succession, the first question many patriarchs and matriarchs think of is who they should pass the baton to. However, they often fail to see the impact of external and internal disruptions on the survival of family firms. As one of the most enduring forms of institution in human history, family businesses have faced evolving external disruptors, from macro-trends such as Industry 4.0 and (de)globalisation, to periodic volatility such as the US-China Trade War and the Covid-19 pandemic. At the same time, family firms are vulnerable to internal disruptions given the conflictual goals inherent in the overlapping family, business and ownership systems, the effects of which are oftentimes amplified in the generational transition. As disruptions become the 'new normal', the key question is: how should family businesses respond to these disruptions and avoid becoming 'a thing of the past'?[1]

This article focuses on how families should break the old lens of succession from the family business angle and explain why reframing relevant issues from the business family perspective can help families navigate the uncharted waters in the disruptive era. We will demystify what a true family legacy means, which should not be the business per se, but the family's entrepreneurial DNA, shared identity and values, and an enduring pool of resources. The latter keeps a business family agile and resilient while facing disruptions. We will discuss how families can prepare themselves for the transition from family business to business family, with the use of a full-service family office to manage a portfolio of companies and with the focus on grooming the rising generation.

Are family businesses doomed?

Amid all the disruptions, Industry 4.0 carries significant impacts on longevity of family businesses. Industry 4.0 combines advanced manufacturing with the Internet of things to create interconnected manufacturing systems to gather and analyse data across machines and to drive smart decisions and actions back into the physical world. The transformation enables more effective processes to produce higher-quality goods at reduced costs. The emergence of wide-ranging disruptive technologies is making existing business models redundant. Research suggested that the business cycle be significantly reduced from 75 years to 15 years.[2] When the rising generation[3] is ready to step up, there may be no more family business for them to succeed to. Our research found that Asian family businesses take about 28 months to identify new disruptive technologies, and then develop and implement relevant response strategies.[4] 'Innovate or perish' is becoming more discernible.

Prior success factors of family businesses, especially those embedded in the emerging economies focusing on cost advantages, have lost their competitive power and are facing various disruptive technologies. Indeed, the past glory may have become a burden because of the family's perceived sunk costs in winding down the business. The perseverance of families to maintain their non-performing legacy business set up by the founder(s) may become a fatal mistake. Families in sunset industries should actively consider exit and harvest the investment for a good offer, but the next generation dare not sell the business due to the family's emotional attachment. The families may miss the golden opportunity to raise the financial capital needed for future transformation.

Breaking the old lens of family business succession

The prevailing lens of 'succession' implies changing of the guard at a particular point, and families often prefer having the rising generation take over the reins. The preference for intra-family succession was especially obvious in Asia and the Middle East, although less so in North America.[5] Following this, one of the greatest succession challenges is that rising-generation members do not want to take charge of their legacy businesses. Our research showed that only 36% of the Asian rising generation are inclined to succeed their family businesses. What intrigued us from our finding is that another 34% of the rising generation want to lead or work in their family businesses while creating their own ventures. This pushes the figure close to 70% of the rising generation, who want to contribute their effort to their families. Whether the rising-generation members can really manage to run both the family business and their own ventures at the same time offers ground for debate, but families should stop dichotomising career options as 'joining the family business' or 'venturing outside'. Families should think about leveraging off talents of the rising generation to create new ventures or spin-offs under the family umbrella. A flexible career presents a real option to the rising generation and one only offered by business families. This opens a new avenue of family succession.

Business family succession: CCKP and 3Ps

As we see the impact of disruptions on succession and family business longevity, the top priority of a business family should not be preserving the business per se, nor creating a century-old operation. The business is only a vehicle of the founder's entrepreneurship, and one of many means that generates value for the family. The primary task of the family is to nurture the rising generation of entrepreneurs as early as possible. We believe the fundamental qualities of the rising generation are what we call 'CCKP'[6]:

- Commitment to sustain the family entrepreneurship;
- Confidence in their own ability to effectuate change;
- Knowledge of the business portfolio and the fast-changing business landscape; and
- Passion for the vision they pursue.

These conditions are necessary yet insufficient for business family succession. Successors should also help their family achieve what we call 'the three preservations' or 'the 3Ps'[7] as follows:

- Preservation of financial wealth, by carefully crafting a portfolio of companies and investments with due consideration of how existing and new ventures create economic values.
- Preservation of family entrepreneurial legacy, values, reputation and social networks, by renewing these non-financial capitals in new venture development and mitigating the loss of these capitals due to cessation of the legacy business.
- Preservation of family harmony and unity, by engaging descendants in new family platforms and ventures other than the legacy business.

The 3Ps try to rebalance and reposition 'the new' and 'the old' as the succession takes place. While the first two Ps are common desires in both East and West, the preservation of family harmony and unity is perhaps more stressed in Asian families – which should however benefit families from different cultural backgrounds. In addition, while disruptive innovation is often criticised as destroying the founders' hard-earned legacy, the reality is that transgenerational entrepreneurship is built on the familial resource pool comprising financial, social and human capital, with appropriate practices, structures and governance mechanisms set up to enhance transgenerational value creation.

Family business versus business family

At this point, it is important to differentiate between family business and business family and understand how succession differs in these two entities.[8,9] Unlike family business, business family always owns one or more companies, which may not be the same one(s) over time. Family business concentrates its resources on sustaining the existing operation – its innovation is mostly focused on improving existing products and services or enhancing its brand. Serving different goals, business family aims to maximise the return of the family portfolio, potentially by acquiring and/or incubating new ventures including but not limited to technological startups. As discussed, many family businesses tend to hold onto their non-performing legacy businesses because of the family's emotional commitment. Facing the exit decision, good business family leaders exercise psychological calmness to evaluate the deal and focus on portfolio value creation. Each business in the portfolio should benefit from the family's involvement or else it should be sold or revamped.

In terms of succession, family business tends to pick the best 'operator'[10] to run the existing show – especially if we are talking about families that treasure meritocracy in the system. From the business family perspective, the best candidate may not be the one who can run the legacy business most effectively, but the one who can balance and maximise the financial and socioemotional returns of the family portfolio as an 'owner'. The candidate should have a thorough understanding of the portfolio, and excel in venture valuation, balancing and exit. Successors to the business family need to be able to make quick and

Family business concentrates its resources on sustaining the existing operation – its innovation is mostly focused on improving existing products and services or enhancing its brand.

informed decisions in family investment, understand the underlying risks and returns and communicate these decisions effectively with all stakeholders. That said, successors at times need to move between the owner's mentality and the operator's mindset, especially at the stage where the family is growing a venture to increase its value before harvesting. Given that managing a family portfolio requires a wider set of talents, successors to the business family should be able to engage different stakeholders in the system, likely through the family values and entrepreneurial DNA. In addition to the financial capital, the owner's mindset also applies to managing the human and social capital. The following table compares family business and business family as informed by various scholarly works.[11]

Transitioning from family business to business family

We anticipate that more family businesses will gradually transition to business families as a natural progression in their development trajectory.[12] Disruptions will accelerate the transition process. Business families stand a better chance of surviving and even thriving in this disruptive era if they can build their capabilities and resources to embrace the following in the transition:

- Emphasise the value of the family portfolio, not that of a particular business, especially when considering the exit of the legacy business.
- Place transgenerational entrepreneurship at the core of the business family to trump the venturing process.
- Focus on the owner's mentality, but balance this with the operator's mindset at appropriate times.
- Build an appropriate organisational structure to accompany the transition with evolving family, business and ownership needs.
- Develop rising-generation leaders who can foster the transition.

Family business and business family

	Family business	Business family
Nature of business	The family has a business that it wants the rising generation to take over.	A portfolio of companies, which may not be the same ones over time. The portfolio is diversified through multiple operating businesses and other investments.
Growth and expansion	Innovation to grow and expand the same business (eg, branding and R&D).	A stronger orientation to develop new businesses, with an emerging trend to focus on technological startups.
Business exit	Strong emotional attachment; Chinese/Asian families tend to hold onto non-performing businesses.	Each business in the portfolio should benefit from the family's involvement or else should be sold or changed.
Key philosophy	'Operator's mindset' – focusing on operational excellence and value creation from within the existing business.	'Owner's mentality' – focusing on value maximisation of the portfolio.
Succession and leadership	Succession depends upon future generations taking over ownership, governance and/or management of the business – usually single leadership with superior ability to operate the business.	Succession depends upon future generations adopting and preserving the family's value system and entrepreneurial spirit in pursuing existing and new opportunities – encouraging distributed leadership to contribute the diverse talents required in managing the portfolio.
Organisational structure	Usually a functional structure under one business organisation.	Likely organised as a multi-business corporation or business group, potentially managed by a family office and/or holding company.

While the first three points are well covered in the prior sections, we will cover the last two points in greater detail below.

Family office: catalysing transition to business family

Family business and business family run on different organisational ethos and structures. While the functional structure of a family business can enhance operational excellence, it may not be able to cope with the rapid decisions required for investments in disruptive times. The family portfolio organised as a multi-business corporation or business group can be managed by a family office or a holding company, which can be seen as an embedded family office. Such a structure can afford flexibility in decision making and subsequent resource deployment. Globally, more families increasingly recognise their private investment offices as family offices, but may lack the vision to manage and transfer socioemotional wealth across generations. We believe that with a much-needed 'upgrade' in their functionalities, family offices can catalyse the transition from a family business to a business family and enhance the odds of successful succession. While families set up their family offices primarily as a one-stop shop for wealth management, they should also embrace governance, education and social functions. We discuss below how these non-investment functions of a family office can advance the vision of a sustainable business family.

Intergenerational governance for agile leadership

Agile leadership, especially when it comes to making financial and investment decisions, is key to survival and post-crisis or even countercyclical growth. As observed in the Covid-19 pandemic, families must make quick decisions to avoid capital chain ruptures or to finance privatisation or M&A projects to benefit from the low asset price. To grow agility in the system, family offices should be tasked to build, execute and oversee an effective investment governance framework, which should be an integral part of the overarching family and corporate governance system. These are built on the family's shared vision and purposes, ground rules of working together as a family team, and mechanisms for collective decision-making. The following governance structure and underlying questions should guide a fruitful discussion within the business family, affording focus on achieving investment agility and succession[13]:

- Guiding principles: Why investing and working together? How can diverging income needs and risk profiles of individual family members be satisfied? How can the family educate the rising generation members as owners and empower them as decision-makers?
- Governance levels and structures: How many levels of governance are necessary? Who should own key decisions? What is the level of autonomy of investment organisations? What metrics should be used to evaluate performance? How do we facilitate focus on investments?
- Roles and responsibilities: Which governing bodies should be responsible for establishing policy and oversight? How can the family make sure that there are checks and balances between the governing and management roles? How can we raise accountability?
- Policies and processes: Who are eligible to participate? How can a member exit? Who can be in the governance and management roles? How can the family clearly communicate trade-offs made? Does the family have clear protocols for risk and crisis management?

The family office should help create an environment conducive to intergenerational governance and engagement. That said, for a number of first-generation entrepreneurs, setting up the family office may represent the first time their personal wealth and business assets are separated. Usually these founders expect more control over investment decisions, and focus on the markets they know. Even where investment decisions are directly made by the entrepreneurs themselves, the family office should assess and codify the underlying decision processes and logic, and perhaps credibility of the social networks. Such knowledge will help the rising generation make quicker decisions if they encounter a similar investment in the future.

Globally, more families increasingly recognise their private investment offices as family offices, but may lack the vision to manage and transfer socioemotional wealth across generations.

> *The transition from family business to business family involves a shuffling of power, and the disruptions may demand a different leader to step up in the process.*

Education for transgenerational value creation and engagement

In addition to coordinating investment education, family offices play a vital role as an 'educator' in several areas of transgenerational value creation:

- First, family offices can help incubate rising-generation startups under the family umbrella. Utilising talents of the rising generation who are digital native presents an essential strategy for sustainable growth. As the rising generation are reluctant to return to their family business for a number of reasons, families should let them spread their wings and create their own ventures. Families can set up an angel fund via the family office to systematically nurture the skills of the rising generation and invest financial, human and social capital in aspiring ventures.
- Second, the family can consider setting up the role of 'chief learning officer' in the family office to coordinate learning as a family, assess future talent needs in the business family, and facilitate opportunities for young siblings and cousins to work together. This can be a concerted effort with relevant committees with the aim of supporting education and career development under the family council.
- Third, family offices can train the rising generation to work with advisers and professionals. Ashby's Law of Requisite Variety states that only variety can absorb variety. Due to the complexity of the disruptions families face, their rising generation need to know how to best work with their advisers and outside professionals, who offer knowledge and expertise not available in the business family system. For instance, family offices can provide a safer platform for the rising generation to collaborate with private equity and venture capital firms, which offer market updates and expertise needed to improve the viability and sales of ventures.

Action learning and other educational opportunities provided by or coordinated via the family office can create transgenerational values. Regardless of the actual practices families adopt, a key principle here is to create opportunities for the rising generation with different levels of expertise and interest in investment to participate in the evolution of their business family. In this way, family offices can become a platform for the rising generation to maintain the close relationship with the family, even though they are not joining the legacy business.

Socialising for sustaining family harmony and unity

The transition from family business to business family involves a shuffling of power, and the disruptions may demand a different leader to step up in the process. All these create a feeling of uncertainty, which may at times stir family conflicts. Timely and transparent communication can reduce the perceived information asymmetry among family members regardless of their roles. Organising social events such as family retreats and honouring the ancestors' and current generation's contribution are ways family offices can take to reduce the anxiety in the system, and help families preserve harmony and unity across generations. Structures such as family council and family assembly in more elaborate governance systems can also play a role here, socialising change with family members. Again, in families which are going through leadership transition from the first to the second generation, the relatively small size of the family may make the complex governance structures look redundant at times. The Western legalistic concept of 'governance' may need a bit of adaptation to be useful for Asian families. That said, families that meet together stay together. The greatest challenge is really to get two generations of the same family to sit together and openly share their own aspirations. Family offices can take the administrative role to facilitate the socialising process, with the help of trusted advisers and family elders.

On preparing the rising generation for the transition

Succession is about the future. Successful succession hinges on growing the rising generation of entrepreneurs who are agile and resilient and on facilitating their continued engagement and contributions to the business family. In addition to developing personal qualities of the rising generation such as CCKP and building capabilities of the full-service family office we advocated, the following should help prepare the rising generation for the transition:

- Seek understanding of strengths, limitations and career aspirations of the rising-generation members. This should be systematically assessed at both individual and family levels, and should be periodically reviewed. Families should analyse whether they have the necessary pipelines of talents to fit the evolving needs of the portfolio, and develop plans to match the gap.
- Encourage the rising generation to build a keen circle of internal and external talents (especially those related to disruptive technologies), through participating in family projects, external education programmes, startup circles and trade associations. Offer startup incubation and counselling for this circle of talents.
- Refocus on the natural strength of long-term orientation and patient capital of families to allow aggressive and sustainable resource commitment to opportunities induced by disruptions.
- Reposition family business tenure so as not to project the image of a life sentence. Exit is a valid and valuable option if well planned. That said, symbiotic bondage between the rising generation and the business family should be lifelong. Families should build platforms to accommodate members of different talents and interests.

Conclusion

Families should recognise that the pursuit of business longevity could be a false proposition in this disruptive era. Transgenerational entrepreneurship will hold a key role in the succession-planning process. Families should adopt a new lens to view succession, focusing on nurturing desirable qualities in the rising generation and transmitting the shared values and entrepreneurial spirit of the business family. Families should embrace the transition from family business to business family. Acting as the family portfolio manager – in a broader sense responsible for growing the family's financial, human and social capital – family offices can be a useful tool to advance the transition and increase the chance of successful succession if they can incorporate governance, education and social functions. While there is no single best model for succession that applies across families, they should benefit from envisioning their own future, engaging and empowering the entire family in the process.

Acknowledgement

The authors would like to thank Edith Ang, Francesca Chan, Marshall Jen and Peter Lee for their kind comments on an earlier draft and Dr Dennis Jaffe and Christian Stewart for their kind inspiration on the topic. All errors rest with the authors.

Roger King, PhD, is Adjunct Professor of Finance and Founding Director and Senior Advisor of the Tanoto Center for Asian Family Business and Entrepreneurship Studies and the Thompson Center for Business Case Studies at The Hong Kong University of Science and Technology.

Jeremy Cheng is Founder of GEN+ Family Business Advisory & Research, and a PhD student at The Chinese University of Hong Kong.

1 CE Aronoff and JL Ward, "Family-owned businesses: A thing of the past or a model for the future?" *Family Business Review*, 1995, 8(2), 121–130.

2 Business Families Foundation (2015), "The Future of Family Business", https://businessfamilies.com/videohome/fostering-intrapreneurship/the-future-of-family-business/.

3 The term 'rising generation' is used instead of the usual phrases of 'next generation', 'incoming generation' or 'young generation'. The term avoids the derogatory, and often destructive, comparison with the current, incumbent or older generation. It contains an affirmative possibility and promotes growth and evolution in the rising generation. For details, see JE Hughes, SE Massenzio and K Whitaker, *The Voice of the Rising Generation: Family Wealth and Wisdom*, Hoboken, NJ: John Wiley & Sons, 2014.

4 R King and CYJ Cheng, *Where Technological Disruptors Meet Asian Family Businesses: Rethinking Next-Generation Leadership and Career*, The Hong Kong University of Science and Technology, and Lombard Odier, 2018.

5 A Calabrò and A Valentino, "2019 global family business survey: The impact of changing demographics on family business succession planning and governance", 2019, available at https://digitalcollections.babson.edu/digital/collection/stepsumrep/id/31/rec/1.

6 Roger King coined the CCKP notion in his earlier work (see R King, WQ Peng and C Stewart, "Family office: the Eastern approach" IFOJ Vol 1(3) [2017] 27–32). The current version is anchored in the same framework, but with adaptation to reflect changes to the disruptive factors.

7 The first author developed the 3Ps in his earlier work (see R King, WQ Peng and C Stewart, "Family office: the Eastern approach" IFOJ Vol 1(3) [2017] 27–32). The current version makes the necessary adaptation to fit the disruptive factors.

8 LP Steier, JJ Chrisman and JH Chua, "Governance challenges in family businesses and business families", *Entrepreneurship Theory and Practice*, 2015, 39(6), 1265–1280.

9 I Le Breton-Miller and D Miller, "Beyond the firm: business families as entrepreneurs", *Entrepreneurship Theory and Practice*, 2018, 42(4), 527–536.

10 For a discussion on 'operator's mindset' and 'owner's mentality', see JA Davis, "What Makes a Family Business Last?", *Harvard Business Review*, 2020, available at https://hbr.org/2020/02/what-makes-a-family-business-last.

11 The idea is grounded in the work of Steier, Chrisman and Chua (2015), Davis (2020), both cited above, and more broadly the portfolio entrepreneurship literature.

12 TM Zellweger, RS Nason and M Nordqvist, "From longevity of firms to transgenerational entrepreneurship of families: Introducing family entrepreneurial orientation", *Family Business Review*, 2012, 25(2), 136–155.

13 Cambridge Associates, *Investment governance for families: lessons learned from advising 200 family portfolios over 30 years*, 2015.

Five things wealthy families can learn from Lee Man Tat

Russell Cohen

In 1954, Lee Man Tat joined the oyster cooking sauce business which his grandfather had founded. He died earlier this year, aged 91 and chairman of LKK – a $17 billion international conglomerate.

There is a Chinese adage (which has its equivalents around the world) that "wealth does not go beyond the third generation". However, by the time Lee Man Tat died every one of his children were involved in the family company and his grandchildren – Generation 5 – were also becoming highly engaged.

What can other wealthy families learn from Lee Man Tat? Here are five tips.

1. Family governance doesn't look after itself

In the late 1990s Lee Man Tat's youngest son threatened to leave the business and Lee Man Tat realised, perhaps for the first time, that he had to take family governance seriously.

Led by Lee Man Tat, the family created a family council which in turn laid the foundations for a family office, a family constitution, a family foundation and a family learning centre. Careful thought was given to the constitution in particular. It was agreed that only those in the bloodline could own shares, but family members would have to work for at least three years in other companies before taking a senior role in the family business. And the constitution could only be changed with a two-thirds majority of leading family members.

More recently, it was identified that members of Generation 5 (Lee Man Tat's grandchildren) were drifting from the family business. They were becoming distracted by alternative careers and the kind of hobbies which require lots of money and time. Measures were taken to secure the engagement. The family business and council introduced a strong emphasis on wellbeing, with the establishment of a Happiness Index, and adopted a more focused pursuit of philanthropy. A programme of regular family retreats was arranged. These would encourage open discussions and the sharing of ideas across generations, as well as the passing of core values down the generations. As Lee Man Tat's son David explained in 2006: "My dad is also learning from us, understanding how we do things, and we're all coming up with ideas. But there are certain principles that just hold true, and my Dad can tell the children about that."

"When there is a deadlock, moving ahead is the most important thing, no matter what direction."

2. Any decision is better than no decision

The family's culture and governance structure encourages a collaborative approach. But the family council also accepts that sometimes any decision is better than no decision. When the family council reach an impasse, it applies a solution which originated from the times when the business was based in Macau – it throws dice. As Charlie, another of Lee Man Tat's sons, has put it: "When there is a deadlock, moving ahead is the most important thing, no matter what direction."

3. Tolerate failure

For much of its 130-year history, the LKK business only made sauces. It took 20 years before it extended its range beyond oyster sauce to shrimp sauce.

The family business is now highly diversified, venturing into herbal medicines and more recently property. In 2017, the family acquired the 'Walkie Talkie' skyscraper in the City of London for a record-breaking $1.3 billion.

But the family understand that, central to the culture of diversification and entrepreneurship, is the tolerance of failure. The family refer to the '6-6-7-7' concept. A family member proposing a new commercial initiative does not have to be to be 100% certain it will be successful; it is sufficient to anticipate a 66% to 77% prospect of success.

4. Think long term, very long term

The label on the LKK oyster sauce says: "since 1888". But the family council's much stated objective is: "the next 1,000 years".

In the 1990s, the family almost tore itself apart. Lee Man Tat and his youngest son, Sammy, started a business selling health supplements in 1992. But the operation was making a loss. There was talk of selling the health supplement business, and even of Sammy being sold the health supplement business in return for giving up his shares in the core sauce business. But after much discussion, Sammy was given a full five years to turn the business around. Since then, LKK Health Products has become the group's main source of revenue.

5. Get lucky

The story goes that Lee Kum Sheung, Lee Man Tat's grandfather, ran a tea stall in Southern China. In 1888, he was serving tea to his customers, and forgot that he was cooking a pot of oyster soup on the stove. On returning to the kitchen, fearing the soup would be spoilt, he discovered it had boiled down into a rich, aromatic paste. He began selling the paste in ceramic jars and a multi-generational business was born.

Russell Cohen is a partner at Farrer & Co LLP, London. He specialises in providing advice on family governance, succession planning, structuring and tax planning.

The next generation of strategic cultural philanthropy – impact, social justice and the opportunities for nextgen donors in the arts

Melissa Cowley Wolf

Having long enjoyed being recipients of robust philanthropic support from generations of high-net-worth individuals, the future of cultural organisations in the United States and across the globe – and indeed the future of arts funding itself – is now uncertain.

Arts funding has been undergoing a profound shift, as several intersecting trends and events are changing both the landscape of philanthropy and wealth management:

- We are undergoing the largest inter-generational transfer of wealth in history. It is estimated that between $40 and $130 trillion will move from one generation to another over a 50-year period.
- As this is happening, philanthropic giving to the arts has been decreasing. In the United States, as total charitable giving rose from $410 billion in 2017 to $428 billion in 2018, total giving to the arts remained stagnant – at $20 billion. Over the past 20 years, total public arts funding decreased by 12.8%, state arts agency appropriations decreased by 25%, local funding contracted by 9%, and federal funds have remained virtually flat. In Europe, government funding has been steadily decreasing, and institutions have therefore become more reliant on local individual giving and fundraising from populations in the United States.
- Simultaneously, the generation inheriting the wealth has an entirely different view of philanthropy than their predecessors. According to one study,[1] rising generation donors rank arts and culture giving fifth in priority, behind education and health.
- And finally, it is predicted that most of these heirs will split with their families' advisers.[2] Wealth managers are looking for new methods to engage these younger clients that are more in line with their values and ideologies.

Rising generation donors have the opportunity to literally remake the model of arts funding. There are very few areas in philanthropy and society for one to contribute to that kind of monumental shift.

And as we can see, the cultural, philanthropic and financial sectors are all affected by this generational turnover. It behooves us all to better understand how the arts present a unique opportunity for these rising donors to make a profound impact with their giving, and have influence over an evolving field and its position in the global landscape.

The trends listed above created a crisis in cultural philanthropy well before the three paradigm-shifting events of 2020 occurred: the global health crisis, the pandemic-induced recession and the growing social justice movement.

As mentioned, giving to the arts had been decreasing. However, there were exciting promises in 2019, as outlined in *Giving USA 2020: The Annual Report on Philanthropy*, the "longest running longitudinal study of the sources and uses of philanthropy in America".[3] Overall charitable giving rose, and the arts and culture sector experienced a long-awaited increase in giving in 2019, mostly due to an incredibly strong S&P and growth in both personal income and GDP – all factors which contribute to a strong philanthropic sector. According to the report, US charitable giving increased by 4.2% from 2018 to $449.64 billion in 2019. Even more impressive, the increase in charitable dollars by individuals grew by 4.7%, and arts and culture saw an increase of 12.6%. (One must note that we did not see more donors entering philanthropy, but an increase in dollars given by fewer donors, continuing a trend all would like to change.)

For those advocating for increased charitable giving across sectors, and especially within arts and culture, these statistics do give some reason to rejoice. But in the first quarter of 2020, charitable giving dropped due to the Covid-19 pandemic, the (then anticipated) recession, stock market volatility and other factors. In March, following a strong opening to 2020, charitable giving decreased by 11% from the 2019 figures in the same month, as reported by the Fundraising Effectiveness Project (conducted by the Association of Fundraising Professionals and the Center on Nonprofits and Philanthropy at the Urban Institute).

Now, with these compounding challenges, the arts and culture sector is facing increased urgency for making its case for support.

A generational shift

While the crises of 2020 are further impacting the flow of capital into the arts, there is another crisis that was already affecting the lack of generational diversity.

The established generation of major donors in the United States came of philanthropic age during the time of post-war American prestige and dominance, especially as it relates to arts and culture. Almost halfway through the last century, the centre of the western art world shifted from Paris to New York, mainly due to two events: the Armory Show of 1913, and the Second World War (particularly the invasion of France). Then, the post-war Abstract-Expressionism movement, centred in New York in the 1940s, put the spotlight on the city as the leader of the western art world. The organisations built since, those that define the arts landscape of New York and other major cities in America, have been examples of civic pride, as well as preservationists of American culture. And the accompanying traditional system of fundraising has consisted of cultivating civic and society leaders – pre-Instagram influencers, if you will – for major gifts. For these contributions, they have been thanked with their names embossed on walls and featured prominently in programmes, at events and on websites. Lavish annual galas have typically brought in the majority of the unearned revenue. And there has been a focus of continuing to engage the wealthiest members of society using these methods.

However, many of these philanthropists – whose contributions, dedication and passion built and sustained some of the most esteemed institutions in American society – have given their final gifts during their lifetime. Many participated in and supported the phenomenon that swept the cultural sector across the world at the end of the last century and beginning of the present – *The Bilbao Effect*. This method of transformational capital construction and cultural investment projects, in the form of cutting-edge architecture by world-famous architects, was a trend that yielded economic resurgence in cities and increased visitorship at museums and performing arts centres. "If you build it, they will come" was true, if the "you" was Frank Gehry (whose Guggenheim Bilbao is the namesake of this term), or architects like Renzo Piano or Zaha Hadid. Those substantial donations supported this trend and created many beloved cultural hubs across America. And they were expensive to build. Civic pride was measured in part by a strong architectural presence in the urban realm, and we have the traditional philanthropic class to thank for some of our greatest national treasures.

But now we find ourselves with outdated models of fundraising, systems that are at odds with two important factors: the values and giving preferences of rising generation high-net-worth individuals, and the significant decline of cultural education, fluency and relevance in recent decades.[4]

A crisis of relevancy

This issue of relevancy and this generational shift is at the core of my work. Operating at the nexus of philanthropy and the arts, I work with philanthropists, arts supporters, nonprofits, financial institutions, cultural leaders, galleries, artists, art fairs, fundraising professionals and others across the globe.

Since January, my conversations with both the nonprofit and market sides of the cultural sector largely revolve around immediate remedies for survival during the Covid-19 crisis, quarantines, and shutdowns of cultural institutions. We also continue to discuss long-term strategies for resiliency and the future of equitable arts funding, particularly to engage the rising generations of philanthropic leaders.

While we exchange a diversity of ideas on how to best evolve arts engagement and funding structures, these conversations share the one particular and vital item: *they all become conversations about relevance, and why the rising generations of high-net-worth individuals are not invested in the arts.*

This was also a subject of conversations when we at the Arts Funders Forum (AFF) conducted interviews with philanthropists and cultural leaders for our 2019 research study into cultural giving trends and preferences.[5] That study had two crucial revelations:

- a majority of art funders (from all generations) and cultural leaders believe that "the arts do a subpar job of expressing the sector's value to society. Art and culture is considered a 'nice to have' not a 'must have'"; and
- there is a definitive "tension between

Civic pride was measured in part by a strong architectural presence in the urban realm, and we have the traditional philanthropic class to thank for some of our greatest national treasures.

The societal benefits of a robust arts and culture system mirror the changes and evolutions this generation wants to see in our society.

generational funding perspectives and habits, with younger generations viewing giving as more process-driven than transactional".

These consensuses, backed up by institutional funding and income analysis, led AFF to report that: "Cultural Institutions are Struggling with an Existential Crisis of Relevance".

The power (and potential) of perception

At a time of such economic uncertainty, this is not a helpful perception of the sector, and not a time to have outdated modes of fundraising. The arts are actively looking to partner with members of the rising generations to redefine and articulate art's power. The cultural economy offers its champions immense possibilities for extensive impact and for developing unique legacies, directly aligned with how rising generation funders want to invest their capital, time and energy.

The societal benefits of a robust arts and culture system mirror the changes and evolutions this generation wants to see in our society.

In the age of a global health crisis and growing social equality movements, now is the best time for nextgen philanthropists and advocates to become invested in the arts.

There is now a new unforeseen opportunity to both democratise arts funding and reshape the narrative of the importance of the arts. Throughout the various stages of the Covid-19 pandemic and quarantines around the world, we witnessed firsthand what some had deemed a cliché – art's power to heal and comfort, to inform and enlighten. One could argue that this made the case for art as a human necessity – just imagine quarantine without film, colouring books, music streaming services, (virtual) operas, ballets, plays, exhibitions, and more.

And yet we know from the giving trends that there is a gap between this innate desired consumption in a time of need and the willingness to support the sector under any circumstances. And that is largely because there needs to be a new narrative developed to articulate to the general public what the art world really is, what it costs to produce great works for art and entertainment, and most importantly – the immense opportunity it presents for impact and legacy building.

By nature, art points out the stark inequities in our society, encourages more civic engagement,[6] and offers solutions to our greatest global challenges. The arts contribute to local and national economies,[7] and frequently the regeneration of depressed cities (eg, Bilbao), and cultural organisations which often complement the work of governments and educational systems,[8] themselves short on funding.

And yet, when I speak with partners and clients in other industries, there is the perception that the fancy international art market events and related social extravaganzas represent the entirety of the art world. This perception of the art world has done a disservice to the sector, and has not appealed to nextgen giving preferences, especially as we know that they are not drawn to these galas and parties. (More on these preferences below.) This perception does not reflect the innovative and entrepreneurial problem solvers that lead and contribute to the arts ecosystem, or the work of the organisations presenting, preserving and archiving these creative and political pursuits. These are natural partners for a generation focused on solving systemic problems and seeking maximum impact.

So, as nextgen donors look for areas where they can make the greatest impact, it is essential that they consider the arts.

The opportunity for nextgen in the arts

The arts are well positioned to address the rising challenges and inequities presented by the pandemic, and the issues at the forefront of the social justice movement.[9] And we know from studies that work in the social justice realm ranks high in priority for nextgen donors.

From music to film to political posters, the arts have always been at the forefront of social change, showing light in the dark places of injustice. Looking just at the 20th and 21st centuries, one of the most prominent anti-war images created is *Guernica*, a 1937 painting by Pablo Picasso portraying the bombing of the Spanish city during the Civil War. American Protest music galvanised a generation of anti-war protesters in the 1960s, and ushered in a new era of political leadership. In the 1980s, the ACT UP (the AIDS Coalition to Unleash Power) posters brought much needed attention to the HIV/AIDS crisis, shifting public opinion and (eventually) government policy. Also in the 1980s, the Guerrilla Girls (an anonymous group of feminist, female artists) aimed to bring gender and racial inequality into focus within the greater arts community, diversifying the pool of artists presented in our institutions. In the 2000s, the HOPE posters of then-candidate Barack Obama, by contemporary street artist and illustrator, Shepard Fairey, presented a clear rallying cry and message.

This type of work has resonated with the coming-of-age generations throughout history, and now it is no different; contemporary art is engaged in a profound critique of our systems, from mass incarceration to health care to the current financial inequities being magnified by the Covid pandemic. As faith in institutions has eroded steadily in previous decades, these institutional critiques are resonating with a rising generation that wants to use their philanthropic capacity to make systemic and lasting change *from the inside*.

AFF research showed that "the emerging class of donors views cultural philanthropy through the lens of social justice. They expressed urgency to develop new methods of listening and learning in historically divested and marginalized communities".[10] The events of 2020 have accelerated the changes that the nextgen had already wanted to see. This presents a timely opportunity for nextgen donors to step in and shape the future of arts funding.

The philanthropic and the arts sector can better partner and engage in innovative matchmaking to help these rising generations achieve their desired monumental impact to contribute to creating a more just society.

Nextgen donor values

We know that as Millennials and Gen Z enter philanthropy in a significant way, they possess the ability to outgive their predecessors. It is estimated that they will give almost half of the transferred wealth away.[11] These nextgen donors will not all be the recipients of vast resources; a large segment will be those who have created their own wealth through entrepreneurial and business ventures, many quite early in their careers. These groups apply the same philosophy to their giving as they do their entrepreneurial ventures – they are focused on concrete results, using new tools to measure the impact of their gifts. They also will begin their philanthropic roles at earlier ages than their predecessors. And their plans to give are vastly different from the preceding generations.

When connecting the dots and looking at these trends in the big picture – the trends in arts giving, the incoming wave of rising philanthropists, and how the values of these nextgens connect with the opportunities of and in the arts – it gives these rising philanthropists a unique opportunity to make their desired impact on cultural philanthropic giving.

The corporate, philanthropic and nonprofit sectors have been very focused on nextgen behaviours, trends and methods of giving and consumption. Big philanthropy has been studying nextgen giving preferences and tracking their entrance into the charitable landscape. Studies and articles abound, as the sectors determine how to best position themselves to engage with this rising donor class.

We know that nextgen donors:

- value issues more than organisations;
- evaluate the achievable impact of their giving more than their predecessors;
- insist on institutional transparency and effectiveness;
- yearn to roll up their sleeves and participate in systemic change-making;
- want organisations to show how they are a conduit to the cause;
- are less interested in the arts' traditional fundraising methods, such as annual galas;
- want to be engaged in peer-funding initiatives and cohorts;
- are focused on local issues and ethical investing;
- insist on clarity about exactly who/what they are funding and impacting; and
- move faster than previous generations.

AFF research shows: "Younger philanthropists view giving as more 'process driven' than 'transaction driven' in contrast with the current donor class. Meaning, they care about 'how' you give not just 'what' you give."[12]

In the arts, there is real ability to make significant change. We know that younger audiences have grown tired and distrustful of organisation's boards (witnessed by the Whitney Museums protests in 2019), labour standards (as seen at the Marciano Art

Studies and articles abound, as the sectors determine how to best position themselves to engage with this rising donor class.

Throughout the pandemic, we have seen operas and ballets stream into homes, and museum collections from around the world now available to a wider audience with lower barriers to entry.

Foundation), and even the current trends in artistic programming (demands for equal representation of women and artists-of-colour).

Cultural organisations of all sizes are actively recruiting these nextgen donors to bring a fresh perspective on how they can equitably function as an institution, and also to their programming; in other words, how they can function to most effectively address the pertinent issues in the communities.

So, what are the particular opportunities for nextgen investment?

How next gen donors can remake the model of arts funding to align with their values

Advancing storytelling through technology
The arts offer an opportunity for the nextgen to participate in showcasing the power of the arts, speaking in their language, to their own generation through their preferred medium. Nextgen donors can advise on how to most effectively use technology to communicate urgency, and work with organisations to tell stories to communicate impact.

Throughout the pandemic, we have seen operas and ballets stream into homes, and museum collections from around the world now available to a wider audience with lower barriers to entry. This is creating an entirely new population to whom artists and organisations can make their case for support.

We know that the rising generations innately understand technology, social media and the power of storytelling. It is worth noting that they were also raised on reality television and documentaries about such wide-ranging subjects as food, fashion and art. These programmes have focused on topics such as examining how food brings people of diverse backgrounds together and how the fashion industry can help mitigate climate change through changes to manufacturing practices. These shows offer behind-the-scenes glimpses into how industries function – how the 'sausage is made' – and therefore have demonstrated that these audiences crave insight into the process. Nextgen audiences do not want to just sit and watch the product; they want to know about the process. They want to see how things are made and the impact on that process.

Right now, organisations could be partnering with nextgen investors to design virtual programming, highlighting both what happens behind the scenes and documenting the direct impact of the efforts.

Developing impact-driven and value-add narratives
The arts offer an opportunity for nextgen donors to craft narratives that illustrate the impact and value-add of their contribution to the arts ecosystem.

Delivering the art for free misses the opportunity, said a rising generation philanthropist I interviewed: "The next gen needs a value-add". Offering art for free during the pandemic-induced quarantines has lowered the initial barrier to entry, but without explaining and assigning value this communicates that there is no value. Nextgen donors can be at the forefront of a movement articulating new metrics and value-adds for one of the world's largest industries.

As noted, giving to education and health ranked higher in priority for nextgen donors. This is partly because those sectors can more clearly communicate the impact of their efforts with traditional metrics, such as graduation numbers or the amount of patients cured by vaccines. How do you measure one's shift in mindset on critical issues after viewing a theatrical production? They also have provided nextgen donors with on-site, roll-up-your-sleeves opportunities, such as coming into classrooms to work directly with students. Nextgen donors can create more of these opportunities within the arts. As a philanthropist and collector I interviewed said: "The value and impact of giving to the arts needs to be appreciated by the rising generations in the same way as giving a child an education".

Bringing an innovative and entrepreneurial mindset to develop a more equitable and democratic system of patronage
The arts provide the opportunity for nextgen donors to bring innovative and entrepreneurial thinking to giving, and specifically to create more collaborative forms of giving and new giving vehicles. As a museum director told me: "There's a tension between the traditional philanthropy model – a small number of uber-wealthy subsidising arts and culture – and some of the newer ideas that spread responsibility among

more individuals, corporations and city and state governments, in addition to earned revenue".

According to Fundraising Effectiveness Project's 2020 First Quarter Report, mid-level gifts and large gifts (those of $1,000 and more) declined 2.2% and 7.4% respectively in the first quarter, but gifts of under $250 increased almost 6%. So while donors at higher levels paused giving (mainly due to stock market decline), those who give smaller amounts continued to give.

This points to the collective power of giving, and bodes well for grassroots fundraising and crowdfunding, two of the ways nextgen donors like to give. And the arts sector is primed and ready for a diversification of funding streams. The AFF research study uncovered that three out of four art funders believe that "collaboration and partnerships" and "new funding vehicles" will have the most significant impact on increasing funding for the arts.[13] While the nextgen has and will continue to use traditional funding vehicles, such as family foundations and donor-advised funds, they are continuously searching for new methods, especially vehicles that stress peer-collective giving and clear, achievable impact.

One such example of a new vehicle is the Boston-based VIA Art Fund. VIA, "a collective, democratic initiative that connects art patrons with cultural producers", represents an innovative philanthropic model that engages a wider audience, includes direct investment into artist and organisational initiatives, and allows donors to better influence impact.

There is enough wealth in our society – and being transferred and made daily – to support both current organisational structures and form new, inventive types of giving models. These types of models are opportunities for the next gen to offer direct support to entities and creatives, where impact can be collectively determined as funds are collectively pooled.

Positioning the arts as a driver of social justice and reform

AFF research shows that "the emerging class of donors views cultural philanthropy through the lens of social justice".

We have seen institutional funders respond to this trend, loosening their restrictions, changing application procedures, and responding quickly in this era of multiple crises. And these funders are well aware of the changing demographics – Darren Walker, president of the Ford Foundation, is spearheading a coalition of foundations to dramatically increase their giving by issuing debt secured by their endowments. Particularly noting the arts are paramount to addressing issues of social justice[14] and showing us the way forward to a more equitable world, Walker articulates the need for increasing giving to arts organisations, as the sector can make a substantial impact.

By nature, the arts are about inclusion and broadening society's views. Therefore, the 21st-century cultural institution is more than just a place for performance and exhibition; it's a gathering space, a 'safe space', a town hall, an educational facility, and a therapeutic necessity. Involvement and giving by nextgen donors can make an extraordinary impact in developing these community centres for dialogue.

Rising generations are focused on equitable access to health, wellness and education. Studies[15] show that a strong cultural presence in a community is proven to improve health and wellness, increase empathy and interpersonal understanding, contribute to greater local economic activity, and inspire conversation and reflection.

The rising generations insist that institutions be most responsible to their largest group of stakeholders – their community. And we are seeing some organisations make this necessary shift. These donors can make this an essential part of the new funding landscape. People want to give to institutions that represent them and address the most pertinent issues in our society. Nextgen can lead a reimagining and evolution of core programming, and even missions. As these funders seek more impact, and 21st-century audiences seek deeper engagement with organisations, the guiding ethos of the rising generation can lead the way.

A donor's checklist

To accomplish the strategies outlined above, here is a brief checklist for nextgen donors to use when beginning to shape their strategies for arts funding:

- Talk to cultural organisations about their plans, and how they want to involve nextgen donors. Ask pointed questions, and never be afraid to push back about their thinking.

There is enough wealth in our society – and being transferred and made daily – to support both current organisational structures and form new, inventive types of giving models.

- Ask to see the strategic plan – see where it overlaps with your area of expertise and interest and offer yourself as a resource and ideas.
- Inquire how the organisation engages directly with its local community – ask about community representation in leadership roles (eg, committees and boards).
- Ask about engagement and education work – find out what is happening alongside the programming (exhibition and/or performance schedule).
- Gather your peers to outline strategies for communal impact at organisations.
- Form your own funding vehicle – create a collective funding mechanism designed to maximise impact and promote a sense of community.
- Talk to specialists who work at the intersection of art and philanthropy.
- Research and invest in works by artists and creatives who are directly addressing issues of social justice.
- Spread the word! Share this knowledge about the impact achievable in the cultural sector with your peers.

Wealth advisers and the arts

As mentioned, the financial sector is impacted by this generational shift and the rising high-net-worth individual's preferences for wealth management. Rising generation donors are looking for ethical investments, strategic impact and also unique experiences with their peer cohorts. In these respects, the arts present a unique opportunity for client retention, in addition to the massive opportunity for impact and legacy. Advisers who can understand and articulate all the benefits of strategic cultural philanthropy will create a sense of client loyalty. In short, investing in the arts offers the following:

New learning experiences and intellectual engagement

- access to museums, artist studios, art schools, art fairs and cultural organisations, where clients can go behind the scenes and learn firsthand how the industry functions and who it impacts;
- fresh and exciting opportunities to learn from creatives about how to think outside the box, and how the arts bring about social change;

Networking and business development

- access to an unparalleled group of professionals and high-net-worth individuals, who share passions for creative pursuits and creating impact (eg, cultural benefactors include several of America's Top Ten Billionaires, and cultural events and conversations bring together these industry leaders, celebrities, musicians, arts, tastemakers and more);

New methods of investment

- new philanthropic and acquisition strategies that benefit both the philanthropist's goals and the cultural sector;
- exposure to a wide network of collecting specialists, auction houses and advisers to grow and build a legacy or investment collection;
- alignment between the philanthropist's vision and forward-thinking and investment-driven organisations, contemporary artists and cultural producers.

Conclusion: the path forward for nextgen and the arts

The time has never been more critical for private philanthropy, and the opportunities to make a change have never been so profound. We are at a turning point where a generational shift can have a paradigm-shifting impact on the evolution of the global cultural ecosystem. The potential is vast for nextgen donors to serve as leaders in this evolution, to create a more democratic and equitable system to address pressing societal challenges.

The nextgen has been telling us how they want to give, and the global events of 2020 can help accelerate the process of remaking the model. By partnering with the arts sector, the rising generation can lead conversations about how the arts can drive social justice to mitigate our biggest global problems, the very problems that this generation is dedicated to solving. They can be at the forefront of redefining arts funding for a new century.

Let me end by saying that amidst this discussion on the significant impact achievable within cultural philanthropy, I would be remiss if I did not remind us that the arts, at their core, offer us a glimpse into our humanity. They are an expression of who we are and a representation of our collective history (both

---

Advisers who can understand and articulate all the benefits of strategic cultural philanthropy will create a sense of client loyalty.

---

good and bad). Art can bring about a transcendental experience that no words can explain and that no system of metrics can quantify. It would be a challenge to find someone who has not been moved to tears – or to tears of joy – by a film, the lyrics or melody of a piece of music, a dancer's grace, the words in a novel or poem, a painting on a museum wall. Whether it's Shakespeare's prose or Spike Lee's dialogue, the arts connect us with our own humanity. Art matters because we matter. Let that also be the legacy the next generation leaves.

Melissa Cowley Wolf is the founder of MCW Projects LLC – www.mcw-projects.com – a consulting firm dedicated to expanding the next generation of cultural philanthropists, audiences and advocates. Melissa advises organisations on philanthropic and narrative strategies to increase relevancy and revenue streams and democratise their supporter base; partners with the financial sector and their clients to highlight the immense and unique impact achievable in the cultural economy; and collaborates across industries to advocate for increased philanthropic support of the arts. She has 20 years' experience in philanthropy and programming for cultural institutions across the United States, and was named in the Artnet 2020 Innovators List as one of 51 global innovators transforming the art industry. Melissa is also the director of the Arts Funders Forum – www.artsfundersforum.com – an advocacy, media, and research platform designed to increase private support for arts and culture.

1 Sharna Goldseker and Michael Moody, *Generation Impact: How Next Gen Donors Are Revolutionizing Giving* (Hoboken, NJ, John Wiley & Sons, Inc, 2017).
2 Ansuya Harjani, "Coming soon: The biggest wealth transfer in history", *CNBC.com*, 13 January 2015, www.cnbc.com/2015/01/13/ coming-soon-the-biggest-wealth-transfer-in-history.html.
3 See https://givingusa.org/.
4 Nick Rabkin and EC Hedberg (NORC at the University of Chicago), "Arts education in America: What the declines mean for arts participation", February 2011, www.arts.gov/sites/default/files/2008-SPPA-ArtsLearning.pdf.
5 Arts Funders Forum's research: a look at what we learned, https://www.artsfundersforum.com/news/our-findings-2019.
6 For Freedoms, https://forfreedoms.org/.
7 The report is the Arts and Cultural Production Satellite Account (ACPSA), produced jointly by the NEA's Office of Research & Analysis and the Bureau of Economic Analysis, US Commerce Department, "Statement on Arts, Jobs, and the Economy", Americans for the Arts, 2017, www.americansforthearts.org/news-room/arts-mobilization-center/statement-on-arts-jobs-and-the-economy.
8 American Alliance of Museums (AAM), Museums and P-12 Education, https://www.aam-us.org/programs/museums-and-p-12-education/.
9 Americans for the Arts, "Art + Social Impact Explorer", www.americansforthearts.org/socialimpact.
10 Arts Funders Forum's research: a look at what we learned, www.artsfundersforum.com/news/our-findings-2019.
11 Goldseker and Moody, *Generation Impact: How Next Gen Donors Are Revolutionizing Giving* (2017).
12 Arts Funders Forum, "Arts Funders Forum's research: a look at what we learned", www.artsfundersforum.com/news/our-findings-2019.
13 Arts Funders Forum, "Arts Funders Forum's research: a look at what we learned", www.artsfundersforum.com/news/our-findings-2019.
14 Arts Funders Forum Virtual Series, "Remake The Model: Ethics & Equity in Cultural Philanthropy with Darren Walker and David Callahan, www.youtube.com/watch?v=LlwK3cj0J-w&feature=emb_err_woyt.
15 Maria Cramer, "Another Benefit to Going to Museums? You May Live Longer", NewYorkTimes.com, 22 December 2019, updated 27 December 2019, www.nytimes.com/2019/12/22/us/arts-health-effects-ucl-study.html.

To understand any generation, we must understand what was happening in the world as they grew up. Until we do, we cannot fully grasp our own roles – as parents, advisers, mentors – in supporting them.

Effective mentoring for the next generation

Jessica McGawley
Dallington Associates

To understand the [person], you have to know what was happening in the world when [they were] twenty.
– Napoleon Bonaparte[1]

1. Introduction

To understand any generation, we must understand what was happening in the world as they grew up. Until we do, we cannot fully grasp our own roles – as parents, advisers, mentors – in supporting them.

Like every generation, 16 to 24-year-olds today – those whom we refer to as Generation Z[2] – differ greatly from their parents and grandparents. They are a generation that have grown up in an era of fast and accessible information; self-directed learning; globalisation; human rights awareness; social media; the visible threat of climate change; fake news; and, most recently, the global COVID-19 pandemic. By and large, they are a socially conscious, inclusive, pragmatic and analytical generation. They are also a generation that like to communicate audio-visually – through images, videos, infographics and voice files.

Unlike their tech immigrant parents, the tech natives of Generation Z have never known a world without the Internet and digital technology.

Taken from the Special Report *Family Business and Responsible Wealth Ownership: Preparing the Next Generation*, published by Globe Law and Business

GENERATION Z

SOCIALLY CONSCIOUS

Gen Z are the most racially diverse, liberal and tolerant generation in history. Gen Zs genuinely value a company's social impact and care strongly about the environment.

EDUCATED

50% of Gen Zs have attended college or university. They proactively seek learning opportunities such as internships and are keener to 'learn before they earn' than their Millennial predecessors.

TECH NATIVES

They are masters of social media, use up to 5 digital devices at one time, and are known as the app generation.

IMPATIENT

Their attention spans are on average 8 seconds, which is 4 shorter than Millennials. They thrive on instant gratification.

26% ARE ANXIOUS

26% of Gen Z suffer from anxiety, as compared to 21% of Millennials, 17% of Gen Xers and 9% of Boomers.

PRAGMATIC

Gen Z have grown up during a global financial crisis and a pandemic. They are cautious with money (57% would choose saving over spending) and want both emotional and financial stability.

Used to having a vast amount of information at their fingertips, they are set to become the most educated generation in history. Understandably, this is also a generation in which many experience feelings of anxiety.

Mentoring young people during these crucial developmental years can significantly improve outcomes for them, equipping them with the knowledge, tools and mechanisms to navigate life and evolve into self-aware, resilient people. In some circumstances, mentoring at this stage can offset the risk or the need for future, and potentially more public, intervention.

This is an age at which young adults are reluctant to openly communicate on certain subjects – and sometimes any subjects – with their parents. It is not unusual for there to be a change in the way that parents and children communicate at this age. However, it can be very difficult for a young person to find an alternative and trusted source from whom to seek the information and guidance that they need. For parents, it can be a particularly challenging time, in which many find themselves second guessing their children and, as a result, being unsure as to what support to offer or what boundaries to set. If you are very close to something or spend too long staring at it, it can be hard to see the solution and – with the best intentions in the world – you risk over-compensating. Although motivated by love and a desire to help, the efforts of parents can sometimes hinder rather than help development at this age.

The generational gap between today's 16 to 24-year-olds and their parents, advisers and employers can be hard to bridge; but this can be made easier. Having someone who can help bridge the gap – someone whom a developing adult can relate to, can ask awkward questions of and can call on in situations of extreme anxiety – can be hugely helpful. In this capacity, a mentor can make all the difference, helping to preserve existing relationships and supporting developing adults in becoming the best versions of themselves.

Mentoring at any age or stage is valuable; although, as with most things, starting young helps to establish a solid foundation to build on. Just as there are no teachers who have not been students, most mentors have themselves been a mentee at some point. The younger we learn, the more we can benefit and the sooner we can pass on our experience. By starting this process earlier in life, the rising next generation can better manage the emotional aspects of succession and, in turn, pass these on to the next generation when it is time.

In this chapter, we look at the particular circumstances facing children of affluence and explore how mentoring can help to develop and prepare them for a life contextualised by wealth, helping them to achieve their goals, develop resilience and autonomy, and become the most fulfilled, capable versions of themselves that they can.

2. Choice, anxiety and the importance of failure

Day by day, what you choose, what you think and what you do is who you become.
– Heraclitus[3]

People today face more choices every day than any preceding generation: from the coffee they drink in the morning to the eco-friendly water bottle they accessorise with, and from the college courses they embark on to the career paths they follow. For children of affluence, the plethora of choices and opportunities are even more diverse, which can be both liberating and sometimes crippling. With so much possibility within reach, how can a young and inexperienced person know that they are making the right, if not the best possible, choices?

Choice brings with it responsibility and, in turn, a pressure to succeed. Although it can feel like it, choice does not equate to control. The trap that many young people from affluent backgrounds fall into is believing that because they have choice, they must succeed; and because they have such a clear advantage, everything must be perfect. Pleasing parents is frequently of paramount emotional importance and failure to achieve perfection is often felt not only as failure in the moment, but also as an indication of failure as a person.

Experiences such as these trigger anxiety and impact confidence. Expressions of anxiety and depression can be perceived as attention seeking if not understood. Left undiagnosed, chronic anxiety can deeply affect an individual's health in the long term. Fear of failure prevents us from being able to make decisions and ultimately from assuming responsibility for, and taking control of, our own lives. But we can choose to frame our view on this differently. We can choose to see our failures as lessons rather than as the object of shame and embarrassment.

Ninety per cent of adults are immune to chickenpox because they had it when they were children. Parents don't tend to protect their children from catching chicken pox, because we know that it is safer for a child to build future immunity by catching the virus than it is to shield them from it and have them catch it as adults, when the risks are greater. The same thinking can and should be applied to failure. By shielding your child from failure, you prevent them from learning

"Choice brings with it responsibility and, in turn, a pressure to succeed. Although it can feel like it, choice does not equate to control."

valuable lessons, building resilience and developing self-esteem. If a person is to become independent, they need to know it's okay to fall down, because it is only by falling down and getting back up again that we learn to walk.

3. The importance of individuation to finding purpose
'Individuation' – a term attributed to Swiss psychiatrist and psychoanalyst Carl Gustav Jung[4] – describes the process of self-realisation: the discovery and experience of meaning and purpose through which one develops their personal identity and becomes who they are. This process can last a lifetime, but can feel at its most intense during the mid to late adolescent years from 16 to 24. These are the years in which we typically forge our identity and enter adulthood. For many of us, the experiences we have, the influences we encounter and the relationships we form during this time are those that we carry into our adult lives and, for better or worse, that impact on our individuation.

Individuation is a process of self-discovery made possible by a shift from the unconscious to the conscious mind. It allows us to see ourselves and to change what we can and accept what we can't. Individuation in itself is not typically a conscious choice, but something that happens to us all, to varying degrees, as we are exposed to the opportunities and challenges of life. These experiences test our boundaries and force us to acknowledge parts of ourselves that we didn't know existed.

If the individuation process stagnates and does not complete (perhaps due to trauma, harmful family dynamics or mental health challenges), a person can become depressed, anxious and overly dependent on others. When our sense of self is shaken, everything can feel like a challenge and anything but praise a criticism. This can often lead to questionable choices, particularly when forming new friendships and romantic or professional relationships, as we seek emotional reinforcement in the wrong places.

If we choose to approach the process of individuation more consciously, with curiosity and a commitment to self-understanding without judgement, then we can truly benefit from it. Doing so can also help to identify our sense of purpose. There are, of course, the lucky few who seem to have been born with an innate sense of purpose – a calling that has determined the course of their lives from a young age. For the vast majority, though, locating purpose is a more involved process and one that demands application. To add to the challenge, purpose can change more than once within a lifetime – for example, when a person becomes a parent. We continue to change and evolve throughout our lifetimes, which is why individuation is a lifelong process.

A mentor acts as a guide on this journey, helping a mentee to realise their personal identity and develop self-esteem, self-awareness and self-reliance. In doing so, we develop independence and autonomy, which is an extremely important part of becoming who we are and standing on our own two feet.

4. Wellbeing is about balance

Like so many lasting concepts, it is the ancient Greeks that we have to thank for the concept of mentoring. When Odysseus left home to fight in the Trojan War and complete his 10-year odyssey thereafter, he entrusted his son to the care of his good friend, Mentor. The results of Mentor's counsel and guidance were so fruitful that his efforts have been remembered throughout history.

Definitions of 'mentoring' have evolved over time, with different models emerging to suit myriad contexts; but one thing they all have in common is the idea of a provider of counsel and guidance to someone less experienced. Something more than a teacher, but without the emotional involvement of a parent.

More often than not, mentoring practice is based on intergenerational counsel and guidance. It makes sense that the older, more experienced

MENTORSHIP

QUALITIES OF A MENTOR

EXPERIENCE BASED

Their guidance and approach will often stem from their own knowledge and experiences.

ACTIVE LISTENER

They are someone who hears both verbal and non-verbal communication and helps the mentee clarify their thoughts.

ENCOURAGING

They encourage mentees in pursuit of their goals, sharing inspirational material and experiences. They are supportive through challenges and perceived failures.

EMPATHETIC

They are able to experience their mentee's thoughts and feelings from their point of view, rather than from their own.

AUTHENTIC

A mentor works in a way that is unique to them and not from a handbook.

A GOOD MENTOR...

BUILDS TRUST

It is about developing a relationship based on trust and bonding. Unlike in therapy or coaching, a mentor will share their experiences including mistakes and failures as they often contain lessons.

STAYS OPEN

A mentee should feel that nothing is inappropriate or off the table to discuss with their mentor.

HOLDS YOU ACCOUNTABLE

The relationship may entail setting goals, clarifying or realigning them, and regularly reviewing the mentee's actions towards these.

LEARNS WITH YOU

The mentor helps the mentee to learn and develop, be that in communication, leadership, knowledge or life skills. This learning is often reciprocal.

PROMOTES INDEPENDENCE

The purpose of mentoring is to get the mentee to a place where they feel confident in their own abilities and no longer need the support.

A MENTOR IS NOT...

AUTHORITATIVE

A mentor will not expect you to learn vicariously through their experience, or tell you what you should or should not do.

JUDGEMENTAL

A mentor will not condemn you for your mistakes, thoughts or views. They will approach these with curiosity and understanding.

A THERAPIST

While a mentor is supportive and trustworthy, they do not work therapeutically or replace the need for psychological support.

A FIXER

One of the mentor's key roles is to help the mentee know themselves. If the mentor falls into the trap of 'fixing', this opportunity for learning is removed.

person should guide the younger, less experienced. We have found that developing adults relate better to mentors who are older than them, but younger than their parents. As a general rule, we match mentees with mentors who are in the region of 10 to 15 years older than themselves. Something else that is very important in a mentoring relationship is reciprocity. The mentoring relationship does not flow in a single direction, as does the relationship between teacher and student. The mentor and mentee learn from each other simultaneously. In this way, the mentor learns from the experiences of the mentee, preventing them from forming assumptions based on their own experience, keeping their understanding of context current and constantly renewing their abilities and credentials as mentors. There is no one-size-fits-all solution in mentoring, so a mentor must learn from their mentees if they are to successfully mentor each and every one of them.

A successful mentoring journey guides an individual towards establishing personal identity and resilience through the development of self-awareness and independence. Abraham Maslow developed a motivational theory based on the fundamentals of human need and how this relates to personal fulfilment.[5] Maslow ranks these needs in a five-tier hierarchy, culminating in human fulfilment. On the bottom

"A successful mentoring journey guides an individual towards establishing personal identity and resilience through the development of self-awareness and independence."

STAGES OF MENTORSHIP

1. BUILDING

Strong foundations are important, so the first thing the mentor and mentee do is get to know each other by discussing interests, sharing experiences and dreams, establishing boundaries and building trust.

2. GOAL SETTING

Sometimes we appropriate the goals of others as our own without realising. Identifying and setting your own goals, and not those of your parents, peers or mentors, is paramount.

3. DEVELOPMENT

This is about achieving goals, drawing on a combination of practical and emotional support. The guidance, tools and support shared help mentees navigate new experiences and events in their lives.

4. REFLECTION

As we develop, the goalposts can often move. Sometimes a plan must be adapted to meet changing needs. It is important to regularly review and realign the development plan, ensuring it places emphasis on the right areas at any given point in the mentoring journey.

5. GRADUATION

Knowing when to let go is important, but doing it too soon can be counterintuitive. A parent always hovers behind their child, arms outstretched, when the training wheels are removed from their first bicycle, just until they are sure the child is steady and can ride alone. A graduated phase-out of the mentoring relationship helps ease the transition to full independence.

rung of the hierarchy sit physiological needs, followed by security, belonging, esteem and, at the pinnacle, self-actualisation – the point at which we become fulfilled beings.

At Dallington Associates, we take a more cyclical approach to needs-based human development and fulfilment, using a model based on the interdependent and interrelational factors of cognitive, emotional, social and physical development. We believe all of these factors to be important, but also recognise that for every mentee, that which takes precedence in any one moment will change over time, influenced by personal development, as well as by outside factors affecting their lives.

5. The wheel of wellbeing

The quadrants in the figure opposite represent the four aspects of development that constitute a person's wellbeing. For a developing adult, all four aspects are significant. It is important to understand that a lag in one area will have an impact on all other areas. Wellbeing is about balance. If a young person – let's call her Lucy – stops exercising and eating properly, she will stop sleeping well, which will affect her cognitive development and ability to study effectively. She will become moody, which will have implications for her social interactions and

"We take a more cyclical approach to needs-based human development and fulfilment, using a model based on the interdependent and interrelational factors of cognitive, emotional, social and physical development."

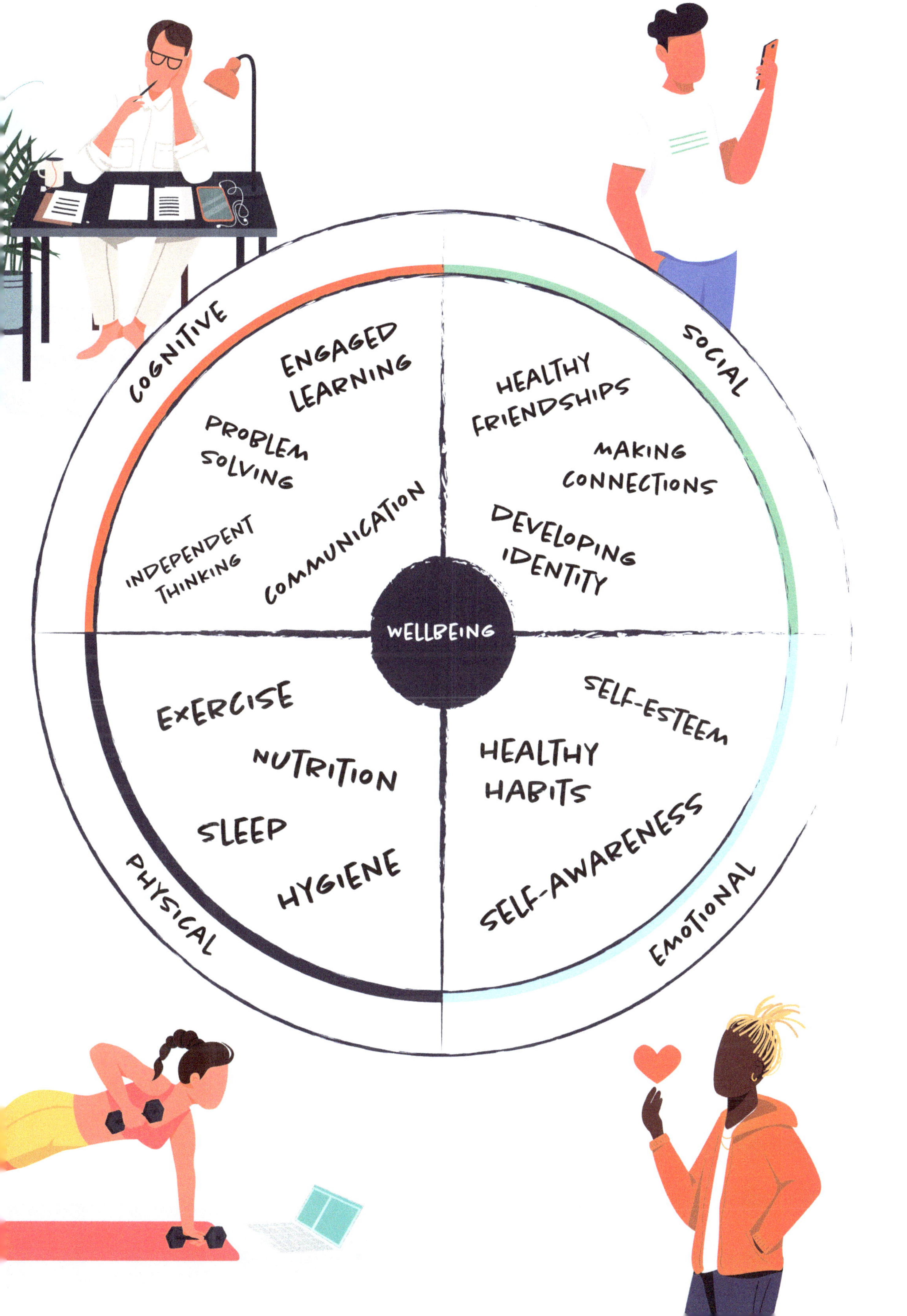
COGNITIVE
ENGAGED LEARNING
PROBLEM SOLVING
INDEPENDENT THINKING
COMMUNICATION
SOCIAL
HEALTHY FRIENDSHIPS
MAKING CONNECTIONS
DEVELOPING IDENTITY
WELLBEING
EXERCISE
NUTRITION
SLEEP
HYGIENE
PHYSICAL
SELF-ESTEEM
HEALTHY HABITS
SELF-AWARENESS
EMOTIONAL

relationships; and this in turn can impact on her mental health. Assessing Lucy's behaviour and progress through the four lenses of cognitive, social, physical and mental wellbeing helps to build a picture of where she is struggling most, which forms the basis of a plan for improvement. What would be even better, though, is if Lucy were able to self-identify her deterioration and form her own plan for improvement.

6. A personalised wheel of wellbeing

Exploring the root cause of Lucy's changing needs helps both Lucy and her mentor to reach a more in-depth understanding of what is going on, based on the interrelational nature of the four quadrants. For example, Lucy may already have been struggling with certain aspects of her life for a while. She is shy and finds it hard to make new friends. She is becoming increasingly paranoid that nobody likes her and that people are talking behind her back. Her self-esteem is very low, so she stops caring for herself. Her diet deteriorates, as do her sleep patterns. The exhaustion and paranoia are affecting her mental health. Lucy creates her personal wheel of wellbeing, as in the figure opposite. The wheel is filled with all of the things that Lucy wants to do in order to lead a more balanced life. By keeping track of her own performance in each of the four quadrants, Lucy can recognise that her mental health is suffering (because she has stopped completing the activities in her social and emotional quadrants), and can ask for help before someone else needs to intervene. Lucy can then update her wheel to reflect her new needs. In this way, the wheel gives Lucy greater control of her own wellbeing. Her ability to identify the issue and be a part of the solution is empowering.

In practical terms, what this means is that to effectively mentor a developing adult, we need to look at the whole person through these four lenses, working with individuals to assess areas for improvement and formulating personal development plans based on these assessments. These plans are not finite. As an individual progresses through the mentoring journey, the balance can shift and the plan may need revising. Some mentees include additional dimensions in their wellbeing plans – for instance, spiritual wellbeing. Certain aspects may need revisiting as dynamics shift. The wheel is not so much cyclical as inter-dimensional and, in hindsight, would possibly be better represented by a three-dimensional model.

7. Boundaries are friends, not foes

Psychologist Erik Erikson's theory of psychosocial development identifies eight stages of development throughout a human being's life.[6] The stages to which he equates the developing adult (spanning adolescence and young adulthood) are those of identity versus role confusion and intimacy versus isolation.

LUCY'S WELLBEING
COGNITIVE
SOCIAL
EMOTIONAL
PHYSICAL
READING TIME
INTENTION SETTING
MORNING STUDY TIME
EXERCISE CREATIVITY
AUTHENTIC CONNECTIONS
VOLUNTEER @RSPCA
BALANCE TIME SPENT ONLINE
JOIN A SOCIETY AT UNI
REMEMBER H-A-L-T BEFORE REACTING
SPEAK UP WHEN FEELING OVERLOOKED
WRITE IN MY DAILY JOURNAL
FOLLOW MORE AUTHENTIC INFLUENCERS
DRINK MORE WATER
PHONE OFF BY 11PM
HOT YOGA 2x A WEEK
DAILY WALK

The formation of identity is a prominent and often challenging theme during teenage-hood and a person's early 20s. For developing adults from affluent backgrounds, and especially for those studying and living abroad, it can be a particularly confusing and often isolating experience. In your earlier years, personal identity is largely tied to family and place. Away from both of these, life can seem complicated. In later years, identity becomes increasingly linked to purpose. Inherited wealth can make it harder for a person to locate their sense of purpose, frequently resulting in feelings of low self-esteem.

Having the freedom to explore one's identity is exciting; but to do so without boundaries or guidance can be overwhelming. Establishing boundaries helps us to feel more secure. Learning the difference between right and wrong, what is acceptable behaviour and what is not, is an essential part of every person's moral and social development. After all, if you're going to choose to break a rule, you've got to know what the rule is. Boundaries help us to make choices that are in our own interest and that do not make us or others vulnerable. Without boundaries, we have no guide, no benchmark; and this can trigger alarming feelings of chronic anxiety.

If you observed a rollercoaster attendant lowering a safety bar for other passengers to keep them safely in their seats and then noticed that they hadn't lowered your own bar, you would ask them to do so or would do so yourself. In this case, the attendant has demonstrated a boundary that you were not previously aware of. Now that you have seen the bar and understand its benefit, you naturally want yours lowered too. If you didn't know that the bar existed, you might ride without it, putting yourself and your companions at great risk. You wouldn't be having fun. You would be vulnerable. Boundaries, by their very nature, encourage a direction of travel towards self-improvement and, until we learn to establish them for ourselves, must be learned from our parents and our teachers, our employers and rollercoaster attendants.

As a developing adult, the testing of boundaries is an important part of the process of individuation. It is a natural instinct to do so. This behaviour is frequently read as dissatisfaction and unhappiness. A parent's natural response is often to acquiesce and even to overcompensate, but this can lead to unrealistic expectations. The world and the people in it will not always bend to someone's will. Giving in to someone's whims and making things easier than they would normally be is setting them up for disappointment. Fast, effortless material gain rarely equates to long-term benefit.

As a parent, learning to say no – or at the very least, delaying gratification – is as important, if not more so, for children as it is for parents. Delayed gratification is an important socialising concept. By choosing to wait for something, saving up for it, working towards it, we understand its value. The realisation that something that is desired is not needed immediately, that without it the world will not fall apart, and that the sense of reward is greater when we do finally receive something or achieve a goal is an important lesson. It teaches a person the difference between need and want, which helps us to master self-discipline and to grasp the true value of things. Delayed gratification also helps a person to develop a richer, more creative internal world, because by not having every desire met with immediacy, they are forced to turn to themselves for satisfaction, distraction and fulfilment.

As we mature, we learn to set our own boundaries for ourselves and for others, creating the space that we need to be able to achieve the things that we need to achieve in the way that we choose to achieve them. This is an important part of forming and maintaining both platonic and romantic relationships.

The next developmental stage in Erik Erikson's theory is that of generativity versus stagnation, addressing the years from 40 to 65, when many of us are parents and most of us are consumed with the

"The world and the people in it will not always bend to someone's will. Giving in to someone's whims and making things easier than they would normally be is setting them up for disappointment."

question of how to make our mark on the world. As we have already explored earlier in the chapter, the process of individuation and the finding of purpose are not finite goals. As we grow and evolve, so do our circumstances and so do our goals and purpose. For this reason, the mentoring relationship at any stage in life must also adapt to keep pace and remain relevant.

8. Independence and autonomy through learned behaviours
Life away from home for the first time holds many adventures, but also many potential pitfalls. Wealthy families often have staff and for a developing adult – let's call him Anil – his arrival at university may be the first time that he has had to think about carrying out certain daily tasks. Anil's family has a driver, a personal assistant, a cook and a cleaner, a housekeeper and security guards. Before he arrived at university, Anil never had to do the grocery shopping, cook his meals, drive himself to appointments or clean his flat. It isn't that Anil can't do these things, but that he hasn't previously had to think about them – and they are time-consuming activities. Doing all these things while staying on top of his studies, keeping track of his day-to-day appointments, exercising regularly and making new friends is challenging. There just isn't enough time in the day. When things get a bit much, Anil is prone to losing things such as his keys, passport or headphones, which is frustrating and makes his life more complicated.

Learning to stay on top of everything takes planning and organisation. There are tools and systems that can help Anil to manage his time and make sure that everything gets done. He doesn't have to be superman, but he does need to adopt some new behaviours.

One of the tools that Anil's mentor helps him to develop is his personalised schedule. This isn't just any schedule, but one informed by the four quadrants of the wheel of wellbeing. Each activity in the schedule is colour coded according to its quadrant. Different schedules will be heavier on some colours, weighted towards the areas in which Anil most needs to develop. Anil's daily action plan helps to build autonomy by helping him to meet his deadlines, take regular exercise, make friends and feel confident. By developing and reinforcing positive behaviours that will last a lifetime, he can learn to rely on himself, make his own choices and take responsibility for his own wellbeing.

These tools and behaviours don't just apply to university students, but are checks and balances that can be applied throughout a lifetime – particularly during periods of flux or trauma in which you might find yourself having to balance and cope with more than usual. As a recent example, the COVID-19 pandemic has forced many of us to reassess our work/life balance and reorganise our lives in order to remain safe and adhere to lockdown regulations. Most of us spread our lives across multiple physical environments on a regular basis – the office, gym, coffee shop, place of worship, club. The restrictions resulting from the pandemic have highlighted the extent to which our health, social and mental wellbeing, as well as our independence and autonomy, are linked to both the activities in which we engage and the environments in which we engage in them. Unable to adhere to our usual routines and behaviours, many of us have experienced misalignment and some depression. What is frustrating is that we can often see this happening, but feel powerless or lack the motivation to take action.

This is the moment at which the tools demonstrated by Lucy and Anil come into play. Using these mechanisms, we can take a step back and apply our four lenses of cognitive, social, physical and emotional wellbeing. Through these lenses, we can begin to understand how to prioritise, reorganise and reimagine a status quo. Using these tools, we can realign ourselves and maintain balance and productivity by developing new behaviours tailored to our new environments.

9. Empathy is empowering

One of the ways in which wealthier families often choose to teach their children about empathy is through philanthropic experience. These projects are beneficial to the communities they serve and are valuable vehicles for teaching a young person set to inherit significant wealth the importance of recognising and engaging with need in the wider world. However, these are often big projects, operating at scale. They don't always offer opportunities for personal engagement with the people they are helping and an opportunity to get to grips with their day-to-day struggles. Projects that involve immersing yourself in a community and walking a mile in other people's shoes are often abroad, and the context is thus far removed and 'other' in nature. It can be difficult for a young person to relate to these experiences and transfer the lessons when back in their own environment. In some sense, the lesson needs to be more literal, more relatable and more granular. One way to achieve this is to encourage young and developing adults to engage with charities or initiatives that are local to them and ideally of personal interest. Engaging in activities closer to home allows them to do more themselves and to directly engage with the people delivering support, as well as with the beneficiaries themselves. Face-to-face contact and the ability to see the results of their efforts first hand make it much easier to relate to the people they are helping, establish empathy and learn useful lessons that they can apply in their own lives.

Understanding value – whether financial or emotional – in relation to yourself or to others is an important part of developing empathy; and empathy is an essential aspect of successful relationships with friends and colleagues. Without empathy, we can have no view of how others experience things, making it incredibly difficult to relate to other people and for them to relate to us.

As well as a creator of opportunity and advantage, inherited wealth can be isolating. Many developing and young adults of affluence experience guilt about their privilege and making friends can sometimes be challenging. On the one hand, a person might feel guilty about the security and advantages afforded to them by wealth. This guilt can be exacerbated by the misplaced assumptions of some peers and colleagues that because they have money, they don't have real problems. It can be difficult to establish intimacy and form genuine attachments if you constantly feel like you have to apologise for your wealth and hide your true self for fear of being exposed to criticism or worse. On the other hand, a developing adult may find themselves in a situation in which they have many friends. In such a scenario, it can be hard to distinguish between genuine friendships and those that are far from genuine. This can make a person vulnerable. Trust is the basic foundation of any relationship. Without trust, genuine relationships cannot flourish.

10. We are who we choose to become

The only person you are destined to be is the person you decide to be.[7]
– Ralph Waldo Emerson

You cannot change the fact that you were born into wealth, but you can choose how you respond to circumstance. By investing time and effort in discovering who you are, overcoming your anxieties, seeking opportunities for improvement rather than perceiving failures and learning to make good decisions, you can create your own winning formula for life and be a better friend, family member, partner, leader and purposeful member of society.

Choosing to use your advantages for positive action rather than apologising for them can be both empowering and liberating. If life is a series of choices, every one of us has the power to choose to be the person that we want to be, starting with the decisions that we make every day. A good mentor helps a mentee to make choices; a great mentor helps to empower a mentee to make those choices independently.

Having themselves experienced the mentoring journey, many mentees become mentors later in life, passing on the wisdom that they have acquired to future generations. As a member of the rising next generation, the opportunity to be guided by someone who truly understands your context is invaluable. After all, who better to be guided by than someone who comes from a background that is not dissimilar; someone who understands the opportunities and pressures, has experienced the challenges and reaped the rewards; someone who is at once immersed and objective.

The mentoring experience is neither linear nor finite. The lessons learned along the way are lessons that can be applied and reapplied throughout a lifetime, whenever a person falls out of equilibrium and finds themselves in need of realignment. Nor does the learning simply flow in one direction. Just as the mentee is guided by the mentor, so must a mentor learn from the mentee. A mentor must always be learning so as to be constantly evolving and avoid stagnation. The world does not stand still: society, ideas and people evolve; and to be relevant and effective, counsel must be rooted in understanding.

Notes

1 Albert Manfred, *Napoleon Bonaparte* (Ediciones AKAL, 1988).
2 'Generation Z' refers to those born between 1995 and 2009. For the purpose of this chapter, we are referring to those within that generation aged 16 to 24.
3 Philip Wheelwright, *Heraclitus* (Colchis Books, 1974).
4 Carl Gustav Jung and Stanley M Dell, *The Integration of the Personality* (Routledge & K Paul, 1963).
5 Joseph E Gawel, Herzberg's *Theory Of Motivation And Maslow's Hierarchy Of Needs* (ERIC Clearinghouse on Assessment and Evaluation, 1997).
6 Patrick H Munley, "Erik Erikson's theory of psychosocial development and vocational behavior", 22(4) *Journal of Counseling Psychology*, pp314–319, 1975.
7 Ralph Waldo Emerson and Edward Waldo Emerson, *The Complete Works of Ralph Waldo Emerson* (AMS Press, 1979).

Jessica McGawley
CEO and founder, Dallington Associates
Jessica@dallingtonassociates.com

Jessica McGawley is a consulting psychologist, family mediator and the CEO and founder of Dallington Associates, a specialist mentorship practice for the rising next generation. She holds an undergraduate degree in ethnomusicology and African culture; a postgraduate diploma in counselling and psychotherapy; and a master's in consulting psychology – psychodynamic and systemic approaches.

Prior to founding Dallington in 2015, Jessica spent seven years as head of operations for London-based consulting firm Oxford Place, where she focused on wealth transition to the next generation.

The youngest-ever board member of United Nations Women London in 2012, Jessica proudly set up its first mentoring scheme. She is a trustee of the Cassandra Learning Centre, a charity that focuses on supporting victims of domestic abuse; and a governor of the Mossbourne Victoria Park Academy in Hackney, London. Jessica is listed as one of the world's top problem solvers in *Tatler*'s High Net Worth Address Book.

Responsible families help all family members to contribute to the stewardship of family businesses and wealth. A focus on issues relevant to women in the family can be a critical, but often neglected, step in the asset protection and succession process.

Women: wealth and self-reliance

Philip Marcovici
The Offices of Philip Marcovici Limited

Caroline Underwood
Philanthropy Company

1. Introduction

Women always end up with the money.
– Philip Marcovici[1]

In earlier chapters, this Special Report has focused on the importance of the grit and resilience needed to live a purposeful life. But if our focus is all about purpose and becoming the best citizens we can be in our families, our communities and our lifetimes, what role does protecting our wealth have in our long-term thinking? And what is wealth protection? Does this go beyond just managing our money?

Responsible families help all family members to contribute to the stewardship of family businesses and wealth. A focus on issues relevant to women in the family can be a critical, but often neglected, step in the asset protection and succession process. Women have a particular contribution to make to families in helping to ensure smooth succession and the protection of family businesses and wealth.

But before a family member can truly contribute to the family group, the 'We' of family, they need to be confident and self-reliant in relation to the 'I' – meaning that it is valuable to focus on ensuring that women in the family are particularly secure and self-reliant regarding family finances.

Taken from the Special Report *Family Business and Responsible Wealth Ownership: Preparing the Next Generation*, published by Globe Law and Business

In an era when equality between the genders has moved so far forward, it seems a bit jarring to write about the specific challenges that exist for women in organising wealth; why on earth is this any different for women than for men?

In other words, why should women think differently from men about wealth and the acquisition of assets?

There are some compelling (and somewhat sad) answers to these questions:

- Women tend to live longer than men;
- In general, women have less ownership of assets than men; and
- Women are often less prepared than men about wealth protection.

But there is a view expressed by one of the authors of this chapter, Philip Marcovici, that women always end up with the money.

Let's take a look at that.

According to the World Health Organization, women generally live longer than men – on average by six to eight years. We say 'generally', but acknowledge of course that in some settings – in particular, in parts of Asia – the biological advantages of women are overridden by discrimination against women so that life expectancy of women at birth is equal to that of men. In more than 35 countries, life expectancy for women is around 80 years old; while in some parts of Africa, it is only 54 and often lower due to HIV/AIDS and maternal mortality.[2]

More baby girls survive to their first birthday than boys. But curiously – and importantly in the context of discussions about wealth – women's longevity most shows itself in old age. Research is not conclusive as to how much of this is due to lifestyle choices or relatively lower rates of cardiovascular disease and cancer. (What is clear is that smoking has a massive impact on reducing lifespan for both genders.) Women living longer means that they are often the inheritors of family wealth and businesses; they therefore often represent the older generation in the family longer than male family members. This carries both risks and opportunities for wealth-owning families.

However, despite the longevity of women, women tend to own less in the way of assets than men. Conversely, women hold a vast amount of wealth in the world. Some estimates show that one-third of the world's wealth is under the control of women.[3] And they are increasing their wealth faster than in previous decades. Apart from ownership of wealth, women play a critical role in the stewardship of wealth: around the world, women are often the decision makers charged with overseeing family finances and dealing with disputes among the younger generation.

Being prepared for these roles is critical.

In his book *The Destructive Power of Family Wealth*, Marcovici points out that "wealth can and should be a positive thing for wealth owning families and the societies they live in".[4] He goes on to discuss some of the issues that he sees as critical for families in relation to women.

Despite increasing gender equality, difficulties still regularly arise, given the lack of knowledge about money that women in families sometimes suffer. Whether in marriages or otherwise, women – like men – need to know and understand the practicalities to do with money to protect themselves and their families.

In a marriage or other relationship, a woman should be asking herself whether she knows exactly what would happen if her partner died or became severely disabled, or if the marriage otherwise came to an end. If a woman has no idea of how much money her husband has and where the money is, in a divorce or on the death of her husband, there is a mess to sort out, and the possibility of the widow or divorced wife

"In a marriage or other relationship, a woman should be asking herself whether she knows exactly what would happen if her partner died or became severely disabled, or if the marriage otherwise came to an end."

being left in difficult financial circumstances becomes a very real and oft-repeated risk. Where the wealth is with the woman, understanding how that wealth can be protected in a divorce or other marriage breakdown is critical.

For wealth-owning families, educating children to understand what they need to know about wealth and marriage and the risks that are inevitable is very important. It is not only daughters who need to know how to protect themselves and how to ensure that they are financially independent in their relationships; all family members need this knowledge, allowing them to be better spouses and better parents as a result.

As we show in this chapter, the information and support to manage your finances and protect your wealth, whoever you are, are easily accessible and well worth the trouble it takes to acquire them.

2. Why is financial and wealth planning advice different for women than for men?

When we started investigating this subject, we assumed that women and men would be pretty equal in their knowledge and management of money in a domestic, business and family wealth setting.

But we were wrong.

It turns out that the traditional view of women knowing about money, particularly in a family or domestic setting, is that men often take the lead in managing money.

Why is advice for women different from men's financial and wealth planning advice? Surely it is the same? Well, yes, it is in broad terms; but our premise is that as women, there are questions that you need to know the answers to. And in families that are still patriarchal, the importance of the women in the family to the long-term sustainability of family wealth and business is not always well respected or understood. This makes it important for the women in the family to sometimes take the lead in asking the right questions: questions that can lead to greater security for both the individual women in the family and the family as a whole – again, the 'I' and the 'We'.

> *My mother, who is still whip smart in her mid 80s, told me that her mother – a prominent professional scientist who authored a book about optometry under a man's name – said to her, "Don't talk about money darling, it is so vulgar."*

This certainly was true – but is it really true for the current generation of young women? Shockingly, it seems so.

"In families that are still patriarchal, the importance of the women in the family to the long-term sustainability of family wealth and business is not always well respected or understood."

Daily assumptions and stereotypes aside, it is true that some women need a little bit more coaching; across many cultures, there is a tendency to 'leave it to the man'. Some even say that there is a tendency in men to think that they know how to run money better than women!

While significant progress has been made in terms of equality, in almost every culture there still seems to be a common thread that women tend not to know as much about family financial affairs as they need to.

3. The challenge of money and family

Family love is messy, clinging, and of an annoying and repetitive pattern, like bad wallpaper.
Friedrich Nietzsche[5]

There is no question of the importance of family and those people lucky enough to have a loving family have a natural advantage in life.

But it is also true that families are, in general, messy – and with the prevalence of divorce, messy in a way that previous generations did not have to unravel.

This makes it even more important to equip yourself with the right information about finances – not just for yourself, but for those around you. As a woman, you should know exactly what your financial situation will be if circumstances change; and sadly that in the main means illness, divorce or death. What will happen financially if your partner becomes seriously ill? What will happen if you become seriously ill?

The very worst time to have money discussions with the family is late at night or at a family occasion. Set aside planned time to sit with the family and discuss money.

It is up to the wealth holders – perhaps Mum and Dad – to make it clear what the situation is. But it is also up to women, as daughters, nieces, wives and sisters, to ask the right questions – and to appreciate that parents or other older generation members may not always have all the answers.

We do not suggest suddenly raising questions at a family event when tensions may already be running high, but instead setting a sensible time to ask questions calmly to get an overall picture of the family assets and finance. Sometimes this is best done between families in

"Engaging an independent and objective expert to help the family work through questions and challenges can be extremely effective – and can help to smooth any emotional outbursts or long-running tensions."

an office setting and for anyone – particularly couples – we recommend that time be put aside to do this calmly, perhaps at the dining table (and without young children present).

Having a discussion that is well facilitated can be extraordinarily helpful; here the dining table discussion might become a 'family retreat' that covers what all family members should know. Engaging an independent and objective expert to help the family work through questions and challenges can be extremely effective – and can help to smooth any emotional outbursts or long-running tensions. The best-prepared wealth-owning families are those that take steps such as these to prepare family members for their roles.

There is no doubt that conversations need to be age appropriate, from teenagers to the older generation. But the point is that women need to understand their own situation and know how to navigate a world with many possible financial pitfalls.

The undeniable truth is that by not making a plan, you are making a plan.

A study conducted by Merrill Lynch Wealth Management Research[6] revealed that 85% of women make day-to-day financial decisions. But the majority of respondents said that the male of the family "takes the lead in all major long term financial decisions like a holiday, a car, a house...".

For wealth-owning families, it is critical to think about the family's asset protection and succession strategies, and to review periodically whether what is in place still meets the family's changing circumstances. But to do this well and to properly keep an eye on advisers, all members of wealth-owning families at the right age – not only women – should be brought into an ongoing programme of learning, leading to responsibility as wealth owners. Whether a son or daughter will be involved in managing a family business or not, they need to be prepared for whatever role they will ultimately have – even if this role is limited to being an owner of the business together with other siblings who may be involved in the day-to-day management of the business. And where there is no business, just having ownership of a portfolio of assets requires preparation and knowledge.

Learning is an ongoing process, and opportunities to learn from other families and their successes and failures can also be instructive.

Everyone in the family needs to be prepared: to resist the thousands of investment scams and poor advice out there; to understand how to navigate difficult divorces and the ever-changing regulatory world; and to work well (and safely) with the advisers they will need to help guide them.

In the case of women, there is a particular need to consider whether they are as prepared as they should be.

4. Making a game plan

So where do you start? We would advise considering some of the really difficult questions – the 'what-ifs'. These are questions about life-changing circumstances – good and bad – and about what would happen in certain situations.

It is never too early to begin to think about the ownership, stewardship and succession process, and to work out what will happen to your assets if you or other family members were to become disabled or to pass away prematurely. A 'stress test' basically means asking the 'what-ifs': "What happens to my assets if I pass away? Is whatever plan I have in place appropriate to my current circumstances and what I would like to see happen? Will what I have put in place in terms of planning be destructive of my family and wealth?"

For people who are early in their lives, perhaps in their 20s – and particularly women – relying on these questions having been raised and addressed by the older generation is often a dangerous assumption. It is up to you to take responsibility and to encourage dialogue on these important issues.

If you or a family member were to pass away suddenly, what happens to the assets owned by that person? This will depend on what structures may be in place to deal with the transition of wealth, including trusts and other vehicles. If there are wills that have been validly executed, these will also come into the picture and the laws relevant to where assets are located will be key.

But who will ensure that the right things are done, and that assets are tracked down and properly looked after and transferred? Is there an inventory of assets that has been kept up to date; and do family members or others who are meant to benefit know where they should go to get information about what to do if something happens to the wealth owner? It is pretty rare for things to run smoothly, and 'stress testing' how assets are owned and whether the asset protection and succession plan works may well mean thinking through exactly what will happen in a number of circumstances, including death, and ensuring that what is intended is what will actually take place.

Part of the stress testing is also to review whether what has been put in place might create problems in terms of those who may have expected to benefit not benefiting or otherwise. If it is intended to exclude or limit the benefit of family members or others, would it be better to clarify this before the death of the wealth owner? Managing expectations between the generations is an important part of ensuring that wealth does not destroy the family.

Stress testing the structures and approaches in place is not limited to considering what happens on death, but also what would happen in the event of disability, divorce and a number of other sudden or life-changing events that affect the assets within the family. Not all challenges to wealth come from within families – the external world is full of risk that needs to be managed and addressed.

5. Knowing what assets are involved and where they are

It is worryingly common for assets to get lost and stolen as wealth owners age and in the process of succession. How family members are meant to track assets down in the event of death or severe disability is important; as is ensuring that those who will be dealing with the assets actually know their value and what intentions there are in relation to them in the event of death.

If there are valuables kept at home or in safety deposit boxes elsewhere, will the right people find them and do the right thing with

"Managing expectations between the generations is an important part of ensuring that wealth does not destroy the family."

"In a complex world, advisers are necessary; but for the safety of the family and its wealth, it is important to ensure that all family members, including women, are in a position to properly supervise advisers."

the assets? The best protection is to ensure that those who are intended to benefit know what they should be looking for. Sometimes this is not always possible or appropriate, given the ages or positions of those involved, and here using trusts or foundations may be the best approach.

But the general guidance is to think about these things – not doing so is almost sure to be problematic at an already critical or distressing time for the family.

6. Working with advisers and family offices

Where large sums of money are concerned, it is advisable to trust nobody.

– Agatha Christie[7]

Every wealth-owning family has, in effect, a 'family office' – one or more people who handle things in and around the assets of the wealth owner. Often, the wealth owner takes care of the assets while the wealth owner is around; but is enough attention being paid to who will take over this function in the event of death or disability?

Excellent tax and succession advice may have been obtained; but are the lawyers and accountants who were involved at the outset still in the picture on an ongoing basis? Very often, the legal or tax adviser is transactional, in the sense that they may have been involved in drafting a will or setting up a trust; but as the years go by, their files become out of date or lost as they retire or move on to other careers or firms. It may be difficult to pick up the trail after the passing or disability of the wealth owner. Even the most sophisticated of families, and ones that have professionally run family offices, may not have everything set up as it should be. While it sounds a bit sad to spend a day going through exactly what would happen in the event of the death or disability of a key family member, this may be the best investment of a day that you ever make. Thinking this through is something that wealth owners should be doing regularly. It is almost inevitable that not everything is arranged as it should be, given the constant changes in assets, in family circumstances and in the regulatory and tax world.

In a complex world, advisers are necessary; but for the safety of the family and its wealth, it is important to ensure that all family members, including women, are in a position to properly supervise advisers. This means knowing how to ask the right questions; monitoring the powers that advisers sometimes seek to implement in trusts, wills and otherwise; and ensuring that the right checks and balances are in place. Simply put, advisers need to be properly supervised and powers need to be in place that allow nominated members of the family to remove and replace them.

We recommend making a list of questions that you would like answered. This list might include questions about inheritance, about financial planning, about your spouse or children. There are some excellent professional advisers who will work with you to develop your thinking, but your own networks may also be helpful. The power of female networks is well known. If you have in your network professionals who will chat with you about the questions that you have, start there. Other families of wealth may also be happy to talk through the challenges with you. Or approach your female friends who are C-suite professionals in the finance and related industries; they may be happy to talk about their own experiences and even to refer you to professional advisers. There are also some really helpful sources of information and membership bodies for you to build your knowledge – for example, SmartPurse[8] and FemaleInvest[9] both provide formal and informal learning online.

7. Communication and avoiding surprises

Know what you own, and why you own it.
– Peter Lynch[10]

Much in the way of bad feeling and risk in relation to succession planning can be avoided through ongoing communication and openness within families regarding how the succession process will proceed. As children grow older, getting their input on the succession process is valuable. The more that those who are to receive assets know about what they are meant to get and where the assets are, the safer the succession process can be.

In complex situations involving second and subsequent marriages and otherwise, avoiding surprises is part of effective planning. The destruction of relationships, litigation that follows the death or disability of the wealth owner and associated problems are more likely to occur when there are surprises that emerge when the wealth owner is gone. When everyone knows what to expect and has been given every opportunity to provide input into the process, there is much less danger of bad feeling and disputes later and, more immediately, of anxiety in the last few months or years of the wealth holder.

A very effective way to address this and ensure that communication and planning are in place is to set up family retreats. Ideally, you will hold these annually; and as younger family members mature, this is an ideal time to bring them into the discussion. The agenda should cover age-appropriate issues and allow for good discussion within families about the assets of the family and how transitions are meant to take place. We all acknowledge that medical and dental check-ups are something that we should undertake regularly; and most people have their car serviced regularly and ideally comprehensively. Assets and wealth should be treated in the same way. As we age, thorough medical check-ups become even more important – and this is also true for asset protection and succession. Looking at things regularly and comprehensively, and involving those who will benefit, are exceptionally important.

8. Navigating tax laws and making choices on asset protection
An investment in knowledge pays the best interest.
– Benjamin Franklin[11]

For many families, legally planning their affairs to minimise tax exposure is an important part of planning. But how far should one go to pay the least amount of tax possible? Is it an ethical obligation of wealth owners to pay headline rates of tax to help address wealth and income inequality and not to take steps to reduce tax exposures? Where is the line between legal tax planning and illegal tax evasion? And what of tax avoidance – something that used to be considered legal and appropriate, but which is increasingly condemned by tax authorities and others?

These are issues that families need to consider and which require good advice and input from professionals who can help wealth owners

"Whatever the view of the wealth owner on how ambitious to be in their tax planning, the key is to make informed decisions and to understand the choices that one has."

to understand the risks as well as, crucially, the legalities. Wealth owners have a responsibility to society to pay their taxes and to help in addressing inequality. However, this does not mean that tax systems and governments always have it right, or that tax systems are always fair in how they work. Wealth owners have choices on where and how they invest, where they live and hold citizenship, and when and how to transfer assets to family members and others whom they wish to benefit with their wealth. Whatever the view of the wealth owner on how ambitious to be in their tax planning, the key is to make informed decisions and to understand the choices that one has.

Is it right and ethical to protect assets from a claim of creditors or from a claim from a spouse on divorce? Should a wealth owner consider all their sons and daughters in law to be gold-diggers, as some do? There really is no obvious right and wrong here. The wealth owner should simply ensure that they understand how things work and how they can go wrong, and then make informed decisions on how best to try to have things work out the way they want them to work out.

For women in the family, it is unsafe to rely on others having asked these and other questions on your behalf. Women in all generations need to understand their own wealth ownership and, importantly, how family wealth and harmony as a whole can best be protected.

9. What Mum and Dad meant

A wise person should have money in their head, but not in their heart.
– Jonathan Swift[12]

Much of the unhappiness that arises in families in and around succession has to do with arguments about what Mum and Dad meant. Misplaced expectations, informal conversations and assumptions can all contribute to a confused understanding of people's intentions.

Dissatisfied with who among the (adult) children gets what, the disgruntled child claims that "Dad actually meant to leave that asset to me" or to have had the business run by the children in a certain way. There is great benefit in ensuring that Mum and Dad make it clear what they mean long before they are not around. Family retreats and discussions in and around the succession process can go a long way towards achieving this; and accompanying these by clear expressions of wishes in wills, trusts and other succession instruments can also be helpful in avoiding future disputes. It is not safe to assume that your children and other heirs know what you mean. Putting things in writing, explaining your thinking while you are around and inviting discussion are better ways to avoid later disputes and unhappiness. And for children, encouraging your parents to take such an approach is sometimes a necessary step.

Too many wealth owners sign will and trust documents that are put in front of them by their legal and tax advisers and do not invest time in explaining to their family the thinking behind the approach implemented. Any planning undertaken with explanations can go a long way towards avoiding later disputes. Wealth owners might also consider recording themselves to outline how they would like to see things go. With the technology to do this easily available today, why not make a video recording of what the wealth owner would like to see happen with their assets, including their businesses, and how they would like to see the next generation carry things forward? This is much more personal than just having formal papers and can help a grieving family to truly understand someone's intentions.

Even more important in the process, however, is to consider a full family discussion on the asset protection and succession plan – a discussion that allows the younger generation both to be prepared for their future roles and to share their own thoughts on how the plan can be strengthened.

10. The realities of emotions and the psychology of wealth
You can only become truly accomplished at something you love. Don't make money your goal. Instead, pursue the things you love doing, and then do them so well that people can't take their eyes off you.
– Maya Angelou[13]

It may sound idealistic to think that communication within families early on can go far to address many potential circumstances of unhappiness and disputes. But communication is critical to avoiding problems. In today's world of wealth owners living longer and longer, it may be worthwhile considering making transfers of wealth to the younger generation earlier, to avoid children waiting to inherit until the death of a parent. Is it right that a child should inherit only at the age of 75 when their Mum or Dad dies at 100?

It may also be idealistic to suggest that children be treated equally, and that money not be used as a means of communicating or signalling favouritism within families. There are many realities that come into this, including specific family issues, such as children who are unable to deal with wealth safely. This may raise many questions: "Is it good to give my money to children early if they are too young to deal with what they get and may squander my hard-earned resources? Is it right to treat my children equally when one of them has really not turned out well and has significant problems with substance abuse or otherwise? Will my children take care of me in my old age if I take advantage of opportunities to save on taxes by making early distributions? Will I be able to pay for the right level of care for myself over many years if I release my assets to my children too soon?"

But some of the limitations on wealth owners doing the right thing are more psychological than real: "Am I afraid that my children will not visit if I don't use my money to keep them interested in me? Am I thinking about treating my children unequally in my succession plan as a way of communicating my disappointment with one of my children?" There is a role, for many families, for psychologists and other health professionals to be part of the succession process and to help navigate the complexities that wealth-owning families face. As such, part of the stress testing of the succession process should involve questions about the psychology of money and its effect on every generation.

Is it easier just to give it all away to charity? Frankly, no... This still causes many issues for families.

Nothing related to money is easy and the work that families need to do with their wealth is ongoing. And women in the family may play a catalytic role in encouraging the kind of dialogue that can be so protective of both family relationships and family wealth.

11. In the case of family businesses

These discussions become even more critical where there is a family business. The plans to transition the business within the family are often discussed with some openness. But clarity on how the next generation's involvement in the business will work day to day seems to be overlooked with alarming frequency.

There are several questions to explore here. How and when might the family business be transitioned to the next generation? Who will run the business, within the family and/or outside the family? What is the role of other family members within the business? And what will your day-to-day role be within the business?

Most importantly, it is not only those family members *in* the business who need to be prepared for their future roles. Family members involved in the ownership or stewardship of the business are critical partners to those family members involved in more active management or ownership roles. Everyone needs to understand their rights and responsibilities if things are to work out well.

12. Divorce and security

A woman's best protection is a little money of her own.
– Clare Boothe Luce[14]

And then there is divorce. No one wants to think about divorce when their relationship is progressing happily. No one wants divorce. But it is a sad fact of life today that the expectations of previous generations of 'one job, one house, one spouse' have long been consigned to the past. Divorce is expensive and the single biggest destroyer of wealth... or is it? Often, the legal rights of spouses on a divorce are such that the divorce can *create* wealth – but does this come at the expense of a family business?

Where finances are well organised and fairly distributed, women can find themselves managing more independent wealth than they had before. Previous generations may not have had the liberty to do this – for example, one of the authors finds it extraordinary that her mother did not know how to write a cheque until her 60s, as her husband had always done this for her!

How do I know if my new partner is a gold digger? A safe answer is to hope for the best and plan for the worst. By understanding how the relevant rules work and the rights that spouses have, we can protect ourselves and the wealth and businesses we may have an interest in. For women holding the money or marrying into the money, understanding how pre-nuptial and post-nuptial agreements work and how to protect themselves and their families is critical.

Inherited assets are vulnerable in divorce, whether or not trusts are in place. It is thus very important to plan things carefully.

Women – and particularly younger women – who may be starting long-term relationships need an understanding of how these rules work and how the steps that they take in relation to their financial affairs can make a difference.

There are planning approaches that can be undertaken to protect assets in the case of divorce, and particularly opportunities for the older generation to do things that will make it difficult for the spouses of their children to make claims against assets deriving from the older generation. But not all of these work; and it is interesting to see how many cases there are of families that have lost control of substantial businesses and wealth through a lack of attention to the risks involved.

Pre-nuptial and post-nuptial agreements play an increasingly important role in the protection of wealth in the case of the break-up of a marriage or other relationship. Although they are not always a perfect fix, the laws of an increasing number of countries do recognise agreements entered into before a marriage (pre-nuptial) or after a marriage (post-nuptial) relating to the economics associated with the dissolution of the marriage.

"Family members involved in the ownership or stewardship of the business are critical partners to those family members involved in more active management or ownership roles."

It is critical to discuss pre-nuptial agreements and their usefulness very early on in the process of discussing family finances and succession within a family. If Mum and Dad put off discussing pre-nuptial agreements until their son or daughter arrives home holding hands with *the one* and, on meeting them, Mum and Dad then tell their son or daughter about pre-nuptial agreements and the necessity for them – "Er, son, can we speak in the kitchen?" – it won't be surprising if the young lover perceives the discussion as a negative judgement of the person they have brought home for their parents to meet. Much more effective is to have the discussion about pre-nuptial agreements well before the man or woman of their dreams is introduced, and to make pre-nuptial arrangements a family requirement that is communicated to potential spouses as part of the overall family governance approach, not something subjective and specifically related to them and their exciting new partner.

A woman needs the financial security to walk away whenever she wants. Make sure that you and your female dependants have enough assets to make free financial decisions at any time in your lives. This gives a feeling of security and happiness.

As a practical matter, what does this suggestion actually mean? Say that my daughter is about to marry into a fabulously wealthy family. I

"A woman needs the financial security to walk away whenever she wants. Make sure that you and your female dependants have enough assets to make free financial decisions at any time in your lives."

may have some assets that I may leave to my daughter on my death, but the amount pales in comparison to the wealth of my daughter's in-laws. In planning for succession to my assets, maybe it makes sense to consider ensuring that assets I leave to my daughter will be available to her in emergency-type circumstances only – through trusts or other planning vehicles, I might restrict her access to what I leave her, so as to ensure that the moneys are available to her throughout her life as a way to ensure that she never becomes financially dependent on her husband. If her marriage continues for 30 years and she gives up her career and only late in life comes to a divorce, my having provided financial security may make the difference in allowing my daughter to exit from a bad situation.

But you should ask yourself the 'what-ifs' about divorce too. This is difficult and painful, but could make a real difference if you find yourself in this unfortunate situation. Talking about money and the financial aspects of a marriage with your partner in advance of the marriage is a healthy thing.

What if:

- *We get divorced?*
- *Because of the divorce I will have to focus on looking after the children and it will be difficult to travel.*
- *Because of the divorce we may have to move.*

13. Finance, mental health and the new norm of living to 100 and beyond

There are many psychological issues that relate to wealth and no amount of wealth overcomes this reality. As with other areas of mental health, open discussion and getting the right assistance to navigate these issues are key. Eminent psychiatrist and author Dr Paul Hokemeyer reflects on some of these issues in his chapter in this Special Report.

Related to issues of mental health are changing demographics and the effects of these on wealth-owning families. Women have a particular role to play in families in this area, for better or for worse. Often, because women live longer, the widow ends up holding the family wealth or family business for the very long term. When assets pass to the younger generation, it may be Mum who ends up being the only survivor in the older generation, playing the role of mentor and arbitrator in disputes among the young generation. But has Mum been well prepared for these roles? And has the family been prepared for Mum taking on these roles?

Women often play the role of caregiver within families, particularly in relation to ageing parents. It is not only death that makes taking care of one's assets impossible; a variety of disabilities – including dementia and other illnesses associated with age – can affect the ability of a wealth owner to look after their affairs. Part of good succession planning is to consider who will be able to make decisions if the wealth owner is unable to make them. Stress testing the succession plan also means considering what happens if the wealth owner becomes disabled and unable to communicate; or if dementia or another disorder makes it impossible for them to make decisions about their healthcare or financial situation. In the absence of clarity on these issues, decisions may fall to those in or out of the family who, under the relevant law, can apply for the ability to make decisions in the place of the wealth owner – but is that always the right person to do this? Has the wealth owner considered that the spouse they were about to divorce may be the one who ends up with the power to make decisions over not only their assets, but whether they remain on life support?

Planning in view of the possibility of living much longer than was the case in the past is also important as a means of addressing some of the real issues that ageing wealth owners face. It is sadly common to see the elderly suffering from forms of dementia, first not remembering where they left things and soon developing a form of paranoia, suspecting staff and family of stealing their possessions. Money becomes something to hang on to, with a sense developing that it is the tie that keeps the younger generation coming to visit.

Families should discuss these dynamics openly at an early stage of their planning and clarify the approach that works best for succession in the context of their family.

14. A changing world, the needs of business and wealth owners and understanding the tools used to address those needs

Being financially literate is a powerful thing, especially for women.
– Otegha Uwagba[15]

There are many issues that women need to be aware of in relation to wealth. The first step in ensuring that you have the knowledge you need (and ensuring that your daughters also have the knowledge they need) is to understand that in a complex world, no one person – whether a professional adviser or otherwise – will have all the answers. An effective adviser will, however, be able to raise the right questions and help the family to find the answers in the right places. Stefan Liniger, an expert on advising wealth owners internationally, addresses some of these important issues in more depth in Chapter VI.

For women in the family, having the objective of being able to ask the right questions is an important step on the journey towards self-reliance. An effective education programme on the subject of women and wealth might cover, among other things, topics such as the following:

- The changing world that we live in affects wealth planning in many ways, and not only in relation to investment returns. Tax transparency and information exchange, political risk, new taxes associated with the post-pandemic world and much more will remain with us for years to come. Self-reliance in relation to wealth requires an understanding of the dynamics affecting not only investments, but also how wealth can be protected and preserved across generations.
- How tax systems work is important to understand, particularly in a world of mobility and where the choices made by the younger generation as to where they might study, live and work can affect family wealth and businesses and more. Tax systems also affect investment choices, as it is the after-tax, not the pre-tax, return that counts. And given that so many investments are cross-border, this requires an understanding of how tax rules apply in the home country, the country of investment and the country in which investment vehicles may be located. We do not all need to become tax experts; but we need to be in a position to ask the right questions and to act on the answers.
- Understanding the holistic needs of the family is important. Wealth-owning families have many needs – some individual to their families, some common to all families – but it is only once needs are identified that they can be attended to. Families must navigate succession laws, which differ from country to country, and which are sometimes affected by religion. Wills, second families, asset protection, multi-jurisdictional families, conflict resolution, family business governance, philanthropy and much more come into the mix.
- The tools of wealth planning include trusts, foundations, companies, partnerships, insurance strategies, safe boxes and much more. All family members need to understand the tools employed in their family asset protection and succession structure and the roles they are meant to play. And for the younger generation – women in particular – asking questions about the checks and balances is key. Will advisers or others 'kidnap' family wealth once the matriarch and patriarch are gone? Or can younger-generation beneficiaries properly keep an eye on them and remove and replace them if necessary? Unless you raise these issues while your parents are around, the chance to influence things may be lost forever.
- In a complex world, advisers are needed; but are family members

equipped not only to ask them the right questions, but also to keep an eye on fees and monitor the work they are doing? Asset managers are good at hiding the revenue they receive and masking some of their conflicts of interest – are family members equipped to manage this?

15. A five-step plan to financial self-reliance

- Know where your wealth is:
  - Make a list of your assets, include your own and shared assets.
  - Talk to your parents or other wealth holders about their financial plans.
  - Understand the plans for the family business and your role in it.
  - Review the 'what-ifs': "What if Mum or Dad passes away? What if my husband and I divorce? What if my daughter marries the wrong man?"
  - If your family asset protection and succession plan includes the use of planning tools such as trusts and foundations, understand how they work, the governance in place and your role going forward.
- Make a game plan:
  - Treat managing your money as you would managing your career.
  - Apply this to inherited and earned money.
  - Consider how you want to spend it over years – not just over months.
  - Include your inheritance plans and your philanthropic plans.
- Fall in love carefully:
  - If you are single and beginning a serious relationship, make a finance plan for yourself – before you fall in love!
  - Uncomfortable as it might seem, have a finance discussion before you are married and if necessary, put a pre-nuptial agreement in place. It may not be very romantic, but it could be game changing.
- Build a group of people you trust:
  - Trusted advisers might come in different roles, but include professional advisers in your game plan.
- Live your life with purpose and joy:
  - Having wealth is a blessing – get organised, protect yourself but above all enjoy it!

Notes

1 Philip Marcovici, *The Destructive Power of Family Wealth: A Guide to Succession Planning, Asset Protection, Taxation and Wealth Management* (John Wiley & Sons Ltd, 2016).
2 World Health Organization, "Global Health Observatory; women and health", www.who.int/gho/women_and_health/mortality/life_expectancy_text/en/.
3 Anna Zakrezewski, Kedra Newsom Reeves, "Managing the Next Decade of Women's Wealth" (BCG 2020), www.bcg.com/publications/2020/managing-next-decade-women-wealth.
4 Philip Marcovici (n 1).

5 Friedrich Nietzsche (1844–1900) was a German philosopher who became one of the most influential modern thinkers. Quote sourced from www.quotes.net/quote/16062.
6 Merrill Lynch, "Seeing the Unseen: The role gender plays in wealth management", www.ml.com/content/dam/ML/Registration/seeing-the-unseen-whitepaper.pdf.
7 Dame Agatha Christie (1890–1976) was an English writer of 66 detective novels and short stories. Quote sourced from Agatha Christie, *Endless Night* (Collins Crime Club, 1967).
8 SmartPurse is a money and coaching toolbox online focused on building the knowledge of women in relation to financial confidence and independence; www.smartpurse.me.
9 FemaleInvest is a financial educator run by women, for women; femaleinvest.com.
10 Peter Lynch (1944–) is an American investor, mutual fund manager and philanthropist. Quote sourced from Novel Investor, "Peter Lynch: The Single Most Important Thing" (11 March 2020).
11 Benjamin Franklin (1706–1790) was one of the Founding Fathers of the United States and a writer, philosopher, politician, statesman. Quote sourced from "The Way to Wealth" (1758), https://en.wikipedia.org/wiki/The_Way_to_Wealth.
12 Jonathan Swift (1667–1745) was an Anglo-Irish satirist, essayist, poet and Anglican cleric. Quote sourced from Jonathan Swift, Thomas Sheridan, John Nichols, *The Works* (1808).
13 Maya Angelou (1928–2014) was an American poet and civil rights activist. Quote sourced from www.goodreads.com/quotes/4749-you-can-only-become-truly-accomplished-at-something-you-love.
14 Clare Boothe Luce (1903–1987) was an American author, politician, and public conservative figure. Quote sourced from Clare Boothe Luce, "The Women" (1936).
15 Otegha Uwagba (1990–) is an author, journalist and speaker, included in the 2018 *Forbes* 30 under 30 list. Quote sourced from Otegha Uwagba, *Little Black Book: A Toolkit for Working Women* (Fourth Estate, 2017).

Philip Marcovici
Principal, The Offices of Philip Marcovici Limited
philip.marcovici@marcoviciasia.com

Philip Marcovici is retired from the practice of law and consults with governments, financial institutions and global families. He was a partner of Baker McKenzie, which he joined in 1982, and practised in the area of international taxation in Hong Kong and Zurich while with the firm. Philip has also practised law in New York and Vancouver, British Columbia. He retired from Baker McKenzie at the end of 2009.

The author of numerous publications, Philip is also the author of *The Destructive Power of Family Wealth* (John Wiley & Sons). Among others, Philip is a member of the Public Policy Committee of STEP and chairs its Responsible Stewardship of Wealth thought leadership group. He holds law degrees from Harvard Law School and the University of Ottawa (*magna cum laude*), and is admitted to practise in Hong Kong, the State of New York, the Province of British Columbia (retired), Canada, England and Wales.

Caroline Underwood
CEO, Philanthropy Company
caroline@philanthropycompany.com

Over nearly three decades, Caroline Underwood OBE has worked with philanthropic individuals and families to achieve positive change, as well as with a wide range of charities and cultural bodies in the UK and worldwide.

Caroline was awarded an OBE for charitable services in the 2017 Queen's Birthday Honours. She is a fellow of the Royal Society of Arts; a trustee of donor-advised fund Our Common Good; a governor of Britain's leading preparatory school, the Dragon School, Oxford; and former vice chair of UNICEF UK.

Today's rising next generation, groomed to take over the family business, have been brought up in the social media era and have really known nothing else. Often classed as Millennials or Generation Z, and broadly born from 1981 onwards, they live in an era in which sharing, posting, liking, tweeting and commenting are all part of life.

Safeguarding the family's digital narrative: how to navigate the challenges of the social media revolution

Charlie Bain
Digitalis

Taken from the Special Report *Family Business and Responsible Wealth Ownership: Preparing the Next Generation*, published by Globe Law and Business

1. Introduction

For Abigail Disney – granddaughter and great-niece of Roy and Walt, who founded the Walt Disney Company – growing up in a family surrounded by untold riches was never entirely comfortable.

Deeply concerned about the remuneration of some of the lowest-paid staff at the company's theme park, Disneyland, she decided to take matters into her own hands and publicly shame the organisation that bears her name and made her extremely wealthy.

Using a combination of her Twitter account and a first-person article in the *Washington Post*, she criticised the $66 million annual pay of Disney's CEO and championed the rights of the employees working in Disney theme parks.[1] In July 2020, she took to Twitter again to criticise Walt Disney's decision to furlough thousands of low-paid workers during the COVID-19 pandemic after paying dividends to shareholders and bonuses to its executives.[2]

Just a few months earlier, in a different boardroom, Rupert Murdoch's 48-year-old son, James, was also taking his family to task. In a very public outburst, he strongly criticised his family's news outlets for downplaying the impact of the climate crisis.[3] It was a rare public attack by a company director on his own group's operations and shed light on the tensions and speculation over his 88-year-old father's succession plans.

What both these examples showed was the tension that often exists when members of very successful and high-profile families break away and cast doubt on their narratives. Both forging their own career paths, but indelibly linked to the family's heritage by name, Abigail Disney and James Murdoch were an intrinsic part of a family history, but their own values and personal views were at odds with the culture they grew up in.

Both made their declarations very publicly and deliberately. But often, such strident views aren't made so openly – especially with private families that don't run listed companies. On many occasions, a family might deal with this internally, but not want it aired to the world. However, what makes this hard is that, unlike 30 or even 20 years ago, we live in a multi-media age in which it is very hard to keep views and opinions private, however hard you try.

Today's rising next generation, groomed to take over the family business, have been brought up in the social media era and have really known nothing else. Often classed as Millennials or Generation Z, and

"Today's rising next generation, groomed to take over the family business, have been brought up in the social media era and have really known nothing else."

broadly born from 1981 onwards, they live in an era in which sharing, posting, liking, tweeting and commenting are all part of life. Inevitably, this has triggered a generational tension between how to preserve the family privacy while adapting to the digital revolution. One question that I am often asked, and which I see play out almost weekly in large families, is how to navigate this new world. What happens if the family's reputation – often built up over many years – is ruined in seconds by one rogue, ill-thought-through posting on the Internet?

What happens when a family name and business brand are synonymous, yet public postings on the Internet are discovered and business interests suffer value destruction as a result?

When does the family unit stop being about the 'We' and become the 'I'? And if you can't prevent that from happening, how can you take steps to make that private from the outside world?

This chapter doesn't attempt to address how to resolve intra-family conflict, but instead examines the critical area of digital privacy. We will look at the dizzying rise of social media and the digital world, and how this is used against some families and the rising next generation to ruin a reputation. We will examine how data collection from apps and 'digital footprints' might affect livelihoods; which new social media platforms to look out for; and the rise of fake news and deepfakes. And above all, we will provide advice and tips on how to traverse this tricky and constantly evolving landscape.

2. A family reputation

Most families that I have had the pleasure of advising are intensely private. Many have built up and passed on the family fortune quietly and beneath the radar. The matriarch and patriarch of the family are typically in their 60s, 70s or 80s (the Silent Generation and Boomers), and grew up in an era when keeping their counsel and not putting their heads above the parapet were the norm. Many do not run public companies, so are not bound to release information into the public domain. Generally, these families don't want a light shone on their business because there is no benefit. The 19th century essayist Walter Bagehot addressed this when talking about the British royal family. He argued that by remaining private to the public, the royals maintained their 'mystery', which is ultimately what the public liked about them.

"We must not let in daylight upon magic," he wrote in *The English Constitution* (1867).[4]

However, the digital revolution has made this hard, as remaining anonymous is impossible today. I always have to pinch myself when I am reminded that Facebook was only launched in its current guise in 2008; for some, it might feel like it's been around for a lot longer. Today, more than half (53%) of the world's population use social media.

The latest figures show that there are 4.2 billion social media users worldwide in 2021 – a 5% increase on a year ago. This is also 920 million more than the number of social media users in 2017, which represents a massive 32.2% jump in just five years. The average annual growth rate over this period is 7.2%.[5]

Figure 1. Global social media use

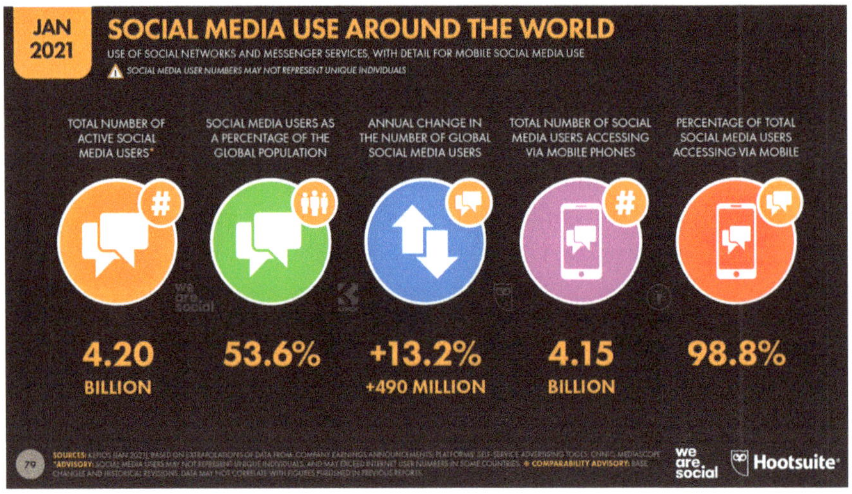

Source: DataReportal – Digital 2021: Global Overview Report

DataReportal's *Digital 2021: Global Overview Report*[6] highlights user figures for some of the most popular apps:

- Facebook – 2.7 billion users;
- Instagram – 1.2 billion users;
- TikTok – 689 million users; and
- Twitter – 353 million users.

According to Global Web Index, the average 16 to 24-year-old spends three hours and one minute on social media a day; while the average 25 to 34-year-old spends two hours and 37 minutes.[7] Compare that with 55 to 64-year-olds, where just 3% of the global population use social media – a figure which drops to around 2% of the over-65s.[8]

Facebook, Twitter and Instagram are now household names. TikTok – a relative newcomer in the social media revolution – is becoming incredibly popular with the under-25s and gaining users by the minute. LinkedIn now has more than 740 million users in 200 countries.[9]

Figure 2. Most-used social media platforms

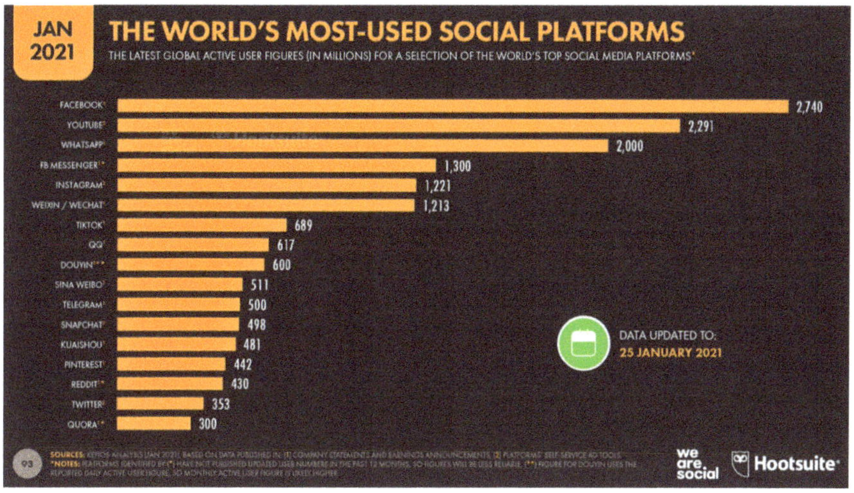

Source: DataReportal – Digital 2021: Global Overview Report

3. The hostile third party

Creating content for or sharing content on a platform has never been easier; and for many, the joy of seeing that content liked or shared is so great that thoughts of privacy go out the window. This feeling is not just limited to teenagers; those a lot older experience it too.

Many studies and articles have been written about the thrill of posting content and seeing the 'likes' or shares flood into your account. The dopamine rush that this generates in the brain is a crucial trigger in encouraging social media users to create content and post it online. And this is where the privacy and reputational aspects come into play.

Many clients that I advise often want to discuss the privacy issues around LinkedIn. LinkedIn, in theory, should be one of the more benign platforms when it comes to sharing content, because it is considered 'grown up' and just limited to business. However, for me, LinkedIn lures us into a false sense of security. Often, a person's entire education, work history, opinions and views are contained on this platform; and critically, their entire network is on show if the right privacy settings are not in place. Boundaries are blurred every day, with personal postings encroaching on the business stories. LinkedIn has also introduced new features that echo Instagram – such as LinkedIn Stories, which enables members and organisations to share images and short videos of their everyday professional moments.

Similar to Facebook, Twitter and Instagram, this 'digital library' of our lives is gold dust to someone with malintent. Whether a journalist, a hostile political activist, a disgruntled former employee of the family business – anybody who wants to cause the family harm can find a way to get hold of that content and highlight the poster and their family in a derogatory way.

One of the critical aspects of digital privacy invasion – which most people forget – is that it is often not the platform that you post on which causes the issue; it's the publication or outlet that spots it, finds the angle and repurposes the content into a damaging story or posting. Why, being part of the well-known family that you are a member of, is your posting a risk? Journalists, for instance, are experts in harvesting information online. If they want to write a derogatory story about a large family, they are likely to start poking around the matriarch or patriarch's digital footprint. Those family members from the Silent Generation are unlikely to have a significant digital presence. But their daughters, sons, grandsons, god daughters – you name it – may well have large digital footprints; and critically, these may contain information about the matriarch or patriarch. This second layer is frequently the weak link in a family trying to preserve a reputation.

The other point about content flying around online and being picked up by interested parties hell bent on causing trouble is that it's often very difficult to put the genie back in the bottle once it's out. I work with some of the best privacy lawyers in the world, who are experts at getting YouTube, Twitter, Facebook and the rest to remove content if it violates their terms or is defamatory. But often, this comes too late – the content has already been picked up and is hurtling around the Web at an alarming speed.

A really interesting example of this was a recent incident involving a documentary on the British royal family. In 1969, the queen agreed for the BBC to film a fly-on-the-wall documentary about the royal family. The 110-minute film was watched by 30 million people and remains one of the United Kingdom's most-viewed television broadcasts.

However, the queen decided that allowing the film to be broadcast was a bad idea and it never saw the light of day again. Since the early 1970s, it was kept under lock and key in an archive. That is, until January 2021, when an unknown user leaked it on YouTube. It was viewed thousands of times before Buckingham Palace and the BBC submitted a copyright claim and YouTube immediately took it down.[10] No real harm done, you might think; YouTube reacted quickly.

However, almost every newspaper globally reported on the leak and took the opportunity to dedicate acres of coverage to the contents of the documentary. It was followed up on blogs and a debate ensued as to who was responsible for leaking it. Some 50 years on, far from being private, it is literally all over the Internet.

4. The rising next generation and jobs

The rising next generation of a family, building their education and lives, should be acutely aware of the risk of content that is posted online either by them or about them coming back to haunt them in years to come. And as the royal family example shows, it need not be recent content; anyone with a grudge can surface content going back years online at any stage.

This not only has an effect on the wider family reputation, but could even cause issues when it comes to people in their 20s, 30s and 40s applying for a job – which in my view is worrying.

In research conducted by Career Builder, it was reported that 54% of employees have decided not to hire a candidate based on their social media profile. A staggering 70% of employers use social media to screen candidates.[11]

But what you post online can not only affect whether you get a job; it can also affect whether you are allowed to enter a country. Nearly all applicants for visas to work or study in the United States must submit their social media details under recently adopted rules. The State Department regulations require people to provide details of their social media accounts and five years' worth of email addresses and phone numbers.[12]

"The rising next generation of a family, building their education and lives, should be acutely aware of the risk of content that is posted online either by them or about them coming back to haunt them in years to come."

In August 2019, it was reported that an incoming Harvard freshman was blocked from entering the United States due to content on his social media pages. Even worse, the content that was deemed problematic was alleged to have come from his friends' activity, rather than his own.

5. How digitally private are the rising next generation?
But are Millennials and Generation Z really that bad when it comes to openly sharing data and social media? This is an interesting debate.

My own anecdotal evidence suggests that they are actually pretty good. When I used to conduct digital privacy audits on behalf of my family office clients five years ago, there would be a sea of open social media accounts with pictures, home addresses and comments, free for all to access. But I have seen a shift in this area, with the 20 to 40-year-old generation in particular becoming much more aware of their online privacy.

One US survey found that, across all age ranges, participants indicated that they do adjust privacy settings where possible. Notably, the team found that the large majority of participants adjust at least some of their account settings, although Millennials make more privacy adjustments on all of their accounts (67% of Millennials versus 50% of

"With the intricate details of our digital lives stored by these platforms, what happens if they fall into the wrong hands and are used inappropriately? What happens if there is a hack or a leak? It doesn't bear thinking about how the worst-case scenario could change lives."

Gen Z participants). Ironically, nearly 60% of Gen Zers – the generation known for having been brought up on technology – said that they had not received education about safety online.[13]

Anna-Sophie Harling is uniquely placed to comment on the rising next generation and privacy. As managing director for Europe at NewsGuard, an online service that rates and ranks news websites for reliability, she is also on the content board of Ofcom. Despite her extensive experience and expertise in all things digital, she is also – critically – under the age of 30.

Harling feels that Generation Z and Millennials are not necessarily that concerned about privacy when it comes to the frenetic need to use social media and share data. "By and large, users are concerned about privacy in the abstract," she told me. "But when it comes to making choices about what personal data to share, they make very little effort to properly read the terms and conditions. A good example is when it recently emerged there were data privacy concerns around WhatsApp; a lot of people instantly moved to Signal and Telegram. But a lot of people did that not because they were overly worried about the privacy of their data, but more because Elon Musk tweeted, 'Use Signal.'"

Sharing data, rather than simply placing it publicly online, is another risk that I am always highlighting to my clients. In October 2020, the House Judiciary Committee issued a report on its investigation of competition in the digital market. The committee found that Facebook, Apple, Google and Amazon have too much market power, and have used this power for anti-competitive purposes. The committee's view of the tech giants' behaviour is best reflected in the following scathing remark: "To put it simply, companies that once were scrappy, underdog startups that challenged the status quo have become the kinds of monopolies we last saw in the era of oil barons and railroad tycoons."[14]

One similarity of platforms such as Facebook, Twitter and Instagram, which many people didn't stop to think about in the early days, is that they are all free. And like many things that are free in life, there is a reason for this: we sign up without paying; they get our data.

For the rising next generation, this is a concern. Some Generation Zs, for instance, have never known a life in which they didn't hand over data to tech giants. With the intricate details of our digital lives stored by these platforms, what happens if they fall into the wrong hands and are used inappropriately? What happens if there is a hack or a leak? It doesn't bear thinking about how the worst-case scenario could change lives. The implications of a massive data leak could take years longer to clean up than an oil spill.

Harling is more confident on this front, believing that regulation and new instruments such as the General Data Protection Regulation and the right to be forgotten are just some of a number of measures that will give us more control over our data in the future.

"Regulation will definitely help in the future," she said. "Regulation could ensure, for example, that when you delete a Facebook or Instagram account, the data will be truly deleted."

6. Disinformation

The other aspect of the Internet that the rising next generation will have to learn to grapple with is how to decipher and navigate disinformation or avoid becoming the victim of it.

When Donald Trump popularised the phrase 'Fake News' in many of his broadcasts and broadsides, he was globalising an emerging phenomenon. Yet propaganda and disinformation are as old as politics itself; they have been around for centuries.

What was new about 'Fake News' was how it was disseminated by social media – driven by short soundbites and tantalising video clips. It preyed on the vulnerability of our short attention spans, especially those of the young. We are now bombarded by so much information that we prefer bite-sized bits of news and analysis, and are likely to digest sometimes hundreds of these a day. If a short video clip of a CEO, a politician or another high-profile person is sent to us, we are likely to view it if it's brief. We may immediately spot it as fake or a joke; but it will still sit in the memory. Or we may believe it. Before we know it, it becomes fact. That's why fake news is so insidious. It disorientates us.

Unsubstantiated and frankly false rumours are flourishing under the radar on the Internet every day, and most of them are easy to spot. However, others aren't, and sharing these rumours is now a major reputational vulnerability.

Let me explain why. The other day, I was called by a family whose son and heir was in his early 40s. One evening, tired after a long day working for the family business, he shared what he thought was an interesting story about how to avoid catching COVID-19 on his Facebook page and wrote a brief comment. The story, unbeknown to him, was in fact fake. Within minutes, the family's PR representative had received a call from the media asking why he was propagating a rumour which was actually a danger to public health. There was also concern from the family that if the story went live, the reputational fall-out would impact on the family's investments. Luckily, the story never appeared; but these are the kinds of extreme reputational issues that families must consider.

Celebrities and high-profile names who shared false rumours online linking 5G to the COVID-19 outbreak were labelled 'super-spreaders' and pilloried in the press. The bottom line is that you don't even need to create the content these days to become a story.

7. Deepfakes

There is a wonderful quote: "A lie can travel halfway around the world while the truth is putting on its shoes." This line perfectly exemplifies the lightning speed at which disinformation can travel in the social media age, before being proved entirely incorrect. With delicious irony, this is supposedly attributed to Mark Twain; yet there has been much debate online (yes, you guessed it) as to whether Twain actually said it or the attribution itself is a lie.

Deepfakes are also a deeply concerning internet phenomenon that the rising generation will have to grapple with in the future. A 'deepfake' is a synthetic video of a person generated by AI software. Except it's not that person – it's a fake. It can enable anyone to create false evidence of someone doing or saying something that they never did or said. A deepfake of a politician can be devastating, and can trigger untold chaos and unrest.

In March 2021, videos circulating online that purported to show Hollywood actor Tom Cruise practising his golf swing, performing a magic trick and telling an anecdote about former Soviet leader Mikhail Gorbachev were revealed as deepfakes. The highly realistic videos went viral across social media platforms, despite the actor having no involvement or even knowledge of the videos until they were released.

The visual effects specialist and creator of the deepfake Tom Cruise videos came forward to say that he wanted to make people aware of what they were watching, adding that the speed at which the technology is advancing could pose problems in the future.[15]

I would say that the word 'problem' is an understatement. This is a huge issue which we will have to address – and fairly rapidly. Synthetic media is on the increase because traditional video production is so unscalable. Why hire actors, a studio and producers when you can make a video using synthetic media for one-third of the cost and in one-tenth of the time?

Apply this to the family office or corporate world. Very soon, I'm convinced that a video of a company CEO addressing stakeholders will be synthetically made, rather than wasting their precious time filming it. Then consider the fact that such software can be used inappropriately. Fraudulent clips of that business leader could highlight a half-truth about the company which could send it out of business.

Fake videos of central bankers could send markets into freefall. Trusted news organisations might scramble to verify that a video is true and reveal whether it is or isn't; but often, by then it's too late. We live in a world where people react immediately.

A private family may have a video made about it and journalists may swarm to the family home to check whether the story is true. By the time they have confirmed it is *not* true, the very fact that the video has been made has become a story in itself. So a low-profile family which has done nothing to get news coverage may suddenly become the centre of scrutiny.

With Generation Z now becoming experts in home video making, we have a whole new stable of humans who can create content such as deepfakes very easily and very quickly. It won't be long before you will be able to access an app on your smartphone and send a deepfake live within minutes. Damian Collins, digital culture and sport select committee chairman in the United Kingdom, warned in February 2019 that deepfakes are "one of the most serious threats that democracy faces".[16] In March 2021, the US Federal Bureau of Investigation warned that they are the next major cyber threat.[17]

Rest assured: you will hear a lot more about deepfakes in the future.

8. The new apps on the block

Leaning quickly about new and emerging social media platforms and their privacy implications will also be critical for the rising next generation.

In the last year or so, we have seen the emergence of several alternative social media apps, such as Parler, Gab, Clubhouse, Rumble, MeWe, CloutHub and DLive. But what exactly are these newcomers and what new digital privacy concerns do they raise? With Facebook and Twitter increasingly banning accounts with far-right narratives, users are being driven to find other platforms in sometimes dark corners of the Internet. The increasing complexity and fragmentation of the online landscape are creating new digital risks, making it crucial to understand the unique political, legal and technical characteristics of each platform.

Clubhouse is an audio-based app that allows users listen to conversations in chatrooms, with an invitation model to attract new users. Any user can start a conversation in a 'private room'. But as I write, there are concerns that hostile third parties could infiltrate a chatroom, listen in, record the conversations and post them online.

"We have a whole new stable of humans who can create content such as deepfakes very easily and very quickly. It won't be long before you will be able to access an app on your smartphone and send a deepfake live within minutes."

9. Tips on how to navigate

So how can the social media active rising next generation avoid ruining the cherished family reputation? What is the best course of action to plan, insulate and protect a family from a quick-fire reputational crisis in the digital age?

One of the first steps is to conduct awareness conversations and training around this. I always think it's a mistake to ban anyone from social media; this is rarely the answer. For many, this is part of their everyday lives, and a ban would merely alienate them from their peer group and make their social lives awkward – especially for the younger generation. No one wants to be asked why they are the only kid not on Snapchat or Instagram.

But talking them through real-life examples of how information posted online can be used against them can change their mindset – albeit very gradually. The Internet can be a force for good, but it can also be a dangerous place. In some cases, understanding the shocking threats makes young people think twice before posting online. For the rising next generation, this is critical not only because it will help to preserve the overall family's reputation, but also if they are thinking of studying in the United States or applying for a job there, because it will make them aware of the importance of their digital footprints. This latter point often chimes with young people. They may feel unconcerned about the family, but they certainly do worry – at a certain stage in life – about themselves. I once heard an expert explain that you should manage your Google profile like you do your financial portfolio. Get rid of the social platforms that don't rank and perform, and launch new ones which can showcase your achievements and further your career. The rising next generation should be continually thinking about their digital footprints, evaluating their content and managing their social media accounts.

The second area of focus should be privacy settings. These should become second nature. I am personally seeing a big shift in this area. People are generally becoming more private and using privacy settings more. But that is not always the case. We are also seeing some generations moving more to what we call 'closed social': communicating via WhatsApp, Telegram, Signal or other chat apps on the market. That's fine; but the risk of information ending up online publicly is still the same: anyone can maliciously take a WhatsApp posting and make it publicly available, especially in chat 'groups' where people are not good friends with all users in the group.

For wealthy families, knowing what is out there online about you in granular detail is essential. A reputational crisis can arise suddenly and, like a wildfire, can spread quickly if you haven't prepared properly and don't know what to do. Knowing all about your digital footprint in intimate detail ahead of a crisis is hugely important, and allows you to respond more confidently and with greater speed. You should know your digital profile as well as you know yourself or your business.

The Deep Web, according to commonly used estimates, contains around 96% of what is out there about us and it is publicly available. The remaining 4% is indexed by search engines. Experts should conduct digital health checks on your Deep Web footprint every six months. Think of it like a check-up with the doctor. There are also great monitoring tools out there which flag content within minutes of it hitting the Internet. Families should continually monitor their footprints so that 'surface' content that appears between health checks is discovered as quickly as possible.

One example of how a family business can very quickly hit the headlines is Italy's Benetton family. It came under reputational attack from politicians and the public following the involvement of one of its companies in the Genoa bridge tragedy in 2018.[18] At least 38 people died when a section of the 1.2 kilometre-long traffic bridge collapsed, sending vehicles hurtling onto buildings and a riverbed. The bridge was part of a toll road operated by a company 88% owned by Atlantia, in which the Benetton family was the largest shareholder. Atlantia's stock devalued more than 25% in the days after the disaster. A report from Bloomberg at the time reported that $2 billion was erased from the family's net worth as the Atlantia stake was its single-largest asset, comprising more than one-third of its $13.3 billion fortune.[19]

The Benetton reputation suffered, with some social media users expressing outrage. The United Colours of Benetton ads were parodied with images of the ruined bridge and the hashtag #BoycottBenetton trended. I often wonder whether the family could ever have envisaged that such a sad tragedy might happen, how quickly it would become so destructive to the family name and how it could have prepared to mitigate this.

Finally, you can put all the measures in place to protect, monitor and mitigate against content that goes online; but there is nothing quite like something that was around long before social media – a good, old-fashioned conversation within the family.

Teaching the rising next generation about the family history, heritage and values that cement a family reputation is the bedrock. Explain the journey to a good reputation. Great families fragment, but they are often glued together by a set of values and a shared purpose. One of those values should be that togetherness cements a reputation. That may not work for Abigail Disney, who clearly has her own views on how the company that operates with her name should act; but it will for others. It is not about the 'I' in the family; it is about the 'We'. All families should think about that the next time their thumbs hover over a new social media post before pressing 'share'.

Notes

1 Yahoo News, "'I was so livid': Disney Heiress visits theme part to see worker conditions", Yahoo News (15 July 2019), https://news.yahoo.com/i-was-so-livid-disney-heiress-visits-theme-park-undercover-to-see-worker-conditions-093000722.html.
2 Jordan Valinsky, "Abigail Disney on Disney furloughs: 'What the actual f—'", CNN Business (23 July 2020), https://edition.cnn.com/2020/04/22/business/abigail-disney-furloughs-bonus-pay-coronavirus-trnd/index.html.
3 Jim Waterson, "James Murdoch criticises father's news outlets for climate crisis denial", The Guardian (14 January 2020), www.theguardian.com/media/2020/jan/14/james-murdoch-criticises-fathers-news-outlets-for-climate-crisis-denial.
4 *Oxford Essential Quotations*, 4th edition (Oxford University Press, 2016), www.oxfordreference.com/view/10.1093/acref/9780191826719.001.0001/q-oro-ed4-00000713#:~:text=Walter%20Bagehot%201826%E2%80%9377&text=Above%20all%20things%20our%20royal.
5 "How Many People Use Social Media in 2021?", www.oberlo.co.uk/statistics/how-many-people-use-social-media.
6 Simon Kemp, "Digital 2021: Global Overview Report", Datareportal (27 January 2021), https://datareportal.com/reports/digital-2021-global-overview-report.
7 Saima Salim, "How much time do you spend on social media? Research says 142 minutes per day", *Digital Information World* (4 January 2019), www.digitalinformationworld.com/2019/01/how-much-time-do-people-spend-social-media-infographic.html.
8 Digital 2021 Global Overview Report, *We Are Social*, https://wearesocial.com/digital-2021.
9 LinkedIn, https://about.linkedin.com/#:~:text=About%20LinkedIn&text=740%20million%20members%20in%20more%20than%20200%20countries%20and%20territories%20worldwide.
10 Sky News, "YouTube deletes fly-on-the-wall royal documentary after it mysteriously resurfaces

50 years on" (29 January 2021), https://news.sky.com/story/youtube-deletes-fly-on-the-wall-royal-documentary-after-it-mysteriously-resurfaces-50-years-on-12201670.
11 Lauren Salm, "70% of employers are snooping candidates' social media profiles", CareerBuilder (15 June 2017), www.careerbuilder.com/advice/social-media-survey-2017.
12 Travel.State.Gov, "Collection of social media identifiers from US visa applications" (4 June 2019), https://travel.state.gov/content/travel/en/News/visas-news/20190604_collection-of-social-media-identifiers-from-U.-S.-visa-applicants.html.
13 Remi Cohen, "Are Gen Z-ers More Security Savvy Online than Millennials?", F5 Labs Application Threat Intelligence (13 February 2020), www.f5.com/labs/articles/threat-intelligence/are-gen-z-ers-more-security-savvy-online-than-millennials-.
14 Adi Robertson and Russell Brandom, "Congress releases blockbuster tech antitrust report", *The Verge* (6 October 2020), www.theverge.com/2020/10/6/21504814/congress-antitrust-report-house-judiciary-committee-apple-google-amazon-facebook.
15 Alex Hern, "'I don't want to upset people': Tom Cruise deepfake creator speaks out", *The Guardian* (5 March 2021), www.theguardian.com/technology/2021/mar/05/how-started-tom-cruise-deepfake-tiktok-videos.
16 Omar Oakes, "'Deepfake' voice tech used for good in David Beckham malaria campaign", *Campaign* (9 April 2019), www.campaignlive.co.uk/article/deepfake-voice-tech-used-good-david-beckham-malaria-campaign/1581378.
17 "FBI warns deepfakes could be the next major cyber threat", *The Global Herald* (13 March 2021), https://theglobalherald.com/news/fbi-warns-deepfakes-could-be-the-next-major-cyber-threat/.
18 Alexandra Newlove and James Beech, "Benetton family targeted over Genoa bridge collapse", CampdenFB/Campden Wealth (17 August 2018), www.campdenfb.com/article/benetton-family-targeted-over-genoa-bridge-collapse.
19 Devon Pendleton and Tommaso Ebhardt, "Benetton wealth Falls $2 billion after Italy bridge collapse", *Bloomberg Quint* (21 August 2018), www.bloombergquint.com/business/benetton-fortune-drops-by-2-billion-after-italy-bridge-collapse.

Charlie Bain
Managing partner, Digitalis
charlie.bain@digitalis.com

Charlie Bain is managing partner at Digitalis, an advisory company that specialises in online reputation management, crisis communications, digital privacy and risk. He is widely recognised as a leading expert in advising clients on their digital footprint and the effect this has on their reputation. During his career, he has helped a number of leading families, global corporates and prominent individuals to understand the nascent field of internet risk and digital crisis communications.

Charlie is on the advisory board of VALUEworks, a multi-family office based in Zurich; and a senior adviser to Dallington Associates, a company that offers specialist mentorship for the rising generation. In addition, Charlie has written for *The International Family Offices Journal* and was a contributor to the book *Advising the Wealthy Client* (Globe Law and Business, 2020), giving an insight into his experience advising family offices.

In 2021, Charlie was recognised as a top recommended specialist in reputation management by *Spear's Magazine*.

About Globe Law and Business

Globe Law and Business was established in 2005. From the very beginning, we set out to create legal books that are sufficiently high level to be of real use to the experienced professional, yet still accessible and easy to navigate. Most of our authors are drawn from Magic Circle and other top commercial firms, both in the United Kingdom and internationally.

Our titles are carefully produced, with the utmost attention paid to editorial, design and production processes. We hope this results in high-quality publications that are easy to read and a pleasure to own.

In 2021, we were very pleased to announce the start of a new chapter for Globe Law and Business following the acquisition of law books under the imprint Ark Publishing. Our law firm management list is now significantly expanded with many well-known and loved Ark Publishing titles.

We are also pleased to announce the launch of our online content platform, Globe Law Online. This allows for easy search and networked access across firms. Key collections include the Private Client Collection. Details of all titles included can be found at www.globelawonline.com. Email glo@globelawandbusiness.com for further details and to arrange a free trial for you or your firm.

We'd very much like to hear from you with your thoughts and ideas for improving what we offer.

Please do feel free to email me at sian@globelawandbusiness.com. Happy reading and thank you for your time.

Sian O'Neill
Managing director
Globe Law and Business
www.globelawandbusiness.com

www.ingramcontent.com/pod-product-compliance
Ingram Content Group UK Ltd.
Pitfield, Milton Keynes, MK11 3LW, UK
UKHW062228150926
8657IPUK00012B/199

9 781787 429949